SCIENCE VISUAL RESOURCES

CHEMISTRY

An Illustrated Guide to Science

The Diagram Group

CHELSEA HOUSE
PUBLISHERS
An imprint of Infobase Publishing

Chemistry: An Illustrated Guide to Science

Copyright © 2006 The Diagram Group

Author: Derek McMonagle BSc PhD CSci CChem FRSC

Editors: Eleanora von Dehsen, Jamie Stokes, Judith Bazler

Design: Anthony Atherton, Richard Hummerstone,
                     Lee Lawrence, Phil Richardson

Illustration: Peter Wilkinson

Picture research: Neil McKenna

Indexer: Martin Hargreaves

Chelsea House
An imprint of Infobase Publishing
132 West 31st Street
New York NY 10001

For Library of Congress Cataloging-in-Publication data, please contact the publisher.

ISBN 0-8160-6163-7

Chelsea House books are available at special discounts when purchased in bulk quantities for businesses, associations, institutions, or sales promotions. Please call our Special Sales Department in New York at 212/967-8800 or 800/322-8755.

You can find Chelsea House on the World Wide Web at
http://www.chelseahouse.com

Printed in China

CP Diagram 10 9 8 7 6 5 4 3 2 1

This book is printed on acid-free paper.

Introduction

Chemistry is one of eight volumes of the **Science Visual Resources** set. It contains eight sections, a comprehensive glossary, a Web site guide, and an index.

Chemistry is a learning tool for students and teachers. Full-color diagrams, graphs, charts, and maps on every page illustrate the essential elements of the subject, while parallel text provides key definitions and step-by-step explanations.

Atomic Structure provides an overview of the very basic structure of physical matter. It looks at the origins of the elements and explains the nature of atoms and molecules.

Elements and Compounds examines the characteristics of the elements and their compounds in detail. Tables give the boiling points, ionization energies, melting points, atomic volumes, atomic numbers, and atomic masses key elements. Plates also describe crystal structures and covalent bonding.

Changes in Matter is an overview of basic chemical processes and methods. It looks at mixtures and solutions, solubility, chromatography, and the pH scale.

Patterns—Non-Metals and **Patterns—Metals** focus on the properties of these two distinct groups of elements. These sections also include descriptions of the industrial processes used when isolating important elements of both types.

Chemical Reactions looks at the essential factors that influence reactions. It includes information on proton transfer, electrolysis, redox reactions, catalysts, and the effects of concentration and temperature.

Chemistry of Carbon details the chemical reactions involving carbon that are vital to modern industry—from the distillation of crude oil to the synthesis of polymers and the manufacture of soaps and detergents. This section also includes an overview of the chemistry of life.

Radioactivity is concerned with ionizing radiation, nuclear fusion, nuclear fission, and radioactive decay, as well as the properties of radiation. Tables describe all known isotopes, both radioactive and non-radioactive.

Contents

1 ATOMIC STRUCTURE

2 ELEMENTS AND COMPOUNDS

3 CHANGES IN MATTER

4 PATTERNS—NON-METALS

5 PATTERNS—METALS

6 CHEMICAL REACTIONS

7 CHEMISTRY OF CARBON

8 RADIOACTIVITY

APPENDIXES

Key words

Big Bang	*supernova*
black hole	*white dwarf*
brown dwarf	
neutron star	
protostar	

Beginnings

- According to the *Big Bang* theory, the universe resulted from a massive explosion that created matter, space, and time.
- During the first thee minutes following the Big Bang, hydrogen and helium were formed as the universe began to cool.

Initial formation

- Stars were formed when gravity caused clouds of interstellar gas and dust to contract. These clouds became denser and hotter, with their centers boiling at about a million kelvins.
- These heaps became round, glowing blobs called *protostars*.
- Under the pressure of gravity, contraction continued, and a protostar gradually became a genuine star.
- A star exists when all solid particles have evaporated and when light atoms such as hydrogen have begun building heavier atoms through nuclear reactions.
- Some cloud fragments do not have the mass to ignite nuclear reactions. These become *brown dwarfs*.
- The further evolution of stars depends on their size (See page 9).
- Stars the size of our Sun will eventually shed large amounts of matter and contract into a very dense remnant—a *white dwarf*, composed of carbon and oxygen atoms.
- More massive stars collapse quickly shedding much of their mass in dramatic explosions called *supernovae*. After the explosion, the remaining material contracts into an extremely dense *neutron star*.
- The most massive stars eventually collapse from their own gravity to *black holes*, whose density is infinite.

Formation of stars

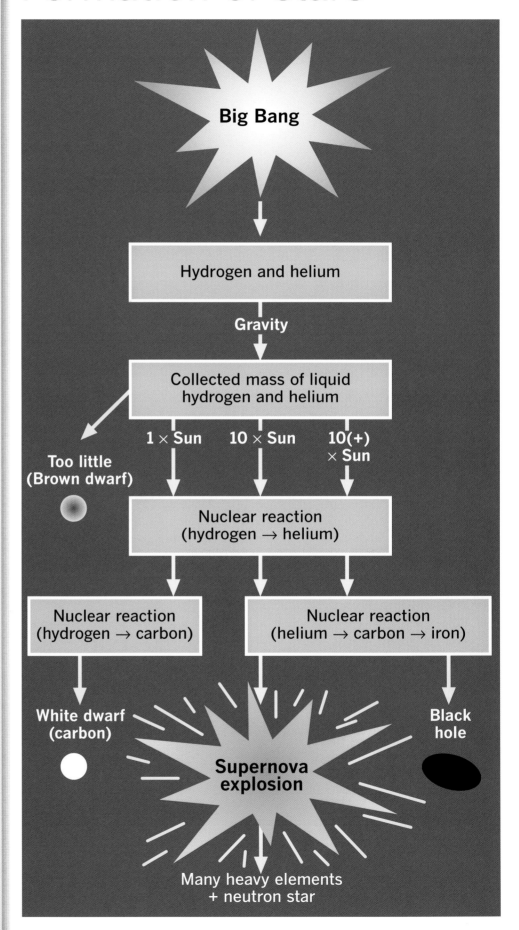

Fate of stars

1 The fate of a star the size of our sun

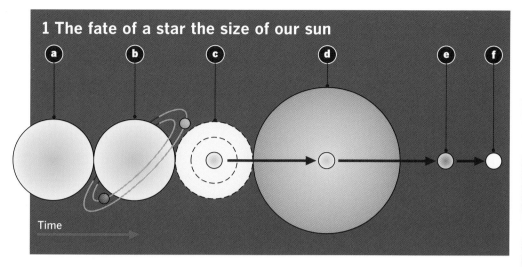

Time

2 Fate of a larger star

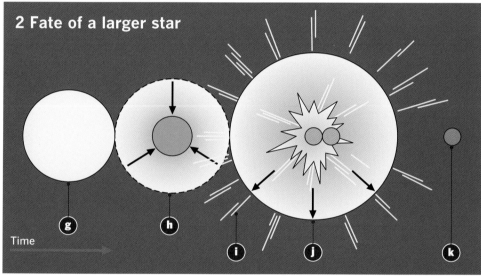

Time

3 Fate of a massive star

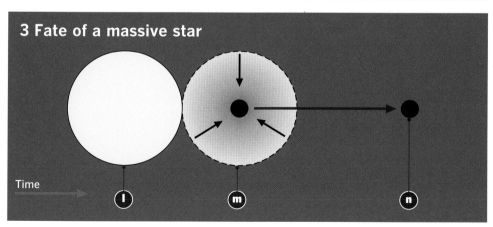

Time

a hydrogen is converted to helium
b planetary system evolves
c hydrogen runs out and helium is converted to carbon
d star cools to form a red giant
e carbon
f star evolves to form a white dwarf
g hydrogen is converted to helium and carbon, and eventually iron
h hydrogen runs out, and star undergoes gravitational collapse

i The collapsed star suddenly expands rapidly, creating a supernova explosion
j creates many different elements
k the core of the dead star becomes a neutron star
l hydrogen converted to many different elements
m hydrogen runs out, and the star collapses to form a black hole
n black hole

Fate of stars

- During most of a star's life, the outward pressure from nuclear fusion balances the pull of gravity, but as nuclear fuel is exhausted, gravity compresses the star inward and the core collapses. How and how far it collapses depends on the size of the star.

1 The fate of a star the size of our sun

- A star the size of our Sun burns hydrogen into helium until the hydrogen is exhausted and the core begins to collapse. This results in nuclear *fusion* reactions in a shell around the core. The outer shell heats up and expands to produce a *red giant*.
- Ultimately, as its nuclear reactions subside, a red giant cools and contracts. Its core becomes a very small, dense hot remnant, a *white dwarf*.

2 Fate of a larger star

- Stars with an initial mass 10 times that of our Sun go further in the nuclear fusion process until the core is mostly carbon. The fusion of carbon into larger nuclei releases a massive amount of energy. The result is a huge explosion in which the outer layers of the star are blasted out into space. This is called a *supernova*.
- After the explosion, the remaining material contracts, and the core collapses into an extraordinary dense object composed only of neutrons—a neutron star.

3 Fate of a massive star

- Stars with an initial mass of 30 times our Sun undergo a different fate altogether. The gravitational field of such stars is so powerful that material cannot escape from them. As nuclear reactions subside, all matter is pulled into the core, forming a *black hole*.

Key words

ammonia
fission
helium
hydrogen
methane

1 Birth of the solar system

- The solar system is thought to have formed about 4.6 billion years ago as a result of nuclear *fission* in the Sun.
- A nebula (cloud) of gases and dust that resulted from the explosion. flattened into a disk with a high concentration of matter at the center.

2 Formation of the inner and outer planets

- Near the Sun, where the temperature was high, volatile substances could not condense, so the inner planets (Mercury, Venus, Earth, and Mars) are dominated by rock and metal. They are smaller and more dense than those farther from the Sun.
- In the colder, outer areas of the disk, substances like *ammonia* and *methane* condensed, while *hydrogen* and *helium* remained gaseous. In this region, the planets formed (Jupiter, Saturn, Uranus, and Neptune) were gas giants.

3 Inner planets

- Inner planets consist of a light shell surrounding a dense core of metallic elements.
- Mercury, the planet closest to the Sun, has a proportionately larger core than Mars, the inner planet farthest from the Sun.

4 Outer planets

- The outer planets have low densities and are composed primarily of hydrogen and helium.
- The outer planets are huge in comparison to the inner planets.
- Jupiter and Saturn, the largest of the gas giants, contain the greatest percentages of hydrogen and helium; the smaller Uranus and Neptune contain larger fractions of water, ammonia, and methane.

The solar system

1 Birth of the solar system

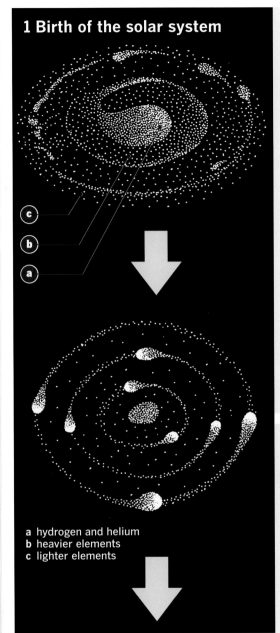

a hydrogen and helium
b heavier elements
c lighter elements

2 Formation of the inner and outer planets

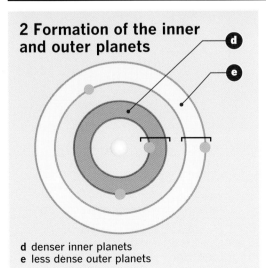

d denser inner planets
e less dense outer planets

3 Inner planets

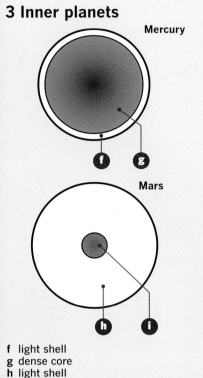

Mercury

Mars

f light shell
g dense core
h light shell
i dense core

4 Outer planets

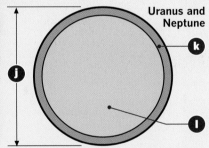

Uranus and Neptune

j diameter = 2 or 3 that of the Earth
k solid water, methane, and ammonia
l liquid water, methane, and ammonia

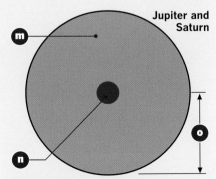

Jupiter and Saturn

m liquid hydrogen and helium
n small rocky center
o radii:
   Jupiter = 11 × radius of Earth
   Saturn = 9 × radius of Earth

Planet composition

Key words

atmosphere   oxide
carbonate   sulfate
crust
mantle
nitrate

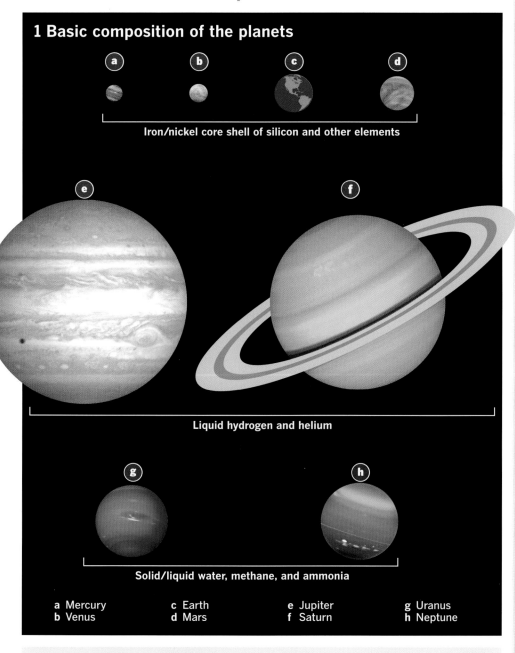

1 Basic composition of the planets

Iron/nickel core shell of silicon and other elements

Liquid hydrogen and helium

Solid/liquid water, methane, and ammonia

| a Mercury | c Earth | e Jupiter | g Uranus |
| b Venus | d Mars | f Saturn | h Neptune |

1 Basic composition of the planets

- The inner planets—Mercury, Venus, Earth, and Mars—consist of an iron–nickel core surrounded by a shell of silicon and other elements.
- The outer planets—Jupiter, Saturn, Uranus, and Neptune—consist largely of solid or liquid methane, ammonia, liquid hydrogen, and helium.
- Pluto is not included in this comparison because it is atypical of the other outer planets, and its origins are uncertain.

2 Composition of Earth

- Earth consists of a dense, solid inner core and a liquid outer core of nickel and iron. The core is surrounded by the *mantle* (a zone of dense, hot rock), and finally by the *crust*, which is the surface of Earth.
- Since most of the materials of Earth are inaccessible (the deepest drilled holes only penetrate a small distance into the crust), we can only estimate the composition of Earth by looking at the composition of the materials from which Earth formed. Meteorites provide this information.
- Oxygen is the most common element on Earth, and about one fifth of Earth's *atmosphere* is gaseous oxygen.
- Oxygen is also present in many compounds, including water (H_2O), carbon dioxide (CO_2), and silica (SiO_2), and metal salts such as *oxides*, *carbonates*, *nitrates*, and *sulfates*.

2 Composition of Earth

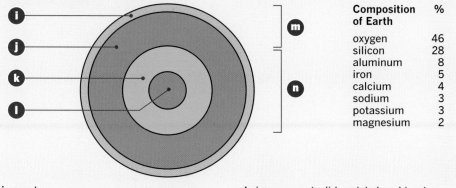

Composition of Earth	%
oxygen	46
silicon	28
aluminum	8
iron	5
calcium	4
sodium	3
potassium	3
magnesium	2

i crust
j mantle (oxygen, silicon, aluminum, iron)
k outer core (liquid – nickel and iron)

l inner core (solid – nickel and iron)
m crust, mantle, and oceans = $2/3$ of mass)
n core = $1/3$ of mass

Key words

atmosphere
carbon dioxide
chlorophyll
photosynthesis

1 Densities and radii of the planets

- The inner planets—Mercury, Venus, Earth, and Mars—are relatively small but have a higher density than the outer planets.
- The outer planets—Jupiter, Saturn, Uranus, and Neptune—are relatively large but have a lower density than the inner planets.

2 Atmospheric composition of the inner planets

- Earth's *atmosphere* was probably similar to that of Venus and Mars when the planets formed. However, the particular conditions on Earth allowed life to start and flourish. With this came drastic changes to the composition of the atmosphere. Of particular importance is the evolution of green plants.
- Green plants contain a pigment called *chlorophyll*. Plants use this pigment to trap energy from sunlight and make carbohydrates. The process is called *photosynthesis*.
- As Earth became greener, the proportion of *carbon dioxide* in the atmosphere fell until it reached the present level of about 0.04 percent.
- The green plants provided a means of turning the Sun's energy into food, which in turn, provided animals with the energy they needed to survive. Thus, animals could evolve alongside plants.
- Conditions on the two planets adjacent to Earth—Venus and Mars— were not suitable for life as we know it, and the atmospheres on these planets have remained unchanged.

Planetary density, size, and atmosphere

1 Densities and radii of the planets

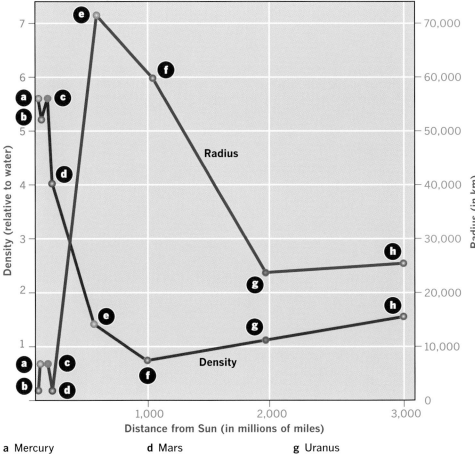

a Mercury
b Venus
c Earth

d Mars
e Jupiter
f Saturn

g Uranus
h Neptune

2 Atmospheric composition of the inner planets

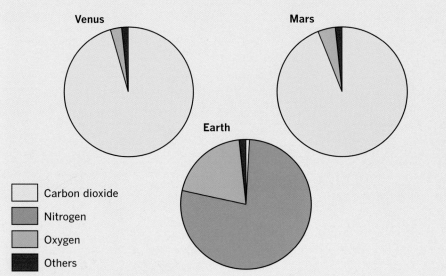

Venus

Mars

Earth

Carbon dioxide

Nitrogen

Oxygen

Others

Atomic structure

1 Principle subatomic particles

Particle	Relative atomic mass	Relative charge
Electron	$\frac{1}{1836}$	–1
Neutron	1	0
Proton	1	1

2 The atom

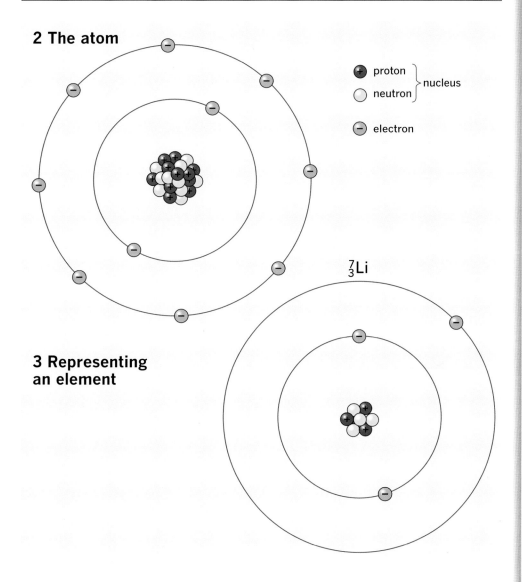

proton ⎱
neutron ⎰ nucleus

electron

$^{7}_{3}$Li

3 Representing an element

4 Isotopes

Hydrogen 1   Hydrogen 2   Hydrogen 3

Key words

atom	neutron
atomic number	nucleus
electron	proton
isotope	subatomic
mass number	particle

1 Principle subatomic particles

- An *atom* is the smallest particle of an element. It is made up of even smaller *subatomic particles*: negatively charged *electrons*, positively charged *protons*, and *neutrons*, which have no charge.

2 The atom

- An atom consists of a *nucleus* of protons and neutrons surrounded by a number of electrons.
- Most of the mass of an atom is contained in its nucleus.
- The number of protons in the nucleus is always equal to the number of electrons around the nucleus. Atoms have no overall charge.

3 Representing an element

- Elements can be represented using their *mass number*, *atomic number*, and atomic symbol:

  $^{\text{mass number}}_{\text{atomic number}}$ Symbol

- The atomic number of an atom is the number of protons in its nucleus.
- The mass number is the total number of protons and neutrons in its nucleus. Thus, an atom of one form of lithium (Li), which contains three protons and four neutrons, can be represented as:

  $^{7}_{3}$Li

4 Isotopes

- All atoms of the same element have the same atomic number; however, they may not have the same mass number because the number of neutrons may not always be the same. Atoms of an element that have different mass numbers are called isotopes. The diagram at left illustrates isotopes of hydrogen.

© Diagram Visual Information Ltd.

Key words

alpha particle
atom
atomic mass

Developing the atomic model

- At end of the 19th century, scientists thought that the *atom* was a positively charged blob with negatively charged electrons scattered throughout it. At the suggestion of British physicist Ernest Rutherford, Johannes Geiger and Earnest Marsden conducted an experiment that changed this view of the atomic model.
- Scientists had recently discovered that some elements were radioactive—they emitted particles from their nuclei as a result of nuclear instability. One type of particle, alpha radiation, is positively charged. Geiger and Marsden investigated how *alpha particles* scattered by bombarding them against thin sheets of gold, a metal with a high *atomic mass*.
- They used a tube of radon, a radioactive element, in a metal block (a) as the source of a narrow beam of alpha particles and placed a sheet of gold foil in the center of their apparatus (b). After they bombarded the sheet, they detected the pattern of alpha particle scattering by using a fluorescent screen (c) placed at the focal length of a microscope (d).
- If the existing model had been correct, all of the particles would have been found within a fraction of a degree of the beam. But Geiger and Marsden found that alpha particles were scattered at angles as large as 140°.
- From this experiment, Rutherford deduced that the positively charged alpha particles had come into the repulsive field of a highly concentrated positive charge at the center of the atom. He, therefore, concluded that an atom has a small dense nucleus in which all of the positive charge and most of the mass is concentrated. Negatively charged electrons surround the nucleus—similar to the way the planets orbit the Sun.

Geiger and Marsden's apparatus

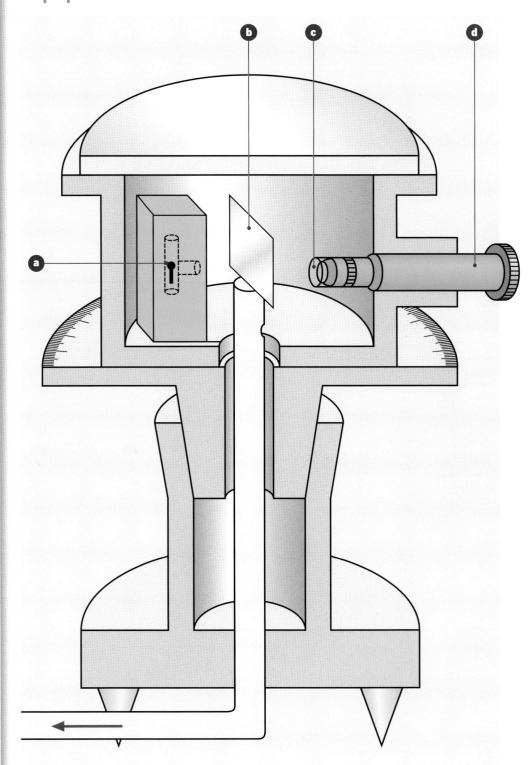

a source of alpha particles (radon tube)
b gold foil
c screen
d microscope

Investigating the electron 1

1 Maltese-Cross tube

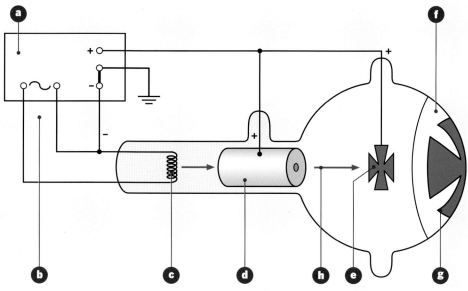

a E.h.t. supply
b low voltage
c heated filament and cathode
d anode

e Maltese-Cross (connected to anode)
g shadow
h invisible cathode rays
f fluorescent screen

2 The Perrin tube

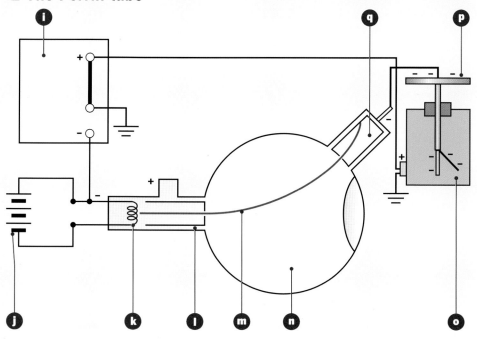

i E.h.t. supply
j 6 V supply
k cathode
l anode
m track of electron beam in magnetic field

n vacuum
o gold-leaf electroscope
p electrons are collected
q insulated metal cylinder

Key words

anode
cathode
cathode rays

electron
fluorescence

Investigating the electron

● During the last half of the nineteenth century, scientists observed that when an electric current passes through a glass tube containing a small amount of air, the air glowed. As air was removed, a patch of *fluorescence* appeared on the tube, which they called *cathode rays*. Scientists then began investigated these streams of *electrons* traveling at high speed.

1 Maltese cross tube

● In the 1880s, William Crookes experimented on cathode rays using a Maltese cross tube.
● The stream of electrons emitted by the hot *cathode* is accelerated toward the *anode*. Some are absorbed, but the majority passes through and travels along the tube. Those electrons that hit the Maltese cross are absorbed. Those electrons that miss the cross strike the screen, causing it to fluoresce with a green light.
● The result of this experiment is that a shadow of the cross is cast on the screen. This provides evidence that cathode rays travel in straight lines.

2 The Perrin tube

● In 1895 Jean Perrin devised an experiment to demonstrate that cathode rays convey negative charge.
● He constructed a cathode ray tube in which the cathode rays were accelerated through the anode, in the form of a cylinder open at both ends, into an insulated metal cylinder called a Faraday cylinder.
● This cylinder has a small opening at one end. Cathode rays enter the cylinder and build up charge, which is indicated by the electroscope. Perrin found that the electroscope had become negatively charged.
● Perrin's experiments helped to prepare the way for English physicist J. J. Thompson's work on electrons a few years later.

Key words

anode	photoelectric
cathode	effect
cathode rays	radiation
electron	

1 J.J. Thomson's cathode ray tube

- In 1897 J.J. Thomson devised an experiment with *cathode rays* that resulted in the discovery of the *electron*.
- Up to this time, it was thought that the hydrogen atom was the smallest particle in existence. Thomson demonstrated that electrons (which he called corpuscles) comprising cathode rays were nearly 2,000 times smaller in mass than the then lightest-known particle, the hydrogen ion.
- When a high voltage is placed across a pair of plates, they become charged relative to each other. The positively charged plate is the *anode*, and the negatively charged plate the *cathode*.
- Electrons pass from the surface of the cathode and accelerate toward the oppositely charged anode. The anode absorbs many electrons, but if the anode has slits, some electrons will pass through.
- The electrons travel into an evacuated tube, where they move in a straight line until striking a fluorescent screen. This screen is coated with a chemical that glows when electrons strike it.

2 Evidence of the photoelectric effect

- The *photoelectric effect* is the emission of electrons from metals upon the absorption of electromagnetic *radiation*.
- Scientists observed the effect in the nineteenth century, but they could not explain it until the development of quantum physics.
- To observe the effect, a clean zinc plate is placed in a negatively charged electroscope. The gold leaf and brass plate carry the same negative charge and repel each other.
- When ultraviolet radiation strikes the zinc plate, electrons are emitted. The negative charge on the electroscope is reduced, and the gold leaf falls.

Investigating the electron 2

1 J.J. Thomson's cathode ray tube

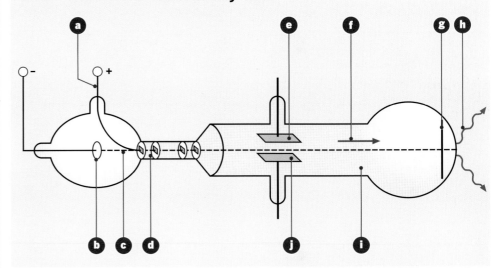

a high voltage	**f** direction of travel of the cathode rays
b cathode	**g** flourescent screen
c gas discharge provides free electrons	**h** light
d anode with slit	**i** evacuated tube
e y-deflecting plate	**j** x-deflecting plate

2 Evidence of the photoelectric effect

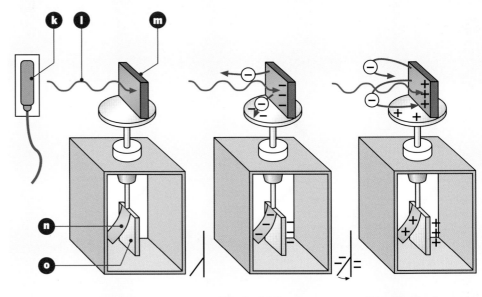

Negatively charged electroscope with zinc plate attached	**The leaf falls as electrons are ejected from the zinc plate**	**If positively charged the electroscope remains charged**

k mercury vapor lamp	**n** gold leaf
l ultraviolet light	**o** zinc plate
m brass plate	

Cathode ray oscilloscope

1 The cathode ray oscilloscope

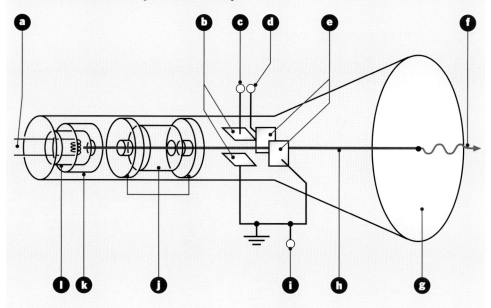

a heater
b y-deflection plates
c y-input terminal
d x-input terminal
e x-deflection plates
f light

g phosphor coating
h electron beam
i common-input terminal
j accelerating and focusing anodes
k grid
l cathode

2 Electron gun

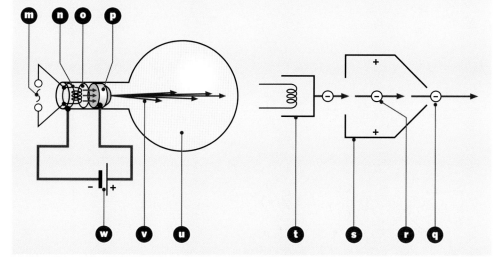

m low voltage
n heater
o cathode
p cyclindrical anode
q high speed electrons
r accelerated electrons
s anode

t cathode
u evacuated tube
v electron beam
w high voltage

Key words

anode
cathode
cathode rays

1 Cathode ray oscilloscope

● The *cathode ray* oscilloscope (CRO) is one of the most important scientific instruments ever to be developed. It is often used as a graph plotter to display a waveform showing how potential difference changes with time. The CRO has three essential parts: the electron gun, the deflecting system, and the fluorescent gun.

● The electron gun consists of a heater and *cathode*, a grid, and several *anodes*. Together these provide a stream of cathode rays. The grid is at negative potential with respect to the cathode and controls the number of electrons passing through its central hole. It is the brightness control.

● The deflecting system consists of a pair of deflecting plates across which potential differences can be applied. The Y-plates are horizontal but deflect the beam vertically. The X-plates are vertical and deflect the bean horizontally.

● A bright spot appears on the fluorescent screen where the beam hits it.

2 Electron gun

● When a current passes through the heater, electrons are emitted from the surface of the cathode and attracted towards an oppositely charged anode. Some will be absorbed by the anode, while others pass through and are accelerated, forming a stream of high-speed electrons.

Key words

electron
radiation

Measuring the charge on the electron

- In the early part of the 20th century, American physicist Robert Millikan constructed an experiment to accurately determine the electric charge carried by a single *electron*.
- Millikan's apparatus consisted of two horizontal plates about 20 cm in diameter and 1.5 cm apart, with a small hole in the center of the upper plate.
- At the beginning of the experiment, an atomizer sprayed a fine mist of oil on to the upper plate.
- As a result of gravity, a droplet would pass through the hole in the plate into a chamber that was ionized by *radiation*. Electrons from the air attached themselves to the droplet, causing it to acquire a negative charge. A light source illuminated the droplet, making it appear as a pinpoint of light. Millikan then measured its downward velocity by timing its fall through a known distance.
- Millikan measured hundreds of droplets and found that the charge on them was always a simple multiple of a basic unit, 1.6×10^{-19} coulomb. From this he concluded that the charge on an electron was numerically 1.6×10^{-19} coulomb.

Measuring the charge on the electron

Millikan's apparatus

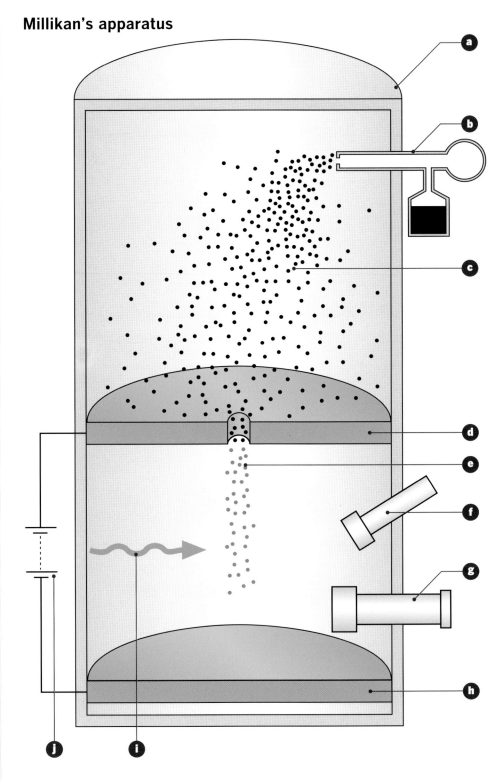

a sealed container
b atomizer
c oil droplets
d charged metal plate (+)
e charged oil droplets

f light source
g viewing microscope
h charged metal plate (−)
i ionizing radiation
j power source

Size and motion of molecules

Key words

Brownian motion
diffusion
molecule

1 Estimating the size of a molecule

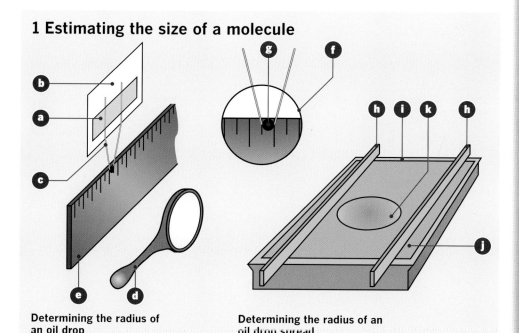

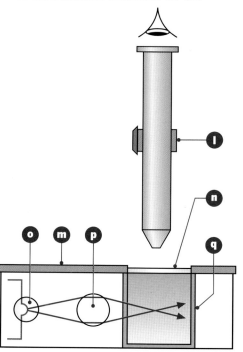

Determining the radius of an oil drop

Determining the radius of an oil drop spread

2 Brownian motion in air

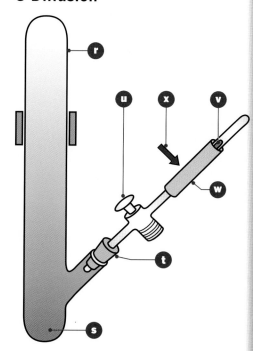

3 Diffusion

a tape	**i** wax-coated tray
b cardboard	**j** lycopodium powder
c fine stainless steel wire	**k** oil patch
d magnifying glass	**l** microscope
e 1/2 mm scale	**m** removable lid
f view through magnifying glass	**n** window
g oil drop	**o** lamp
h waxed sticks	**p** glass rod for converging light

q glass smoke chamber	
r glass diffusion tube	
s liquid bromine capsule	
t rubber stopper	
u tap	
v bromine capsule	
w rubber tube	
x point at which pressure is applied to break capsule	

1 Estimating the size of a molecule

- Scientists can estimate the size of a *molecule* by dividing the volume of a sphere by the volume of a cylinder.
- In the example in the diagram, the volume of a spherical oil drop of radius, r_s, is given by:

$$\frac{4 \times \pi \times r_s^3}{3}$$

- When the oil drop spreads across the surface of water, it takes the shape of a cylinder of radius, r_c, and thickness, h. The volume of such a cylinder is:

$$\pi \times r_c^2 \times h$$

- If we assume that the layer of oil is one molecule thick, then h gives the size of an oil molecule.
- When spread on water the drop of oil will have the same volume therefore:

$$h = \frac{4 \times \pi \times r_s^3}{3} \times \frac{1}{\pi \times r_c^2}$$

$$h = \frac{4\,r_s^3}{3\,r_c^2}$$

2 Brownian motion in air

- *Brownian motion* is the random motion of particles through a liquid or gas. Scientists can observe this by using a glass smoke chamber.
- Smoke consists of large particles that can be seen using a microscope.
- In the smoke chamber, the smoke particles move around randomly due to collisions with air particles.

3 Diffusion

- *Diffusion* is the spreading out of one substance through another due to the random motion of particles.
- The diagram illustrates how scientists use a diffusion tube to observe this. Initially the color of the substance is strongest at the bottom of the tube.
- After a period of time, as a result of diffusion, the particles of the substance mix with air particles, and the color becomes uniform down the length of the tube.

© Diagram Visual Information Ltd.

Key words

anode	mole
Avogadro's	
constant	
electrolysis	
Faraday constant	

Defining Avogadro's constant

- *Avogadro's constant* is the number of particles in a *mole* of a substance. It equals 6.023×10^{23} mol^{-1}.
- It is **F**, the *Faraday constant*—96,500 coulombs per mole, the amount of electric charge of one mole of electrons—divided by 1.60×10^{-19} coulomb—the charge on one electron (expressed as **e**).
- Thus, the Avogadro constant, **N**, is given by: $N = \dfrac{F}{e}$

or:

$$\frac{96,500}{1.60 \times 10^{-19}} = 6.023 \times 10^{23} \text{ mol}^{-1}$$

Determining the Constant

- The number of molecules in one mole of substance can be determined by using electrochemistry.
- During *electrolysis*, current (electron flow) over time is measured in an electrolytic cell (see diagram). The number of atoms in a weighed sample is then related to the current to calculate Avogadro's constant.

Illustrating the Procedure

- The diagram illustrates the electrolysis of copper sulfate. To calculate Avogadro's constant, the researcher weighs the rod to be used as the *anode* before submerging the two copper rods in copper sulfate. She then connects the rods to a power supply and an ammeter (an instrument used to measure electric current). She measures and records the current at regular intervals and calculates the average amperage (the unit of electric current). Once she turns off the current, she weighs the anode to see how much mass was lost. Using the figures for anode mass lost, average current, and duration of the electrolysis, she calculates Avogadro's constant.

Determination of Avogadro's constant

Determination of Avogadro's constant

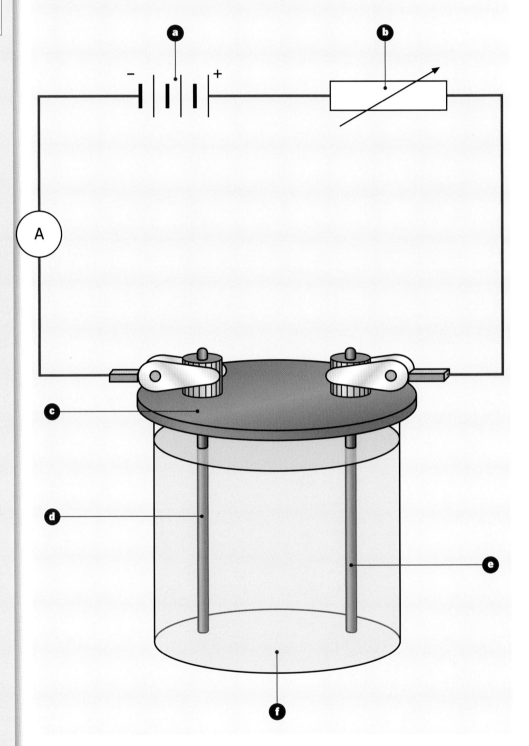

a power supply with ammeter
b rheostat
c hardboard or wooden electrode holder
d copper rod cathode
e copper rod anode
f copper sulfate solution

The mole

1 Defining a mole

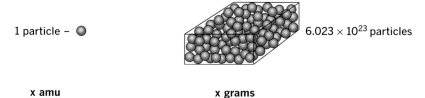

1 particle – ●

x amu

6.023 × 10²³ particles

x grams

2 Moles of gas

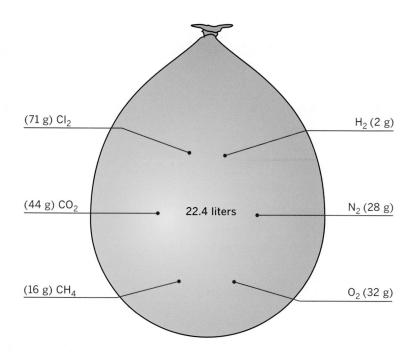

(71 g) Cl₂

H₂ (2 g)

(44 g) CO₂

22.4 liters

N₂ (28 g)

(16 g) CH₄

O₂ (32 g)

3 Molarity

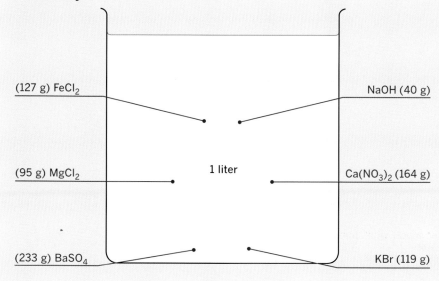

(127 g) FeCl₂

NaOH (40 g)

(95 g) MgCl₂

1 liter

Ca(NO₃)₂ (164 g)

(233 g) BaSO₄

KBr (119 g)

1 Defining a mole

- Because *atoms*, *ions*, and *molecules* have very small masses, it is impossible to count or weigh them individually. As a result, scientists use *moles* in a chemical reaction.
- A mole is the amount of substance that contains as many elementary entities (atoms, molecules, ions, any group of particles) as there are atoms in exactly 0.012 kilogram of carbon-12. This quantity is Avogadro's constant $(6.023 \times 10^{23} \text{ mol}^{-1})$.
- The significance of this number is that it scales the mass of a particle in atomic mass units (amu) exactly into grams (g).
- Chemical equations usually imply that the quantities are in moles.

2 Moles of gas

- One mole of any gas occupies 22.4 liters at standard temperature and pressure, (which is 0 °C and atmospheric pressure).
- The diagram shows the mass in grams of one mole of the following gases: chlorine (Cl_2), carbon dioxide (CO_2), methane (CH_4), hydrogen (H_2), nitrogen (N_2), and oxygen (O_2).

3 Molarity

- *Molarity* is concerned with the concentration of a solution. It indicates the number of particles in 1 liter of solution.
- A 1 molar solution contains 1 mole of a substance dissolved in water or some other solvent to make 1 liter of solution.
- The diagram shows the mass in grams of one mole of the following substances: iron(II) chloride ($FeCl_2$), magnesium chloride ($MgCl_2$), barium sulfate ($BaSO_4$), sodium hydroxide ($NaOH$), calcium nitrate ($Ca(NO_3)_2$), and potassium bromide (KBr).

Key words

atomic emission spectrum
wavelength
infrared
spectrum
ultraviolet

Atomic spectrum

● The *atomic emission spectrum* of an element is the amount of electromagnetic radiation it emits when excited. This pattern of wavelengths is a discrete line *spectrum*, not a continuous spectrum. It is unique to each element.

Investigating hydrogen

● Toward the end of the nineteenth century, scientists discovered that when excited in its gaseous state, an element produces a unique spectral pattern of brightly colored lines. Hydrogen is the simplest element and, therefore, was the most studied. Hydrogen has three distinctively observable lines in the visible spectrum—red, blue/cyan, and violet.

Series

● In 1885 Swiss mathematician and physicist Johannes Jakob Balmer proposed a mathematical relationship for lines in the visible part of the hydrogen emission spectrum that is now known as the Balmer series.
● The series in the *ultraviolet* region at a shorter *wavelength* than the Balmer series is known as the Lyman series.
● The series in the *infrared* region at the longer wavelength than the Balmer series is known as the Paschen series.
● The Brackett series and the Pfund series are at the far infrared end of the hydrogen emission series.

Atomic emission spectrum: hydrogen

Emission spectrum in the near ultra-violet and visible Balmer series

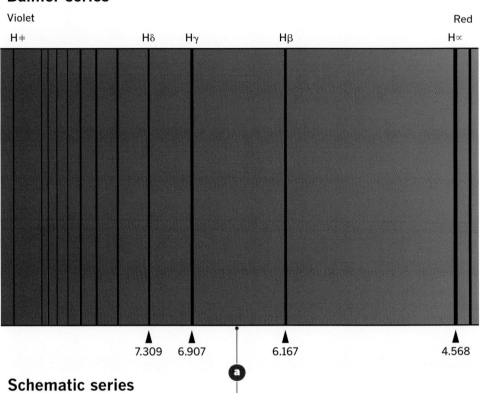

a frequency (×10¹⁴Hz)

Schematic series

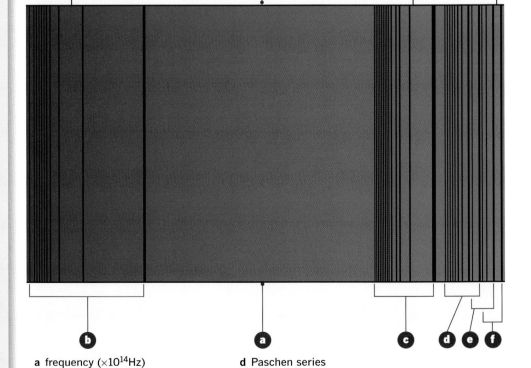

a frequency ($\times 10^{14}$Hz)
b Lyman series
c Balmer series
d Paschen series
e Bracket series
f Pfund series

Energy levels: hydrogen atom

Energy-level schematic

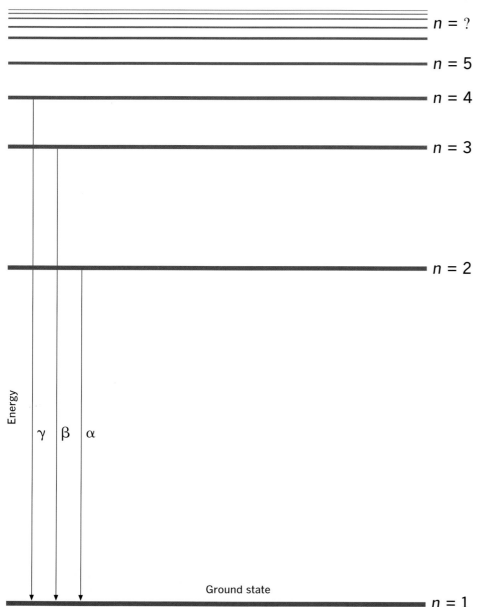

Line spectrum

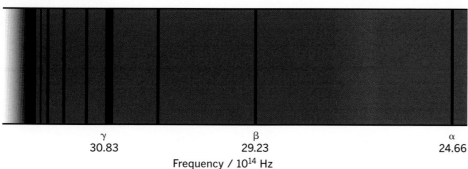

© Diagram Visual Information Ltd.

Key words

ground state
orbital
quantum number
shell
ultraviolet

Energy levels

- Electrons are arranged in definite energy levels (also called *shells* or *orbitals*), at a considerable distance from the nucleus.
- Electrons jump between the orbits by emitting or absorbing energy.
- The energy emitted or absorbed is equal to the difference in energy between the orbits.

Energy levels of hydrogen

- The graph shows the energy levels for the hydrogen atom. Each level is described by a *quantum number* (labeled by the integer **n**).
- The shell closest to the nucleus has the lowest energy level. It is generally termed the *ground state*. The states farther from the nucleus have successively more energy.

Transition from n level to ground state

- Transition from **n=2** to the ground state, **n=1**:
  Frequency =**24.66 x 10^14 Hz**
- Transition from **n=3** to the ground state, **n=1**:
  Frequency =**29.23 x 10^14 Hz**
- Transition from **n=4** to the ground state, **n=1**:
  Frequency =**30.83 x 10^14 Hz**

Line spectrum

- This radiation is in the *ultraviolet* region of the electromagnetic spectrum and cannot be seen by the human eye.

Key words

fluorescence
luminescence
phosphorescence

1 Luminescence

- *Luminescence* is the emission of light caused by an effect other than heat.
- Luminescence occurs when a substance is stimulated by radiation and subsequently emits visible light.
- The incident radiation excites electrons, and as the electrons return to their ground state, they emit visible light.
- If the electrons remain in their excited state and emit light over a period of time, the phenomenon is called *phosphorescence*.
- If the electrons in a substance return to the ground state immediately after excitation, the phenomenon is called *fluorescence*.

2 Fluorescence

- In this diagram, a fluorescent light tube contains mercury vapor at low pressure. Electrons are released from hot filaments at each end of the tube and collide with the mercury atoms, exciting the electrons in the mercury atoms to higher energy levels. As the electrons fall back to lower energy states, photons of ultraviolet light are emitted.
- The ultraviolet photons collide with atoms of a fluorescent coating on the inside of the tube. The electrons in these atoms are excited and then return to lower energy levels, emitting visible light.

Luminescence

1 Luminescence

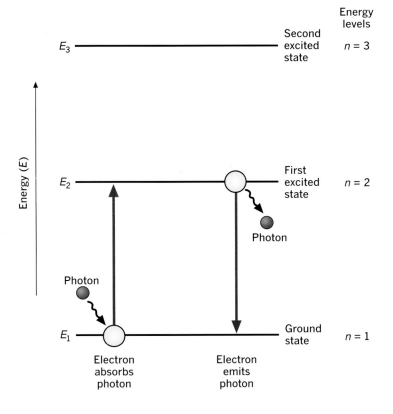

2 Fluorescence

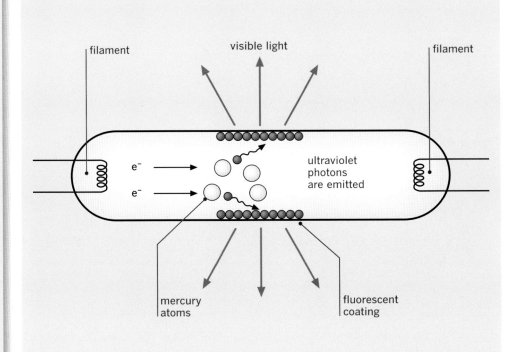

Organizing the elements

1 Antoine Lavoisier

Group 1	Group 2	Group 3	Group 4
heat	sulfur	copper	lime
light	phosphorus	tin	baryta
oxygen		lead	magnesia
nitrogen		zinc	alumina
			silica

2 Johann Dobereiner

Triad			Relative atomic mass		
Li	Na	K	7	23	39
S	Se	Te	32	79	128
Cl	Br	I	35.5	80	127
Ca	Sr	Ba	40	88	137

3 John Newlands

H	Li	Be	B	C	N	O
1	2	3	4	5	6	7
F	Na	Mg	Al	Si	P	S
8	9	10	11	12	13	14
Cl	K	Ca	Cr	Ti	Mn	Fe
15	16	17	18	19	20	21

4 Lothar Meyer

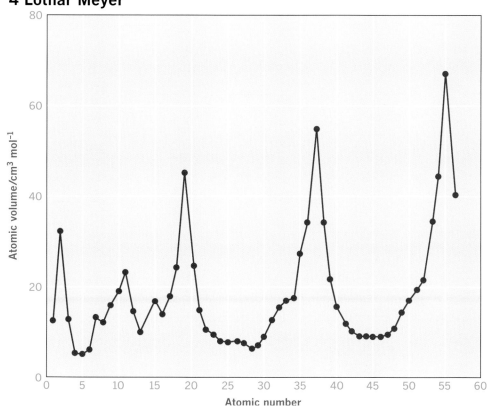

Key words

atomic mass
atomic volume
element

1 Antoine Lavoisier
- In 1789, French chemist Antoine Lavoisier organized what he believed were the *elements* into four groups: Group 1 gases, Group 2 non-metals, Group 3 metals, and Group 4 earths.

2 Johann Dobereiner
- In 1817, German chemist Johann Dobereiner noticed that the *atomic mass* of strontium was about half way between that of calcium and barium. After further study, he found that he could organize other elements into similar groups based on the same relationship to each other. He called these groups triads. Subsequently, scientists attempted to arrange all of the known elements into triads.

3 John Newlands
- In 1864, English chemist John Newlands noticed that if the elements were arranged in increasing order of atomic mass, the eighth element after any given one had similar properties. He likened this to an octave of music and called the regularity the "law of octaves."
- Newlands's arrangement worked well for the first 17 elements but broke down thereafter. Consequently, it was not well received by other scientists.

4 Lothar Meyer
- In 1870, German chemist Lothar Meyer plotted a graph of *atomic volume* against atomic mass.
- He found a pattern in which elements of similar properties appeared in similar positions on the graph.

The periodic table

1 Mendeleyev's periodic table

- The modern *periodic table* is based on that developed by Russian chemist Dmitry Mendeleyev in the 1860s.
- He arranged the *elements* in order of increasing *atomic mass*. He called the horizontal rows *periods* and the vertical columns *groups*. He grouped the elements on the basis of their properties.
- Mendeleyev made a separate group for those elements that did not appear to fit the pattern. He also left spaces where there was no known element that fit the pattern and made predictions about the missing elements.
- There were some problems with Mendeleyev's table. For example, iodine was placed after tellurium on the basis of its chemistry, even though its atomic mass was lower than tellurium. Also, there was no obvious place for the *noble gases*. These problems were subsequently resolved when, in 1914, English physicist Henry Moseley showed that the elements could be arranged in a pattern on the basis of their *atomic number*.

2 The modern periodic table

- Metals occupy positions to the left and center, while non-metals are found to the right. Hydrogen is the exception to this pattern. The atomic structure of hydrogen would indicate that it belongs at the top left of the table; however, it is a non-metal and has very different properties from the *group 1* elements.

1 Part of Mendeleyev's periodic table

Period	Group							
	I	II	III	IV	V	VI	VII	VIII
1	H							
2	Li	Be	B	C	N	O	F	
3	Na	Mg	Al	Si	P	S	Cl	
4	K	Ca	*	Ti	V	Cr	Mn	Fe Co Ni
	Cu	Zn	*	*	As	Se	Br	
	Rb	Sr	Y	Zr	Nb	Mo	*	Ru Rh Pd
5	Ag	Cd	In	Sn	Sb	Te	I	

Spaces were left for elements that had not been discovered. They were candium, gallium, germanium, and technetium.

2 Modern Periodic Table

Metals

Semi-metals

Non-metals

1 H																	2 He
3 Li	4 Be											5 B	6 C	7 N	8 O	9 F	10 Ne
11 Na	12 Mg											13 Al	14 Si	15 P	16 S	17 Cl	18 Ar
19 K	20 Ca	21 Sc	22 Ti	23 V	24 Cr	25 Mn	26 Fe	27 Co	28 Ni	29 Cu	30 Zn	31 Ga	32 Ge	33 As	34 Se	35 Br	36 Kr
37 Rb	38 Sr	39 Y	40 Zr	41 Nb	42 Mo	43 Tc	44 Ru	45 Rh	46 Pd	47 Ag	48 Cd	49 In	50 Sn	51 Sb	52 Te	53 I	54 Xe
55 Cs	56 Ba	57- 71	72 Hf	73 Ta	74 W	75 Re	76 Os	77 Ir	78 Pt	79 Au	80 Hg	81 Tl	82 Pb	83 Bi	84 Po	85 At	86 Rn
87 Fr	88 Ra	89- 103	104 Rf	105 Db	106 Sg	107 Bh	108 Hs	109 Mt	110 Ds	111 Rg	112 Uub	113 Uut	114 Uuq	115 Uup	116 Uuh		

57 La	58 Ce	59 Pr	60 Nd	61 Pm	62 Sm	63 Eu	64 Gd	65 Tb	66 Dy	67 Ho	68 Er	69 Tm	70 Yb	71 Lu
89 Ac	90 Th	91 Pa	92 U	93 Np	94 Pu	95 Am	96 Cm	97 Bk	98 Cf	99 Es	100 Fm	101 Md	102 No	103 Lr

First ionization energies of the elements

Key words

electron	lanthanide series
element	mole
group 1	nucleus
ion	period
ionization energy	shell

The first ionization energies of the elements, arranged by period (1–6) and group, with values given below each element symbol:

Period	1	2	(transition metals)										13	14	15	16	17	18
1	H 1310																	He 2370
2	Li 520	Be 900											B 800	C 1090	N 1400	O 1310	F 1680	Ne 2080
3	Na 500	Mg 740											Al 580	Si 790	P 1010	S 1000	Cl 1250	Ar 1520
4	K 420	Ca 590	Sc 630	Ti 660	V 650	Cr 650	Mn 720	Fe 760	Co 760	Ni 740	Cu 750	Zn 910	Ga 580	Ge 760	As 950	Se 940	Br 1140	Kr 1350
5	Rb 400	Sr 550	Y 620	Zr 660	Nb 660	Mo 680	Tc 700	Ru 710	Rh 720	Pd 800	Ag 730	Cd 870	In 560	Sn 710	Sb 830	Te 870	I 1010	Xe 1170
6	Cs 380	Ba 500	La 540	Hf 680	Ta 760	W 770	Re 760	Os 840	Ir 880	Pt 870	Au 890	Hg 1010	Tl 590	Pb 720	Bi 700	Po 810	At	Rn

First ionization energy

- The first *ionization energy* of an element is the energy needed to remove a single *electron* from 1 *mole* of atoms of the *element* in the gaseous state, in order to form 1 mole of positively charged *ions*.
- Reading down *group 1*, there is a decrease in the first ionization energies. This can be explained by considering the electronic configuration of the elements in the group. Reading down, the outer electron is further from the positively charged *nucleus*, and there is an increasing number of complete *shells* of inner electrons, which to some extent, shield the outer electron from the nucleus. The result is that less energy is needed to remove the outer electron. A similar situation exists in other groups.

Increase in ionization energy

- There is a general increase in the first ionization energies across a *period*. This increase is due to electrons at the same main energy level being attracted by an increasing nuclear charge. This charge is caused by the increasing number of protons in the nucleus. The increase makes it progressively more difficult to remove an electron; thus more energy is needed.
- The diagram illustrates this principle using the first six periods minus the *lanthanide series*.

Elements whose ionization energies are the greatest in their period

He	Helium
Ne	Neon
Ar	Argon
Kr	Krypton
Xe	Xenon
Rn	Radon

Key words

ionization energy
noble gases
period
periodicity
shell

First ionization energies

- The graph shows a repeating pattern, or *periodicity*, corresponding to reading down the *periods* of the periodic table.
- Within a period, it becomes increasingly more difficult to remove an electron due to the increasing nuclear charge. The graph peaks at the last element in each period, which is a *noble gas* (labeled on the graph).
- The noble gases have complete outer *shells* of electrons. This electron configuration provides great stability, and consequently, the noble gases are very unreactive. Some are totally unreactive. The first *ionization energies* of the noble gases are very high.

Variation of first ionization energy

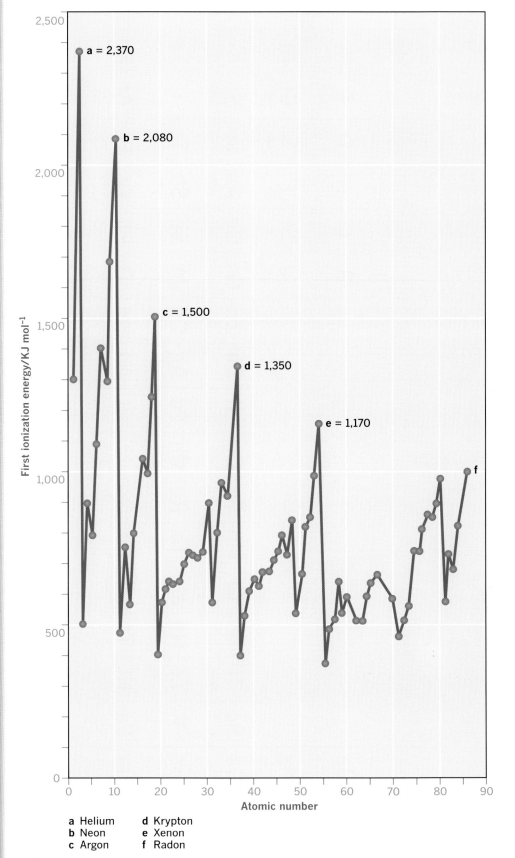

a Helium   d Krypton
b Neon   e Xenon
c Argon   f Radon

Melting points of the elements °C

Period	1	2	3	4	5	6	7	8	9	10	11	12	13	14	15	16	17	18
1	H −259																	He −270
2	Li 181	Be 1278											B 2300	C 3700	N −270	O −218	F −220	Ne −248
3	Na 98	Mg 649											Al 660	Si 1410	P 44	S 119	Cl −101	Ar −189
4	K 63	Ca 839	Sc 1541	Ti 1660	V 1890	Cr 1857	Mn 1244	Fe 1535	Co 1495	Ni 1455	Cu 1083	Zn 420	Ga 30	Ge 937	As 817	Se 217	Br −7	Kr −157
5	Rb 39	Sr 769	Y 1522	Zr 1852	Nb 2467	Mo 2610	Tc 2172	Ru 2310	Rh 1966	Pd 1554	Ag 962	Cd 321	In 156	Sn 232	Sb 631	Te 450	I 114	Xe −112
6	Cs 29	Ba 725	La 921	Hf 2227	Ta 2996	W 3410	Re 3180	Os 2700	Ir 2410	Pt 1772	Au 1064	Hg −39	Tl 304	Pb 328	Bi 271	Po 254	At 304	Rn −71

Key words

group	noble gases
group 1	period
lanthanide series	solid
liquid	transition metals
melting point	

Melting points

- The *melting point* is the point at which the solid and *liquid* phase of a substance is in equilibrium at a given pressure.
- In a *solid*, the particles are held in a rigid structure by the strong forces of attraction that exist between them. They vibrate but cannot move position. When a solid is heated to its melting point, the particles gain sufficient energy to overcome these forces of attraction, and the particles are able to move position.
- Within *groups* of metallic elements, the melting point decreases down the group. The converse is true for non-metals, where the melting point increases down the group.
- Reading across *periods* 2 and 3, the elements follow a pattern of metallic structure, giant covalent structure, and simple covalent structure. The melting point increases until a maximum is reached with the element that exists as a giant covalent structure.
- The more reactive metals in *group 1* are soft and have low melting points. *Transition metals* (elements that have an incomplete inner electron structure) are generally harder and have higher melting points.
- The *noble gases* exist as single atoms with only weak forces of attraction between them. Consequently, their melting points are very low.
- Using the first six periods minus the *lanthanide series*, the diagram highlights the element with the highest melting point in a period.

Elements whose melting points are the greatest in their period

C	Carbon
Si	Silicon
V	Vanadium
Mo	Molybdenum
W	Tungsten

© Diagram Visual Information Ltd.

Key words

element
melting point
period
periodicity
periodic table

Melting points

- The graph shows a repeating pattern, or *periodicity*, corresponding to reading down the *periods* of the *periodic table*.
- The structure of periods 2 and 3 with regard to the nature of the *elements*, is:
  Elements having a metallic structure: *melting point* increasing
  Elements having a giant covalent structure: melting point maximum
  Elements having a simple covalent structure: melting point decreasing
- In general, the melting point increases at the start of these periods, corresponding to elements that have metallic structure. The melting point is at maximum for elements that have a giant covalent structure (labeled on the graph). After this, the melting point rapidly falls to low values, corresponding to those elements that have a simple covalent structure.

Variation of melting points

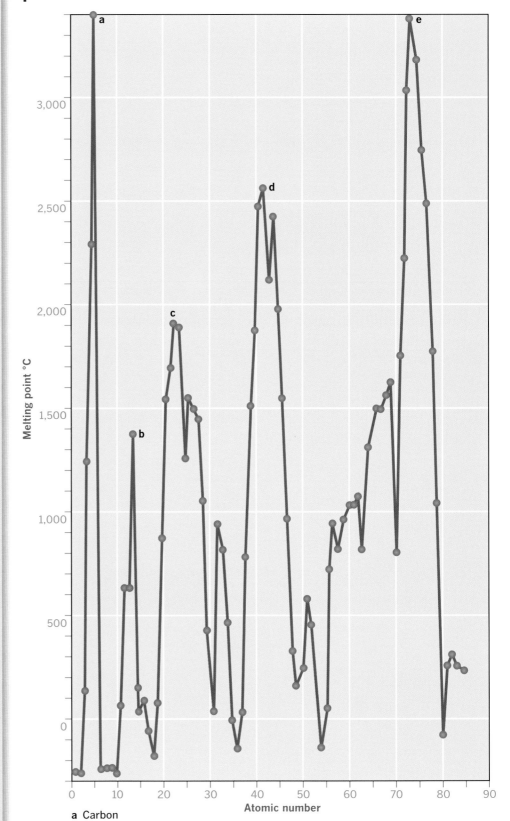

a Carbon
b Silicon
c Vanadium
d Molybdenum
e Tungsten

Boiling points of the elements °C

Period	1	2											13	14	15	16	17	18
1	H −253																	He −269
2	Li 1342	Be 2970											B 2550	C 4827	N −196	O −183	F −188	Ne −246
3	Na 883	Mg 1107											Al 2467	Si 2620	P 280	S 445	Cl −35	Ar −186
4	K 760	Ca 1484	Sc 2831	Ti 3287	V 3380	Cr 2670	Mn 1962	Fe 2750	Co 2870	Ni 2730	Cu 2567	Zn 907	Ga 2403	Ge 2830	As 613	Se 685	Br 59	Kr −152
5	Rb 686	Sr 1384	Y 3338	Zr 4377	Nb 4742	Mo 5560	Tc 4877	Ru 3900	Rh 3727	Pd 2970	Ag 2212	Cd 765	In 2080	Sn 2260	Sb 1750	Te 990	I 184	Xe
6	Cs 669	Ba 1640	La 3457	Hf 4602	Ta 5427	W 5420	Re 5627	Os 5297	Ir 4130	Pt 3827	Au 3080	Hg 357	Tl 1457	Pb 1740	Bi 1560	Po 962	At 337	Rn −62

Boiling points

- The *boiling point* is the temperature at which a *liquid* becomes a *gas*.
- The particles in a liquid are held together by the strong forces of attraction that exist between them. The particles vibrate and are able to move around, but they are held closely together. When a liquid is heated to its boiling point, the particles gain *kinetic energy*, moving faster and faster. Eventually, they gain sufficient energy to break away from each other and exist separately. There is a large increase in the volume of any substance going from a liquid to a gas.
- Within *groups* of metallic elements, the boiling point decreases down the group. The converse is true for non-metals: the melting point increases down the group.
- The more reactive metals in *group 1* have relatively low boiling points. *Transition metals* generally have very high boiling points.
- The *noble gases* exist as single atoms with only weak forces of attraction between them. Consequently, their boiling points are very low because it takes relatively little energy to overcome these forces.
- Using the first six periods minus the *lanthanide series*, the diagram highlights the element with the highest boiling point in a period.

Elements whose boiling points are the greatest in their period

C	Carbon
Si	Silicon
V	Vanadium
Mo	Molybdenum
Re	Rhenium

Key words

boiling point
gas
group 1
group 2
transition metals

Variation of boiling point

● The majority of non-metallic elements are *gases* at room temperature and atmospheric pressure. Most non-metallic elements have simple covalent structures and have very low *boiling points*.

● Elements with metallic and giant covalent structures have very high boiling points (see diagram). The boiling points of *transition metals* are generally much higher than those of the *group 1* and *group 2* metals.

Variation of boiling points

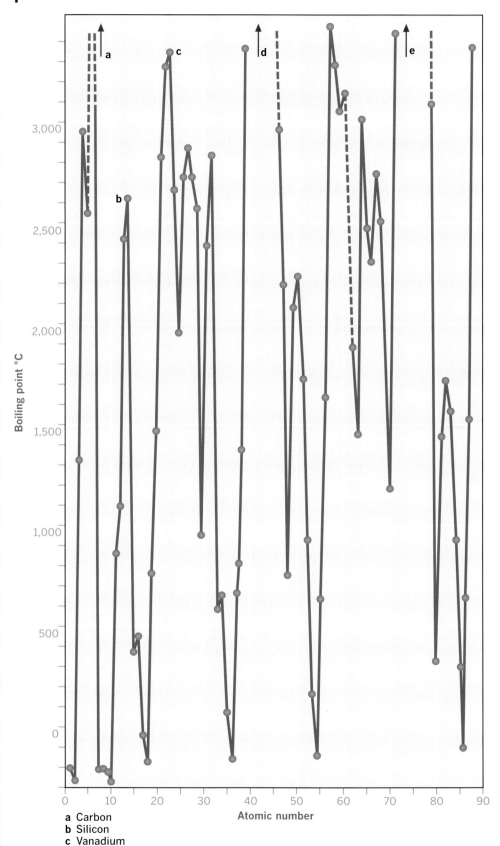

a Carbon
b Silicon
c Vanadium
d Molybdenum
e Rhenium

Atomic volumes of the elements

Key words

atomic mass	group 8
atomic volume	lanthanide series
density	mole
element	noble gases
group	period

Period	1	2	3	4	5	6	7	8	9	10	11	12	13	14	15	16	17	18
1	H 14.1																	He 31.8
2	Li 13.0	Be 4.9											B 4.3	C 5.4	N 17.3	O 14.0	F 17.1	Ne 16.8
3	Na 23.7	Mg 14.0											Al 10.0	Si 11.6	P 16.9	S 15.5	Cl 18.7	Ar 24.2
4	K 44.9	Ca 26.0	Sc 14.7	Ti 10.6	V 8.9	Cr 7.3	Mn 7.4	Fe 7.1	Co 6.6	Ni 6.6	Cu 7.1	Zn 9.2	Ga 11.8	Ge 13.3	As 13.1	Se 16.5	Br 25.6	Kr 32.2
5	Rb 55.7	Sr 34.0	Y 16.1	Zr 14.2	Nb 10.9	Mo 9.4	Tc 8.5	Ru 8.1	Rh 8.3	Pd 8.8	Ag 10.3	Cd 13.0	In 15.8	Sn 16.4	Sb 18.2	Te 20.4	I 25.6	Xe 42.9
6	Cs 71.0	Ba 39.2	La 22.6	Hf 13.5	Ta 10.9	W 9.6	Re 8.9	Os 8.5	Ir 8.6	Pt 9.1	Au 10.2	Hg 14.8	Tl 17.2	Pb 18.3	Bi 21.4	Po 22.23	At	Rn 50.5

Atomic volume

- The *atomic volume* is the volume of one *mole* of the atoms of an *element*. It can be found by dividing the *atomic mass* of one mole of atoms by the density of the element:

$$\text{Atomic volume} = \frac{\text{Atomic mass}}{\text{Density}}$$

- Since there are 6.023×10^{23} atoms per mole of atoms, it would seem possible to use the atomic volume to calculate the volume of a single atom, and thus its radius. However there are two problems with doing this. First, the state of an element, and therefore its density, changes with temperature and pressure. Second, using the atomic volume to calculate the volume of a single atom assumes that an element consists of atoms that are not bonded to each other. This is true only of the *group 8* elements (*noble gases*). For these reasons, it is not possible to consider the volume of an atom in isolation, but only as part of the structure of an element.
- In general, atomic volume increases down a *group*. Across a *period*, it decreases and then increases.
- The diagram highlights the element with the highest atomic volume in the first six periods (minus the *lanthanide series*).

Elements with peak atomic volumes

He	Helium
K	Potassium
Rb	Rubidium
Cs	Cesium
Rn	Radon

Key words

atomic mass
atomic number
atomic volume
periodicity

Periodicity

● As early as the Middle Ages, scientists recognized that elements could be differentiated by their properties and that these physical and chemical properties were periodic.

● The German chemist Lothar Meyer demonstrated *periodicity* by plotting *atomic volumes* against atomic weights (the term *atomic mass* is now used).

● This periodicity is better shown by plotting atomic volumes against *atomic number*.

● You can see periodicity most clearly by the pattern between potassium (b) and rubidium (c), and between rubidium (c) and cesium (d) in the diagram. These correspond to the changing values across period 4 and period 5, respectively.

Variation of atomic volumes

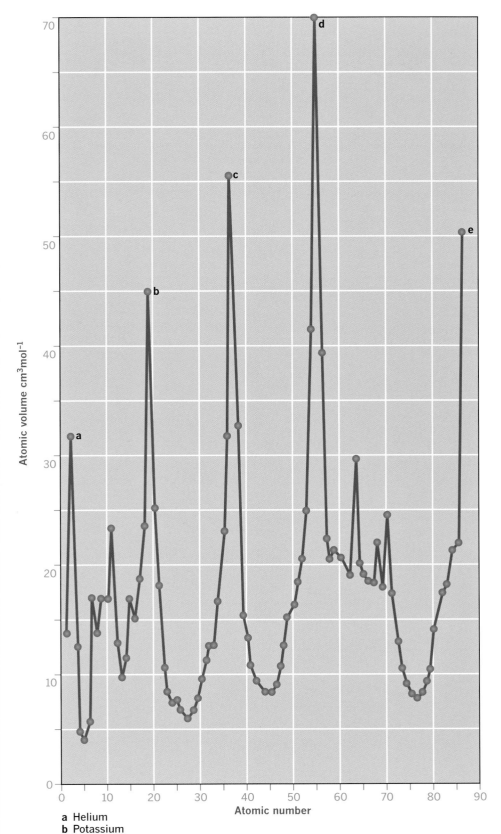

a Helium
b Potassium
c Rubidium
d Cesium
e Radon

Atomic mass

1 Carbon-12

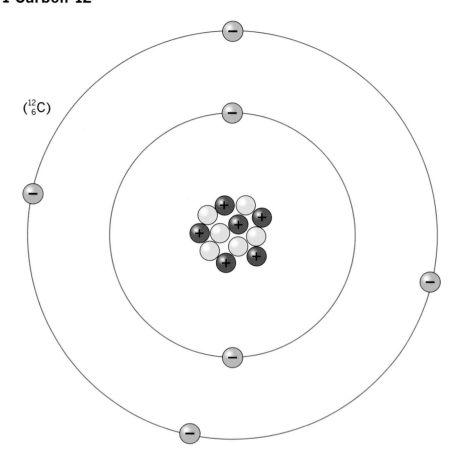

$(^{12}_{6}C)$

2 Lithium

Isotope		Natural abundance
Lithium-6	$(^{6}_{3}Li)$	7.5%
Lithium-7	$(^{7}_{3}Li)$	92.5%

The relative atomic mass of lithium is given by:

$$\frac{(6 \times 7.5) + (7 \times 92.5)}{100} = 6.925$$

3 Chlorine

Isotope		Natural abundance
Chlorine-35	$(^{35}_{17}Cl)$	75.77%
Chlorine-37	$(^{37}_{17}Cl)$	24.23%

The relative atomic mass of lithiumis given by:

$$\frac{(35 \times 75.77) + (37 \times 24.23)}{100} = 35.4846$$

Key words

atomic mass
isotope

1 Carbon-12
- To compare the masses of different atoms accurately, scientists need a standard mass against which all other masses can be calculated. Masses are given relative to this standard.
- The *isotope* carbon-12 is used as the standard. On this scale, atoms of carbon-12 are given a mass of exactly 12. The *atomic masses* of all other atoms are given relative to this standard.
- If an element contained only one isotope, its atomic mass would be the relative mass of that isotope. However, most elements contain a mixture of several isotopes in varying proportions.
- Natural abundance gives the proportion of each isotope in a sample of the element.
- If more than one isotope of an element is present, the atomic mass is calculated by taking an average that takes into account the relative proportion of each isotope. Diagrams 2 and 3 illustrate how the atomic mass of common isotopes of lithium and chlorine would be calculated.

2 Lithium
- There are two common isotopes of lithium: lithium-6 and lithium-7.
- The atomic mass of lithium is 6.925, but for most calculates a value of 7 is sufficiently accurate.

3 Chlorine
- There are also two common isotopes of chlorine: chlorine-35 and chlorine-37.
- The atomic mass of chlorine is 35.4846, but for most calculations a value of 35.5 is sufficiently accurate.
- Rounding the atomic mass of chlorine to the nearest whole number would lead to significant errors in calculations.

Key words

atomic mass
atomic number
element
isotope

Atomic mass

- The *atomic mass* of an *element* is the average of the relative masses of its *isotopes*. It provides the relative mass of an "average" atom of the element, which is useful for calculations.
- The atomic mass is represented by the symbol $A(r)$
- The atomic mass of an isotope is its mass relative to the isotope carbon-12.
- The atomic mass of an isotope is the sum of the protons and neutrons in its nucleus.
- The atomic masses of the elements are presented below the element on the periodic table at right.

Atomic number

- The *atomic number* of an element is the number of protons in its nucleus.
- The atomic number is usually represented by Z.
- The number of neutrons in the nucleus of an isotope is:
  $A(r) - Z$
- The atomic numbers of the elements are presented above the element in the periodic table at right.

Periodic table with masses and numbers

1	2	3	4	5	6	7	8	9	10	11	12	13	14	15	16	17	18
1 **H** 1.008																	2 **He** 4.00
3 **Li** 6.94	4 **Be** 9.01											5 **B** 10.81	6 **C** 12.01	7 **N** 14.01	8 **O** 16.00	9 **F** 19.00	10 **Ne** 20.18
11 **Na** 23.00	12 **Mg** 24.31											13 **Al** 27.00	14 **Si** 28.08	15 **P** 30.97	16 **S** 32.06	17 **Cl** 35.45	18 **Ar** 39.95
19 **K** 39.10	20 **Ca** 40.08	21 **Sc** 44.96	22 **Ti** 47.87	23 **V** 50.94	24 **Cr** 52.00	25 **Mn** 54.94	26 **Fe** 55.84	27 **Co** 58.93	28 **Ni** 58.69	29 **Cu** 63.55	30 **Zn** 65.41	31 **Ga** 69.72	32 **Ge** 72.64	33 **As** 74.92	34 **Se** 78.96	35 **Br** 79.90	36 **Kr** 83.80
37 **Rb** 85.47	38 **Sr** 87.62	39 **Y** 88.90	40 **Zr** 91.22	41 **Nb** 92.91	42 **Mo** 95.94	43 **Tc** 98.00	44 **Ru** 101.07	45 **Rh** 102.90	46 **Pd** 106.42	47 **Ag** 106.90	48 **Cd** 112.41	49 **In** 114.82	50 **Sn** 118.71	51 **Sb** 121.76	52 **Te** 127.60	53 **I** 126.90	54 **Xe** 131.29
55 **Cs** 132.90	56 **Ba** 137.33	57–71	72 **Hf** 178.49	73 **Ta** 180.95	74 **W** 183.84	75 **Re** 186.21	76 **Os** 190.23	77 **Ir** 192.22	78 **Pt** 195.08	79 **Au** 196.97	80 **Hg** 200.59	81 **Tl** 204.38	82 **Pb** 207.20	83 **Bi** 208.98	84 **Po** 210	85 **At** 210	86 **Rn** 220
87 **Fr** 223	88 **Ra** 226	89–103	104 **Rf** 261	105 **Db** 262	106 **Sg** 266	107 **Bh** 264	108 **Hs** 277	109 **Mt** 268	110 **Ds** 271	111 **Rg** 272	112 **Uub** 285	113 **Uut** 284	114 **Uuq** 289	115 **Uup** 288	116 **Uuh** 292		

57 **La** 138.90	58 **Ce** 140.12	59 **Pr** 140.91	60 **Nd** 144.24	61 **Pm** 145.00	62 **Sm** 150.36	63 **Eu** 151.96	64 **Gd** 157.25	65 **Tb** 158.92	66 **Dy** 162.50	67 **Ho** 164.93	68 **Er** 167.26	69 **Tm** 168.93	70 **Yb** 173.04	71 **Lu** 174.97
89 **Ac** 227	90 **Th** 232.04	91 **Pa** 231.03	92 **U** 238.03	93 **Np** 237	94 **Pu** 244	95 **Am** 243	96 **Cm** 247	97 **Bk** 247	98 **Cf** 251	99 **Es** 252	100 **Fm** 257	101 **Md** 258	102 **No** 259	103 **Lr** 262

Calculating the molecular mass of compounds

1 Diatomic molecule (chlorine)

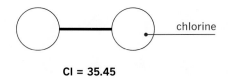

chlorine

Cl = 35.45

2 Covalent compound (ethanol)

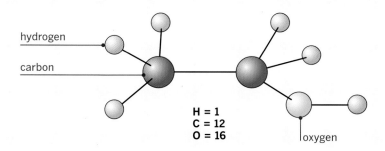

hydrogen

carbon

H = 1
C = 12
O = 16

oxygen

3 Ionic compound (sodium chloride)

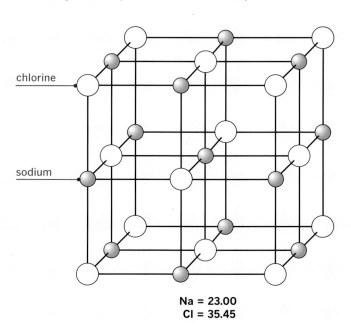

chlorine

sodium

Na = 23.00
Cl = 35.45

Calculating molecular mass

You calculate the *molecular mass* of a compound the same way regardless of structure:

1. Multiply the number of atoms in an element by its *atomic mass*.
2. Repeat this process for each element in the compound, then
3. Add the numbers.

1 Diatonic molecule (chlorine)

- The element chlorine exists as a *diatomic molecule* Cl_2.
  Atomic mass of chlorine = 35.5
  Molecular mass of chlorine
  = 2 x 35.5 = 71

2 Covalent compound (ethanol)

- Ethanol is a simple *covalent compound* that has the formula C_2H_5OH.
  Atomic mass of carbon = 12; hydrogen = 1; oxygen = 16.
  Molecular mass of ethanol
  = (2 x 12) + (6 x 1) + (1 x 16) = 46

3 Ionic compound (sodium chloride)

- *Ionic compounds* do not exist as molecules but as a giant *lattice* composed of ions in a fixed ratio. The formula mass of an ionic compound is the sum of the atomic masses of the ions in their simplest ratio.
- Sodium chloride consists of an ionic lattice in which the ions are present in the ratio 1:1. Therefore, the formula of sodium chloride is taken to be **NaCl**.
  Atomic mass of sodium = 23; chlorine = 35.5.
  Formula mass of sodium chloride
  = 23 + 35.5 = 58.5

© Diagram Visual Information Ltd.

Key words

anion	ionic crystal
bond	ion
cation	lattice
coordination number	

Ionic crystals

- In an *ionic crystal*, each *ion* is surrounded by a number of oppositely charged ions in a *lattice* structure.
- There are several types of ionic structures.
  Simple: The atoms form grids.
  Body centered: One atom sits in the center of each cube.
  Face centered: One atom sits in each "face" of the cube.
- The lattice structure is determined by two factors:
  1. the ratio of the number of *cations* (positively charged ions) to *anions* (negatively charged ions)
  2. the ratio of the radii of the ions.
- In general, the higher the value of the radius ratio the higher the *coordination number* of the lattice. The coordination number is the number of atoms, ions, or molecules to which *bonds* can be formed.

1 Simple cubic structure (CsCl)

- In cesium chloride, the radius ratio is 0.94 (due to the large cesium ion). The coordination is 8:8. Each ion is surrounded by 8 oppositely charged ions.

2 Face-centered cubic structure (NaCl)

- The radius ratio in the sodium chloride lattice is 0.57. The coordination is 6:6. Each ion is surrounded by 6 oppositely charged ions.

3 Body-centered cubic structure (CaF₂)

- In calcium fluoride the radius ratio is 0.75. The coordination is 8:4. Each calcium ion is surrounded by 8 fluoride ions, while each fluoride ion is surrounded by 4 calcium ions.

Structure of some ionic crystals

1 Simple cubic structure (CsCl)

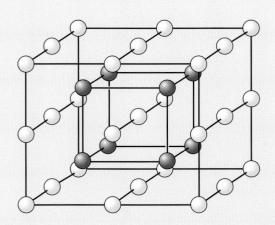

- cations
- anions

2 Face-centered cubic structure (NaCl)

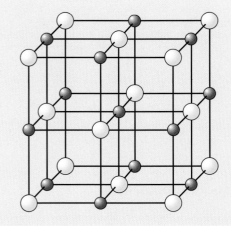

- cations
- anions

3 Body-centered cubic structure (CaF₂)

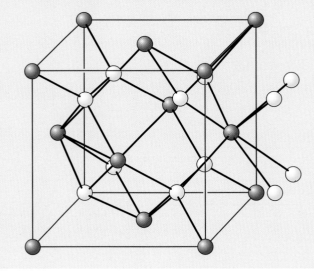

- cations
- anions

Crystal structure of metals: lattice structure

Key words

body centered
cubic packing
crystal
face-centered
cubic close
packing

hexagonal close
packing
lattice
unit cell

1 Hexagonal close packing

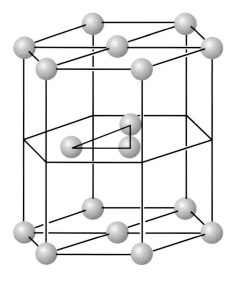 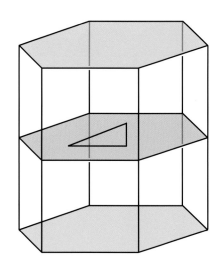

Metallic crystals

● Like all other *crystals*, metallic crystals are composed of *unit cells*, sets of atoms, ions, or molecules in orderly three dimensional arrangements called *lattices*.

1 Hexagonal close packing

● When arranged in a single layer, the most efficient method of packing the ions is in the form of a hexagon in which each ion is surrounded by six other ions.

● In *hexagonal close packing*, a second layer is positioned so that each ion in the second layer is in contact with three ions in the first layer. The third layer is placed directly above the first, and the fourth layer directly above the second, etc. This arrangement is sometimes represented as ABABAB.

2 Face-centered cubic close packing

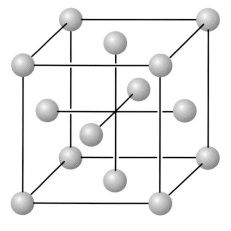 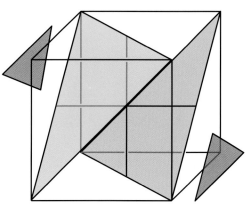

2 Face-centered cubic close packing

● Here the third layer does not sit directly above either the first or second layers. The pattern is repeated after three layers, giving rise to an ABCABCABC arrangement.

3 Body-centered cubic packing

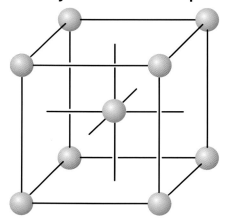 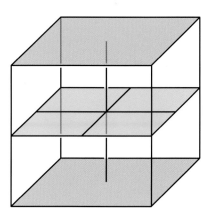

3 Body-centered cubic packing

● Here the layers are formed from ions arranged in squares. The second layer is positioned so that each sphere in the second layer is in contact with four spheres in the first layer. The third layer sits directly above the first layer, giving rise to an ABABAB arrangement.

Key words

body-centered cubic packing	hexagonal close packing
coordination number	
face-centered cubic close packing	

1 Efficient packing

- Both *hexagonal close packing* and *face-centered cubic close packing* may be considered as efficient packing since the spheres occupy 74 percent of the available space. In both arrangements, each sphere is in contact with 12 others, and is said to have a *coordination number* of 12.

2 Less efficient packing

- *Body-centered cubic packing* is less efficient than hexagonal and face-centered cubic close packing. Spheres occupy only 68 percent of the available space. Each sphere is in contact with eight others (four in the layer above and four in the layer below) and, therefore, has a coordination number of eight.

Metals showing hexagonal close packing

- Cobalt
- Magnesium
- Titanium
- Zinc

Metals showing face-centered cubic close packing

- Aluminum
- Calcium
- Copper
- Lead
- Nickel

Metals showing body-centered cubic packing

- Group 1 metals
- Barium
- Chromium
- Iron
- Vanadium

Crystal structure of metals: efficient packing

1 Efficient packing
Hexagonal close packing

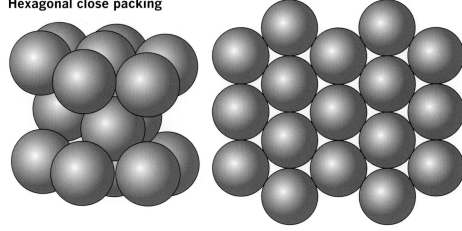

Face-centered cubic close packing

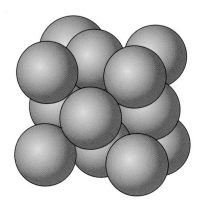
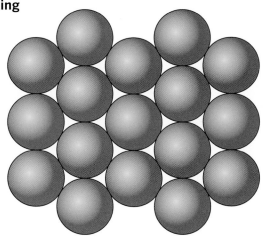

2 Less efficient packing
Body-centered cubic packing

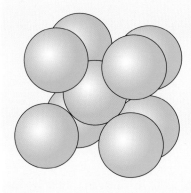
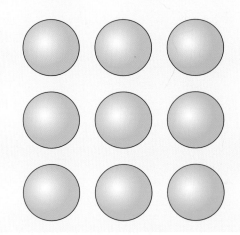

Chemical combination: ionic bonding

1 Formation of sodium chloride (NaCl)

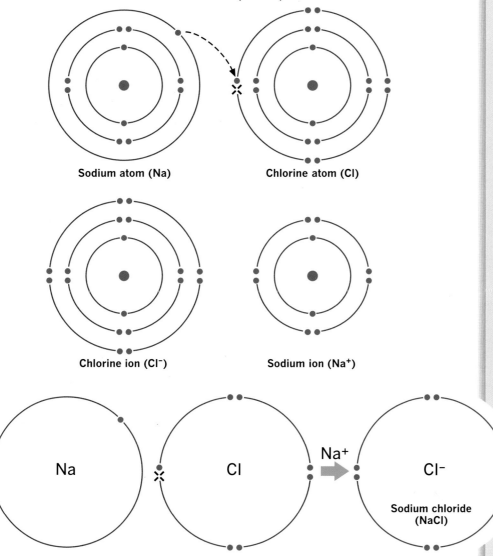

Sodium atom (Na)   Chlorine atom (Cl)

Chlorine ion (Cl⁻)   Sodium ion (Na⁺)

Na   Cl   Na⁺   Cl⁻

Sodium chloride
(NaCl)

2 Formation of magnesium oxide (MgO)

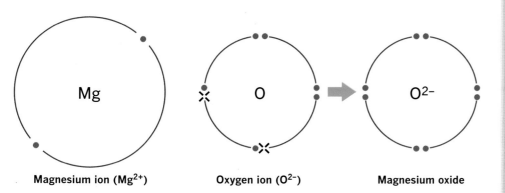

Mg   O O^{2-}

Magnesium ion (Mg^{2+})   Oxygen ion (O^{2-})   Magnesium oxide

Ionic bonding

- Ionic *bonds* are formed by the attraction of opposite charges.
- In *ionic bonding*, the atoms in a compound gain, lose, or share electrons so the number of electrons in their outer *shell* is the same as the nearest *noble gas* on the periodic table.
- Non-metals gain electrons to give negatively charged ions (*anions*).
- Metal atoms loose electrons to give positively charged ions (*cations*).

1 Formation of sodium chloride (NaCl)

- A sodium atom has one electron in its outer shell. The easiest way it can attain a complete outer shell is by losing this electron to form a sodium ion, Na^+.
- A chlorine atom has seven electrons in its outer shell. The easiest way it can attain a complete outer shell is by gaining one more electron to form a *chloride* ion, Cl^-.

2 Formation of magnesium oxide (MgO)

- A magnesium atom has two electrons in its outer shell. It loses these electrons to form a magnesium ion, Mg^{2+}.
- An oxygen atom has six electrons in its outer shell. It gains two electrons to form an *oxide* ion, O^{2-}.

Electronic configuration

Na (sodium atom)	2.8.1
Na⁺ (sodium ion)	2.8
Cl (chlorine atom)	2.8.7
Cl⁻ (chloride ion)	2.8.8
Mg (magnesium atom)	2.8.2
Mg²⁺ (magnesium ion)	2.8
O (oxygen atom)	2.6
O²⁻ (oxide ion)	2.8

Key words

carbonate	resonance
ion	structure
limiting form	sulfate
nitrate	
radical	

Radicals

- A *radical* is a group of atoms that cannot be represented by one structural formula. It can pass unchanged through a series of chemical reactions. Radicals include the *carbonate* ion, CO_3^{2-}, the *nitrate* ion, NO_3^-, and the *sulfate* ion, SO_4^{2-}.

1 Carbonate ion

- The carbon atom is bonded to three oxygen atoms. By transferring electrons, it is possible to write three *limiting forms* for this *ion*. (Limiting forms are the possibilities for the distribution of electrons in a molecule or ion.)
- Electrons are continually being transferred in the ion. Thus its exact form is constantly changing. The ion is best represented as a *resonance structure* (the average of the limiting forms) in which dotted lines indicate that the charge on the ion, 2-, is spread over all three of the carbon–oxygen bonds.

2 Nitrate ion

- The nitrogen atom is bonded to three oxygen atoms. This ion has three limiting forms.
- It is best represented as a resonance structure in which dotted lines indicate that the charge on the ion, 1-, is spread over all three of the nitrogen–oxygen bonds.

3 Sulfate ion

- The sulfur atom is bonded to four oxygen atoms. This ion has three limiting forms.
- The ion's exact form is constantly changing. It is best represented as a resonance structure in which dotted lines indicate that the charge on the ion, 2-, is spread over all four of the sulfur–oxygen bonds.

Chemical combination: ionic radicals

1 Carbonate ion

limiting forms

resonance structure

2 Nitrate ion

limiting forms

resonance structure

3 Sulfate ion

limiting forms

resonance structure

Chemical combination: covalent bonding

1 The hydrogen molecule

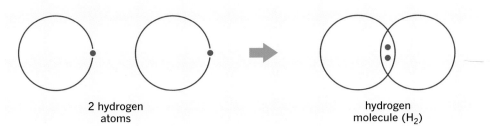

2 hydrogen
atoms

hydrogen
molecule (H₂)

3 The ammonia molecule

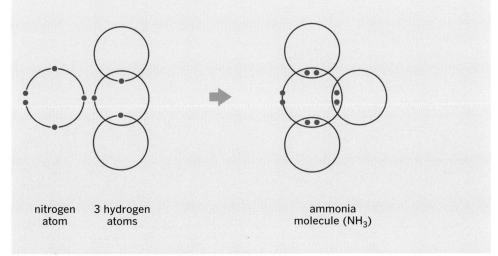

nitrogen   3 hydrogen
atom   atoms

ammonia
molecule (NH₃)

4 The methane molecule

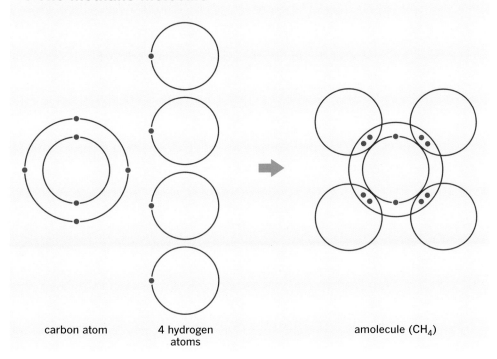

carbon atom   4 hydrogen
               atoms

amolecule (CH₄)

Key words

ammonia	methane
bond	nitrogen
carbon	shell
hydrogen	
ionic compound	

Covalent bonding

● Atoms gain stability by having a complete outer *shell* of electrons. In *ionic compounds*, this is achieved by the transfer of electrons. In covalent bonding, atoms share electrons.

1 The hydrogen molecule

● A *hydrogen* atom has one electron in its outer shell. In a hydrogen molecule, two hydrogen atoms each donate this electron to form a *bond*. Each hydrogen atom can be thought of as having control of the pair of electrons in the bond. Thus, each can be thought of as having a full outer shell of electrons. The single bond is shown as H-H.

2 The ammonia molecule

● A *nitrogen* atom has five electrons in its outer shell and needs another three electrons to complete the shell. In *ammonia*, three hydrogen atoms each donate one electron to form three N-H bonds. The nitrogen atom now has control of eight electrons and has a complete outer shell, while each hydrogen atom has control of two electrons and also has a complete outer shell.

3 The methane molecule

● A *carbon* atom has four electrons in its outer shell and needs another four electrons to complete the shell. In *methane*, four hydrogen atoms each donate one electron to form four C-H bonds. The carbon atom now has control of eight electrons and has a complete outer shell, while each hydrogen atom has control of two electrons and also has a complete outer shell.

Key words

ammonium ion	covalent
coordinate	compound
bonding	hydronium ion
covalent bond	lone pair

Coordinate bonding

● *Coordinate bonding* is a particular form of covalent bonding in which one atom provides both electrons that the two atoms share.

1 Ammonium ion

● There is a non-bonding or *lone pair* of electrons on the nitrogen atom of an ammonia molecule. Nitrogen uses this lone pair to form a coordinate bond with a hydrogen ion, forming the *ammonium ion*, NH_4^+.

2 Hydronium ion

● The *hydronium ion*, H_3O^+, forms in a similar way.

3 Aluminum chloride

● The Al^{3+} ion is very small and carries a high charge. It attracts electrons so strongly that aluminum chloride is a *covalent compound*. It exists as Al_2Cl_6 molecules in which two $AlCl_3$ molecules are linked by coordinate bonds formed by the donation of lone pairs of electrons from two chlorine atoms.

4 Ionic compounds with covalent character

● The ions in a sodium chloride lattice are perfectly spherical. Thus the bonds in this compound are said to be perfectly ionic.

● But in an ionic compound consisting of a small, highly charged positive ion and a large negative ion such as lithium iodide, the positive ion attracts electron charge away from the negative ion. The result is that the negative ion becomes distorted, and electron density becomes concentrated between the ions, creating a bond similar to a *covalent bond*. Compounds like lithium iodide are said to be ionic with covalent character.

Chemical combination: coordinate bonding

1 Ammonium ion

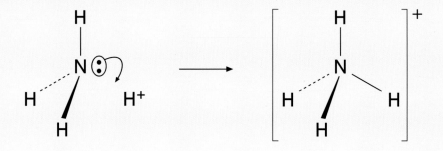

2 Hydronium ion

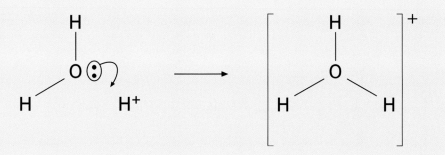

3 Aluminum chloride

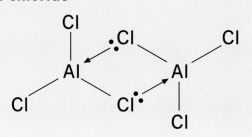

4 Ionic compounds with covalent character

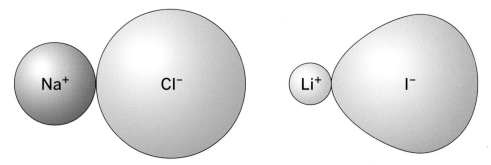

Mixtures and solutions

Producing a solution

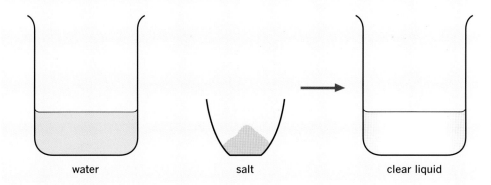

water   salt   clear liquid

Producing a suspension

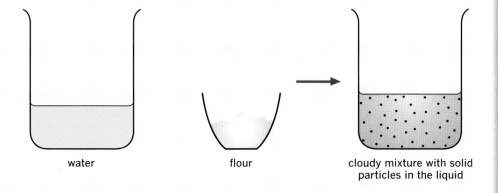

water   flour   cloudy mixture with solid particles in the liquid

Producing an emulsion

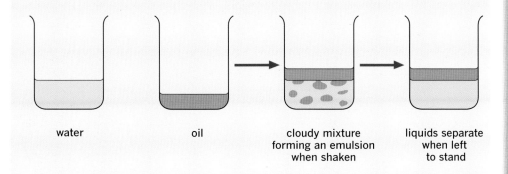

water   oil   cloudy mixture forming an emulsion when shaken   liquids separate when left to stand

Key words

emulsion   suspension
ionic compound
mixture
soluble
solution

1 Solutions

- A *solution* is a homogeneous *mixture* of substances. Particles in solutions are very small and cannot be seen. The particles may be atoms, ions, or molecules, and their diameters are typically less than 5 nm. Salt dissolves in water to form a clear colorless solution.
- Many, but not, all *ionic compounds* are *soluble* in water.
- A small proportion of organic compounds are soluble in water. However, organic compounds are generally more soluble in organic solvents such as hexane and ethanol.

2 Suspensions

- A *suspension* is a heterogeneous mixture of two components. The particles will settle out over a period of time. Suspended particles have diameters that are typically 1,000 nm or more.
- When flour is mixed with water, it forms a white suspension. Tiny particles of flour are suspended in the water. The flour particles can be filtered off from the suspension.

3 Emulsions

- An *emulsion* is a colloidal dispersion of small droplets of one liquid in another (See page 46).
- When oil and water are mixed, they form an emulsion. Oil is less dense than water and forms the upper layer.
- Tiny oil droplets are suspended in the water. After a while, the oil droplets join together, and two layers are formed.
- The mixture of oil and water can be separated using a separating funnel.

Key words

aerosol	gel
colloid	sol
emulsion	solution
filtration	suspension
foam	

Colloids

- A *colloid* is a substance made of particles whose size is intermediate between those in *solutions* and *suspensions*.
- The particles in a suspension have a diameter of typically 1,000 nm or more. The particles in a suspension will settle over a period of time.
- The particles in a colloid are approximately 500 nm or less in diameter and do not settle on standing.
- The particles in a colloid cannot be separated from the dispersion medium by ordinary techniques like *filtration* and centrifugation.
- A colloid consists of a dispersing medium and dispersed substance. These terms are analogous to the terms solute and solvent.
- Colloids are classified according to the original phases of their constituents. The main types are: *aerosols*, *foams*, *emulsions*, *sols*, and *gels*.
- Aerosols are extremely small solid or liquid particles suspended in air or another gas.
- Foams form when a gas is suspended in a liquid or a solid.
- Emulsions form when small particles of a liquid are suspended in another liquid.
- Sols form when solid particles are suspended in a liquid.
- Gels are solid particles arranged as a fine network in a liquid to form a jelly.

Colloids

1 In Air

aerosol

1 Colloid type	2 Phase of dispersing medium	3 Phase of dispersed substance	Examples
aerosol	gas	liquid	clouds, fog, insecticide spray
aerosol	gas	solid	dust, smoke

2 In liquids

paint

1 Colloid type	2 Phase of dispersing medium	3 Phase of dispersed substance	Examples
foam	liquid	gas	froth, whipped cream
emulsion	liquid	liquid	milk, salad dressing
sol	liquid	solid	milk of magnesia, paint

3 In solids

cork   polystyrene

1 Colloid type	2 Phase of dispersing medium	3 Phase of dispersed substance	Examples
solid foam	solid	gas	cork, polyurethane
gel	solid	liquid	agar, geletine, jelly
solid sol	solid	solid	alloys

Simple and fractional distillation

Key words

boiling point
distillation
fractional
  distillation
mixture

Simple distillation of sea water

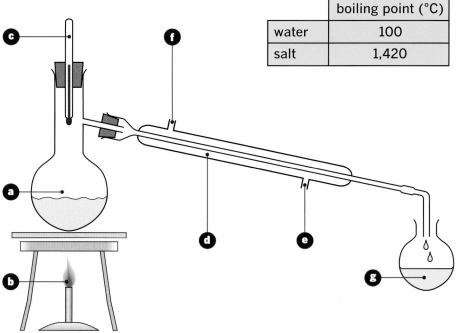

	boiling point (°C)
water	100
salt	1,420

Fractional distillation of ethanol

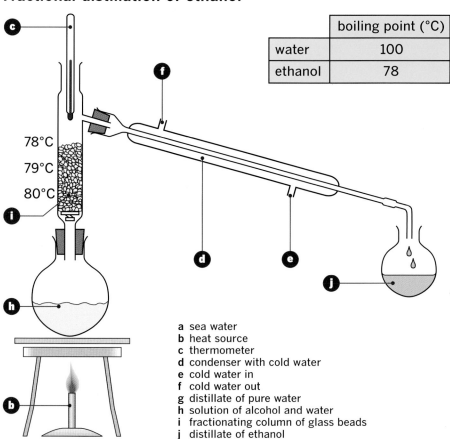

	boiling point (°C)
water	100
ethanol	78

a sea water
b heat source
c thermometer
d condenser with cold water
e cold water in
f cold water out
g distillate of pure water
h solution of alcohol and water
i fractionating column of glass beads
j distillate of ethanol

1 Simple distillation

● *Distillation* is a process in which a *mixture* of materials is heated to separate the components.

● Simple distillation is used when the *boiling points* of the components are widely separated.

● In the diagram, salt water is placed in a round-bottom flask. Water boils at 100°C and becomes water vapor.

● A condenser consists of an inner tube surrounded by a jacket of cold water. This jacket ensures that the inner tube remains cool.

● The vapor passes into the condenser, where it is cooled and changes back into liquid.

● The water runs out of the condenser and is collected in a second flask.

● The salt remains in the round-bottomed flask.

2 Fractional distillation

● *Fractional distillation* is used to separate components whose boiling points are similar.

● Ethanol boils at 78°C and turns to vapor. Because the boiling point of water is only 100°C, a significant amount of water also becomes vapor as a result of evaporation.

● The fractionating column contains glass beads, which provide a large surface area for vapor to condense and the resulting liquid to subsequently boil.

● As the vapor mixture moves up the fractionating column, it condenses and then boils again to become vapor. Each time, the proportion of ethanol in the mixture increases.

Key words

filtrate	soluble
immiscible	solvent
insoluble	
mixture	
residue	

1 Separating a mixture of two solids

- Sugar is *soluble* in ethanol, while salt is *insoluble*. When a *mixture* of sugar and salt is mixed with ethanol, the sugar dissolves while the salt does not.
- When the mixture is filtered, the undissolved salt remains as the *residue* in the filter. The *filtrate*, sugar solution, passes through the filter.
- If the filtrate is left open to the air, the ethanol evaporates, and solid sugar remains.

2 Separating two solutes in solution

- Salt dissolves in water but not in carbon tetrachloride.
- Iodine is slightly soluble in water but is far more soluble in carbon tetrachloride.
- When a mixture of salt and iodine is shaken in a mixture of water and carbon tetrachloride, the salt dissolves in the water and the iodine in carbon tetrachloride.
- Water and carbon tetrachloride are *immiscible*, they do not mix, and form two layers in a separating funnel. Carbon tetrachloride is more dense than water and forms the lower layer.
- When the layers are run into separate evaporating basins and left, the *solvents*—carbon tetrachloride and water—evaporate, leaving salt and iodine respectively.

Separating solutions

1 Separating a mixture of two solids

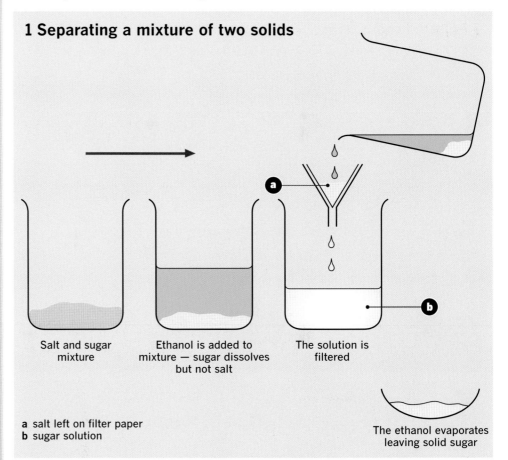

Salt and sugar mixture

Ethanol is added to mixture — sugar dissolves but not salt

The solution is filtered

a salt left on filter paper
b sugar solution

The ethanol evaporates leaving solid sugar

2 Separating two solutes in solution

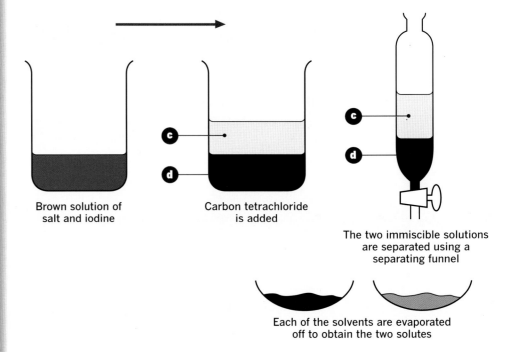

Brown solution of salt and iodine

Carbon tetrachloride is added

The two immiscible solutions are separated using a separating funnel

Each of the solvents are evaporated off to obtain the two solutes

c salt solution in water
d purple solution of iodine in carbon tetrachloride

Paper chromatography

1 Paper chromatography

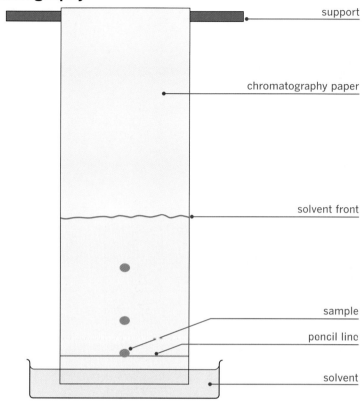

support

chromatography paper

solvent front

sample

poncil line

solvent

2 R_f value

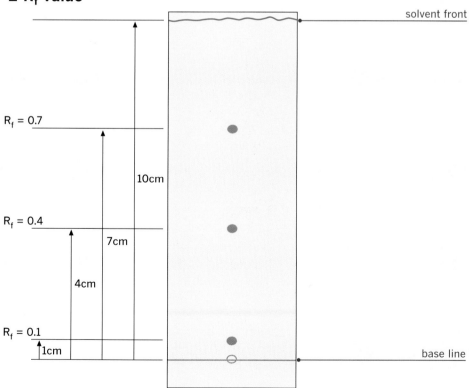

solvent front

$R_f = 0.7$

10cm

$R_f = 0.4$

7cm

4cm

$R_f = 0.1$

1cm

base line

1 Paper chromatography
- *Chromatography* is a technique for separating and identifying *mixtures* of *solutes* in *solutions*.
- In paper chromatography, absorbent paper is suspended on a support so that only the bottom rests in the *solvent*.
- A base line is drawn in pencil above the level of the solvent. (If ink were used, the dyes in the ink would separate during the process and mix with the sample.)
- A concentrated solution of the sample mixture is made by dissolving as much as possible in a very small volume of solvent.
- A small amount of the concentrated solution is spotted onto the base line. The chromatography paper is suspended over the solvent.
- The solvent rises up the chromatography paper.

2 R_f value
- The R_f *value* is the ratio of the distance moved by a substance in a chromatographic separation to the distance moved by the solvent. The greater the attraction between a substance and the solvent molecules, the greater the R_f value.
- The molecules of each substance in a mixture are attracted both to the chromatography paper and to the solvent molecules.
- The greater the attraction between a substance and the solvent molecules, the quicker it will be carried up the chromatography paper. Dyes that are very soluble in the solvent are carried up to the top of the paper, while those that are less soluble remain lower down.
- The R_f value is independent of the height of the solvent front but is dependent on the solvent used.

Key words

alkane	mass
chromatography	spectrometry
gas-liquid	mobile phase
chromatography	stationary phase

1 Gas-liquid chromatography

- In chromatography, substances are partitioned between a *stationary phase* and a *mobile phase*. The stationary phase is the substance that retards the components of the sample. The mobile phase is the components of the sample.
- In *gas-liquid chromatography*, the stationary phase, packed into the column, consists of a high-boiling point liquid, such as a long-chain *alkane*, supported by a porous inert solid, such as charcoal or silica.
- The mobile phase consists of a carrier gas—usually nitrogen, hydrogen, helium, or argon.
- A sample mixture is injected into the chamber where it vaporizes and is carried through the column by the carrier gas. Various compounds in the sample pass through the column at different rates due to their attraction to the stationary phase.
- The separated compounds pass to a detector or directly into a mass spectrometer.

2 Mass spectrometry

- *Mass spectrometry* is a technique used to identify the chemical constitution of a substance by means of analyzing its ions.
- The sample passes into the ionization chamber, where it is bombarded by electrons and forms a series of positive ions.
- The ions are accelerated by an electric field and deflected along a circular path by a magnetic field. The lighter the ions, the greater the deflection.
- The intensity of the ion beam is detected electrically, amplified, and finally recorded.
- Each compound gives a characteristic spectrum from which it can be identified.

Gas-liquid chromatography and mass spectrometry

1 Gas-liquid chromatography

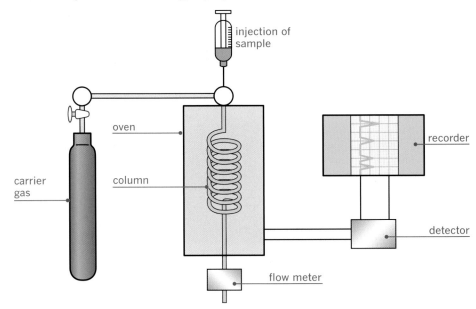

2 Mass spectrometry

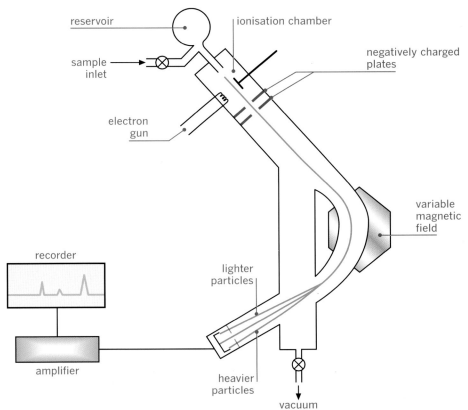

The pH scale

Key words

acidity
alkalinity
pH
pH meter

1 pH scale

[H$^+$]/mole dm^{-3}

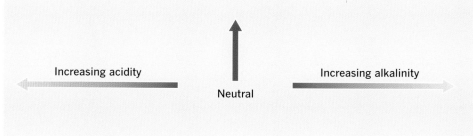

1	10^{-1}	10^{-2}	10^{-3}	10^{-4}	10^{-5}	10^{-6}	10^{-7}	10^{-8}	10^{-9}	10^{-10}	10^{-11}	10^{-12}	10^{-14}	10^{-14}
0	1	2	3	4	5	6	7	8	9	10	11	12	13	14

pH

Increasing acidity ← | ↑ Neutral | → Increasing alkalinity

Lower pH/sronger acid ← | → Higher pH/sronger alkali

1 pH scale

- *pH* is a measure of the *acidity* or *alkalinity* of a solution. The term pH was originally introduced by the Danish biochemist Søren Sørensen in 1909 while working on methods of improving the quality control of beer. The letters pH stand for "potential of hydrogen."
- Acidic solutions always have a pH of less than 7, and alkaline solutions always have a pH of more than 7. The lower the pH value, the more acidic the solution; conversely, the higher the pH value, the more alkaline the solution.
- The pH of a solution is the logarithm to base 10 of the reciprocal of the numerical value of the hydrogen ion concentration:
  $$pH = lg(1/[H^+]0 = -lg [H^+]$$
- The pH of a neutral solution can be calculated directly from the ionic product (K_w) of water:
  $$K_w = [H^+][OH^-] = 10^{-14} \text{ mol}^2 \text{ dm}^{-6}$$
  For a neutral solution:
  $$[H^+] = [OH^-] = 10^{-7} \text{ mol dm}^{-3}$$
  therefore the pH of a neutral solution = 7.
- The pH scale is logarithmic, so hydrogen ion concentration increases or decreases by a power of 10 for each step down or up the scale.

2 Schematic of a pH meter

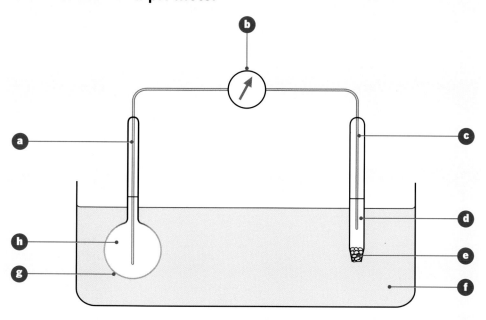

a platinum wire
b sensitive voltmeter
c silver wire coated with silver chloride (AgCl)
d saturated potassium chloride (KCl)
e capillary opening with porous plug
f solution of unknown pH
g Thin glass membrane through which H$^+$ ions can pass
h solution of fixed acid pH

2 pH meter

- A *pH meter* is an electrochemical cell consisting of an electrode, such as a glass electrode, which is sensitive to hydrogen ion concentration, and a reference electrode.
- The emf (electromotive force) of the cell can be measured using a high-resistance voltmeter. A pH meter is a high-resistance voltmeter calibrated with the pH scale.

© Diagram Visual Information Ltd.

Key words

acid	equilibrium
acid-base	titration
indicator	universal
alkali	indicator
end point	

1 Common indicators

● *Acid-base indicators* are substances that are different colors in *acids* and *alkalis* so they "indicate" whether a solution is an acid or alkali.

2 Changing equilibrium

● Acid-base indicators are usually weak acids that disassociate to give an ion that is a different color than the acid. A change in pH causes a change in the position of the equilibrium of the reaction and, therefore, the color of the solution.

● Phenolphthalein is such an indicator. It is a colorless, weak acid that dissociates in water, forming pink anions. Under acidic conditions, the *equilibrium* of the reaction is to the left, and the concentration of the anions is too low for the color to be visible. Under alkaline conditions, the equilibrium is to the right, and the concentration of anions is high enough for the pink to be seen.

3 Universal indicator

● In contrast to an indicator such as phenolphthalein, which is able to show whether a substance is an acid or base only in the broadest terms, a *universal indicator* has a range of colors that indicate how acidic or how alkaline a solution is.

4 pH range of indicators

● Most indicators do not change color when the pH of a solution is exactly 7. This means that the *end point* of the *titration*, the point at which the indicator undergoes the maximum color change, occurs at a different time to the equivalence point of the titration, the point at which there are equivalent amounts of acid and alkali.

● The suitability of an indicator for use in a titration depends on what combination of strong and weak acid and alkali is to be used.

Indicators

1 Table of common indicators

Indicator	Color in acid	Color in alkali
litmus	red	blue
methyl orange	red	yellow
phenolphthalein	colorless	pink

2 Changing equilibrium (phenol phthalein)

colorless
(acid)

pink
(base)

3 Universal indicator

pH														
0	1	2	3	4	5	6	7	8	9	10	11	12	13	14
red					orange	yellow	green	blue			purple			
Color														

4 Table of pH range over which acid–base indicators change color

Indicator	Color		pH range over which color change occurs
	Acid	Alkali	
bromocresol green	yellow	blue	3.8–5.4
bromothymol blue	yellow	blue	6.0–7.6
methyl orange	red	yellow	3.2–4.4
methyl red	yellow	red	4.8–6.0
phenolphthalein	colorless	pink	8.2–10.0
phenol red	yellow	red	6.8–8.4

Titration of strong acids

1 Titration of strong acid against strong alkali

(pH changes during the titration of 50 cm^3 of 0.1M HCl with 0.1M NaOH)

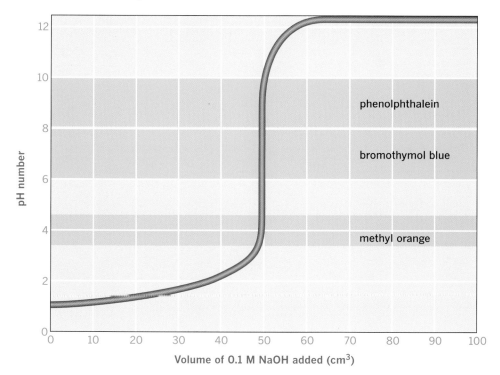

1 Titration of strong acid against strong alkali

- At the *end point* of strong *acid*–strong *base alkali titration*, the *pH* changes by 5 or 6 pH units when only 1 drop of acid or alkali is added.
- Methyl orange, bromothymol blue, and phenolphthalein are all suitable indicators for this titration because they all change color within a very small change in volume of sodium hydroxide solution.

2 Titration of strong acid against weak alkali

- At the end point of a strong acid–weak alkali titration, the pH change for the addition of one drop of acid or alkali is significant. However, the pH at equivalence (when there are equivalent amounts of acid and alkali) is less than 7. A suitable indicator should change color below or around pH 7. Thus both methyl orange and bromothymol blue would be suitable indicators because they change color between pH 3.2 and 7.6. Within this range, the pH of the titration mixture changes significantly for a very small change in volume of sodium hydroxide solution.
- Phenolphthalein would not be a good choice of indicator because it changes color between pH 8.2 and 10.0. In order to change the pH of the titration mixture over this pH range, a significant volume of sodium hydroxide solution must be added. The result would be an overestimate of the volume of sodium hydroxide solution needed to neutralize the acid.

2 Titration of strong acid against weak alkali

(pH changes during the titration of 50 cm^3 of 0.1 M HCl with 0.1 M NH$_3$)

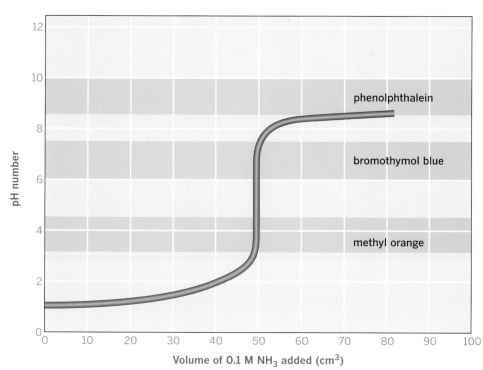

Titration of weak acids

Key words

acid	titration
alkali	
end point	
equivalence point	
pH	

1 Titration of weak acid against strong alkali

- At the *end point* of a weak *acid*–strong *alkali titration*, the *pH* change for the addition of one drop of acid or alkali is significant. However, the pH at equivalence (when there are equivalent amounts of acid and alkali) is greater than 7. A suitable indicator should change color above pH 7. Thus phenolphthalein would be a good choice because it changes color between pH 8.2 and 10.0. Within this range, the pH of the titration mixture changes significantly for a very small change in volume of sodium hydroxide solution.
- Conversely, bromothymol blue and methyl orange would not be good choices because they change color between pH 3.2 and 7.6, which is before the *equivalence point* of the titration is reached. The result would be an underestimate of the volume of sodium hydroxide solution needed to neutralize the acid.

2 Titration of weak acid against weak alkali

- The pH changes too slowly around the equivalence point to give a color change with the addition of one drop of acid or alkali. The use of methyl orange, bromothymol blue, or phenolphthalein would not give accurate results.
- It is not usual to titrate weak acids with weak alkali, but if it must be done, a pH meter is necessary to find the equivalence point accurately. There is no suitable indicator for this type of titration.

1 Titration of weak acid against strong alkali

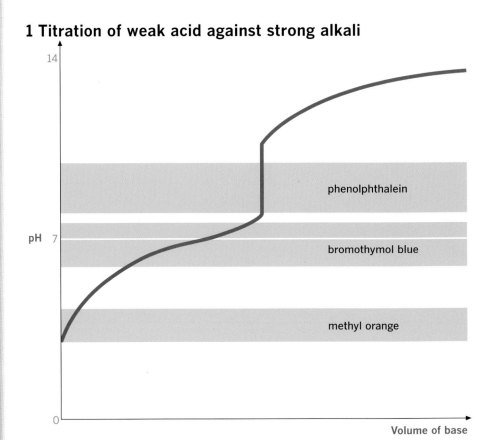

2 Titration of weak acid against weak alkali

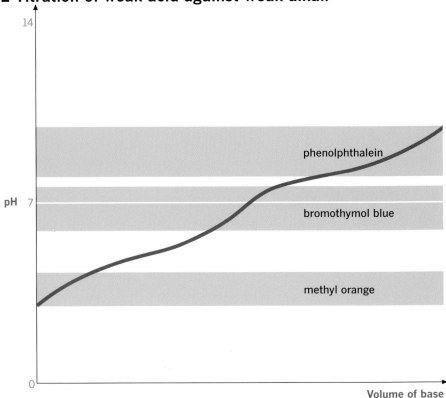

pH and soil

1 Soil classification

pH	Description
< 5.5	strongly acid
5.5 – 5.9	medium acid
6.0 – 6.4	slightly acid
6.4 – 6.9	very slightly acid
7.0	neutral
7.1 – 7.5	very slightly alkaline
7.6 – 8.0	slightly alkaline
8.1 – 8.5	medium alkaline
> 8.5	strongly alkaline

2 pH range of common fruit and vegetables

Fruit or vegetable	Soil pH range
cabbage	6.0 – 7.5
cauliflower	6.5 – 7.5
celery	6.5 – 7.5
cucumber	5.5 – 7.0
potato	5.0 – 6.0
peas	6.0 – 7.5
strawberry	5.0 – 6.0
tomato	5.5 – 7.0

3 Elements needed by plants

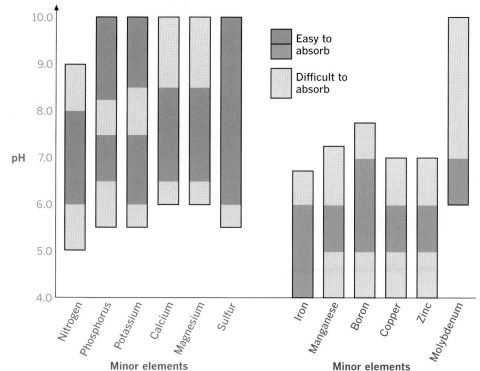

Key words

pH

1 Soil classification

- Soil can be classified according to its *pH*.
- Soils naturally tend to become more acidic due to organic acids being released into the soil as a result of the decay of organic material.
- The acidity of soil can be reduced by spreading slaked lime (calcium hydroxide) or lime (calcium carbonate).

2 pH range of common fruits and vegetables

- Most plants grow best in soil that is slightly acidic, with a pH value between 6.3 and 7.2. Plants will grow outside this range but not as well. This has serious implications for food crops.
- The soil pH is an important consideration in preparing soil to grow crops.

3 Elements needed by plants

- Plants need a number of major and minor elements in order to grow well, and they obtain these from the soil. The minerals dissolve in soil water and are absorbed into the plant through the roots.
- The pH of the soil determines how easily minerals containing these elements can be absorbed. At soil pH values between 6.0 and 7.0, all major elements and minor elements can be absorbed, although some are absorbed more easily than others. In very acidic or very alkaline soils, relatively few plants prosper because they cannot absorb all of the minerals needed for healthy growth.

© Diagram Visual Information Ltd.

Key words

atmosphere
convection
 current

The water cycle

- Earth's water is always moving in a cycle called the hydrologic or water cycle.
- The Sun provides the energy driving the cycle.

1 Evaporation

- Heat energy causes water to evaporate from the surface of the oceans, leaving all dissolved substances behind. The rate of evaporation is greater in areas of Earth where the seas are warmer.
- Water vapor rises into the *atmosphere*, where it eventually condenses to form clouds. These are dispersed by winds, which carry them to the colder regions of Earth.

2 Transportation

- When clouds reach landmasses, they are carried up on *convection currents*. As they rise, the temperature decreases, and eventually the water vapor condenses, forming precipitation, which falls to Earth.
- Rainwater contains dissolved gases, which makes it slightly acidic.

3 Deposition

- The fresh water flows over rocks and through soils before gathering in streams and rivers. As the water flows through the ground, solids dissolve in it.
- Water is removed from rivers for both industrial and domestic use. Much of this water is ultimately returned to the rivers. Finally, the water flows out to sea, thus completing the cycle. Any dissolved solids are carried in it and eventually deposited in the oceans.

The water cycle

1 Evaporation

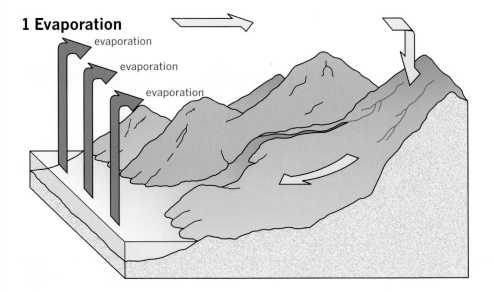

evaporation
evaporation
evaporation

2 Transportation

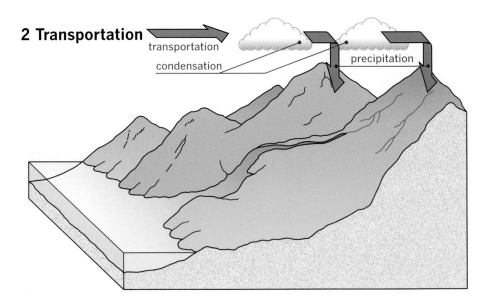

transportation
condensation
precipitation

3 Deposition

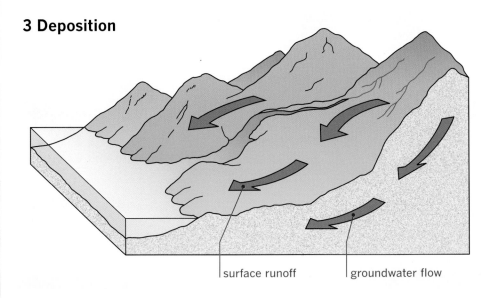

surface runoff   groundwater flow

Treatment of water and sewage

Key words

methane
oxidizing agent
sewage

1 water treatment

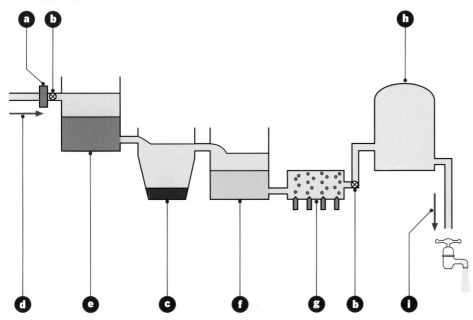

2 Sewage treatment

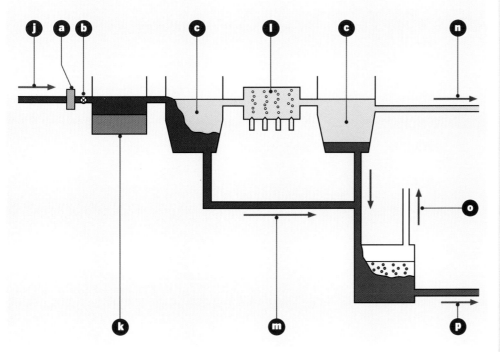

a screen	**i** to homes and factories
b pump	**j** sewage in
c sedimentation tank	**k** settling tank
d water in	**l** digester aeration tank
e coarse sand filter	**m** sludge collected
f fine sand filter	**n** clean water to river
g chlorine added	**o** methane out
h covered storage tank	**p** digested sludge out

1 Water treatment

- Particles are removed from water by passing it through a series of sand filter beds and sedimentation tanks. The filter beds also contain bacteria, which break down and destroy micro-organisms in the water.
- Chlorine is a powerful *oxidizing agent* that is used to kill any remaining microorganisms in the water before is stored ready for distribution. Storage tanks are covered to prevent the entry of foreign bodies.

2 Sewage treatment

- Raw *sewage* cannot be released into rivers because of the threat to health and the effects on the environment. The waste materials it contains must first be broken down by the action of decomposing bacteria.
- Solids are removed from the sewage by a series of screens and settling tanks. The remaining liquid passes into a digester, where bacteria break down the waste products. Streams of air are blown into the tank in order to provide the bacteria with the oxygen needed to survive and to keep the mixture circulating.
- After settling, the clean water is allowed to pass into the river, while the sludge undergoes further digestion during which *methane* is released. The digested sludge contains nitrogenous compounds and is often used as a fertilizer.

Key words

bond	oxygen
covalent	
compound	
hydrogen	
lone pair	

1 A covalent compound
- Water is essentially a *covalent compound* formed by two atoms of *hydrogen* and one atom of *oxygen*.

2 The water molecule
- The oxygen atom in a water molecule has two pairs of bonding electrons (sometimes called shared pairs) and two pairs of non-bonding electrons (sometimes called *lone pairs*).
- These four pairs of electrons are directed toward the corners of a tetrahedron. However, the tetrahedral shape is distorted. The non-bonding pairs of electrons repel each other more strongly than the bonding pairs of electrons. Repulsion between these and the bonding pairs of electrons reduces the angle between the oxygen–hydrogen bonds to 104.5 °.

3 The polar nature of the molecule
- Oxygen is more electronegative than hydrogen and, therefore, has a stronger attraction for the electrons in the oxygen–hydrogen *bond*. The result is that the electrons in the bond reside closer to the oxygen atom. Since electrons are negatively charged, this leaves the oxygen atom slightly negative and the hydrogen atom slightly positive. This is shown using δ notation; oxygen is δ- and hydrogen is δ+.

The water molecule

1 A covalent compound

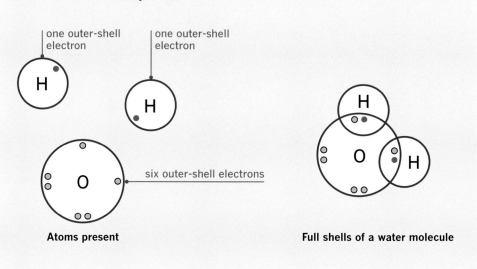

one outer-shell electron

one outer-shell electron

six outer-shell electrons

Atoms present

Full shells of a water molecule

2 The water molecule

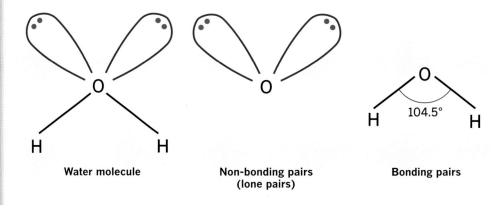

104.5°

Water molecule

Non-bonding pairs (lone pairs)

Bonding pairs

3 The polar nature of the molecule

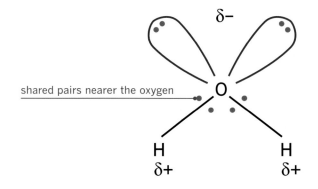

δ-

shared pairs nearer the oxygen

H
δ+

H
δ+

Water as a solvent of ionic salts

Key words	
anion	hydration
body-centered cubic	ionic crystal
cation	lattice
face-centered cubic	

1 Ionic lattices

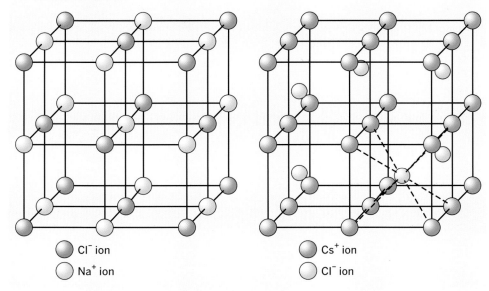

⬤ Cl⁻ ion
◯ Na⁺ ion

◯ Cs⁺ ion
◯ Cl⁻ ion

2 The effect of water on an ionic lattice

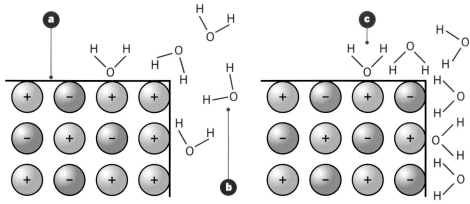

Ionic lattice put into water

The ions attract the water molecules

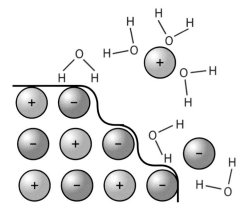

The lattice starts to split up

a lattice
b water molecules

c charged ends of molecules attracted to ions of opposite charge

1 Ionic lattices

● The ions in an *ionic crystal* are arranged in a *lattice*. Each ion is surrounded by a number of oppositely charged ions. The lattice structure is determined by:
- the ratio of the number of positively charged ions (*cations*) to negatively charged ions (*anions*)
- the ratio of the radii of the ions (r_{cation} / r_{anion})

● The radius ratio in sodium chloride is 0.57. The ions are arranged in a *face-centered cubic* structure in which each sodium ion is surrounded by six chloride ions, and each chloride ion is surrounded by six sodium ions.

● The radius ratio of cesium chloride is 0.94 (due to the larger cesium ion). The ions are arranged in a *body-centered cubic* structure in which each cesium ion is surrounded by eight chloride ions, and each chloride ion is surrounded by eight cesium ions.

2 The effect of water on an ionic lattice

● When an ionic compound is placed in water, the water molecules collide with the lattice. If the water molecules collide with sufficient energy to overcome the forces of attraction between the oppositely charged ions, *hydration* occurs, and the compound will dissolve, forming a solution.

© Diagram Visual Information Ltd.

Key words

anion	lattice
bond	transition metals
cation	
ion	
ionic compound	

Ionic solutions

- Ionic solutions are *ionic compounds* dissolved in water.

1 Stabilizing free ions

- Due to the uneven sharing of electrons in the oxygen–hydrogen *bonds* of a water molecule, the oxygen atom is slightly negatively charged and the hydrogen atoms are slightly positively charged.
- Water molecules surround and stabilize the *ions* in the compound: positively charged *cations* are stabilized by the negative oxygen atoms, and negatively charged *anions* are stabilized by the positive hydrogen atoms.

2 Transition metals in solution

- *Transition metal* ions form complexes with water.
- Transition metals have an incomplete outer shell and can fill this with the electric charge on the water molecule. Non-bonding pairs of electrons from the water molecules are donated to form coordinate bonds.
- The bonds between the metal ions and water are so strong that they remain when solids are obtained from their solutions.

3 Production of silver chloride

- When silver nitrate solution and sodium chloride solution are mixed, insoluble silver chloride forms a white precipitate.

$$Ag^+(aq) + Cl^-(aq) \rightarrow AgCl(s)$$

- The silver ions and chloride ions are more stable when bonded together in an ionic *lattice* than existing apart surrounded by water molecules.

Ionic solutions

1 Stabilizing free ions

negatively charged oxygen atom

positively charged hydrogen atom

2 Transition metals in solution

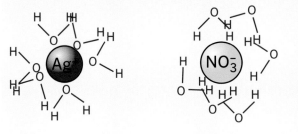

3 Production of silver chloride when a metal chloride is added to silver nitrate solution

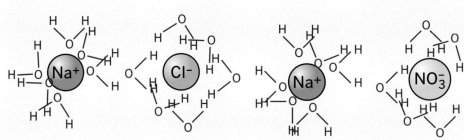

Silver nitrate solution and sodium chloride solution

After reaction, clusters of water molecules have been forced away from aqueous silver and chloride ions to leave solid silver chloride

Solubility

1 Table of solubility of ionic compounds

Soluble	Insoluble
all salts of ammonium, potassium, and sodium	
all nitrates	
most bromides, chlorides, and iodides	lead and silver bromides, chlorides, and iodides
most sulphates (calcium sulfate is slightly soluble)	barium and lead sulfate
ammonium, potassium, and sodium carbonate	most other carbonates
ammonium, potassium, and sodium hydroxides (calcium hydroxide is slightly soluble)	most other hydroxides

2 Table of the most abundant compounds in seawater

Name of compound	Formula of compound	Percentage of solids in seawater
sodium chloride	NaCl	78
magnesium chloride	$MgCl_2$	9
magnesium sulphate	$MgSO_4$	7
calcium sulphate	$CaSO_4$	4
potassium chloride	KCl	2
calcium carbonate	$CaCO_3$	less than 1
magnesium bromide	$MgBr_2$	less than 1

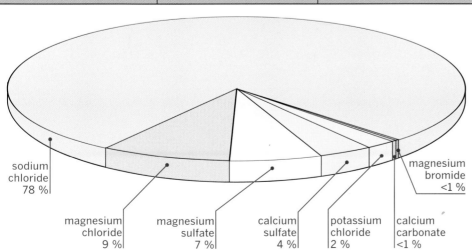

sodium chloride 78 %

magnesium chloride 9 %

magnesium sulfate 7 %

calcium sulfate 4 %

potassium chloride 2 %

calcium carbonate <1 %

magnesium bromide <1 %

Key words

ionic compound
insoluble
soluble

1 Solubility of ionic compounds

- All *ionic compounds* are *soluble* in water to some extent. However the solubility of some is so low that they are best regarded as *insoluble*. Solubility generally follows the following rules.
- All ammonium, potassium, and sodium salts are soluble.
- All nitrates are soluble.
- With the exception of lead and sliver bromides, chlorides, and iodides, bromides, chlorides, and iodides are soluble.
- Most sulfates are soluble, with the exception of barium and lead sulfate.
- Most carbonates are insoluble, with the exception of ammonium, potassium, and sodium carbonate.
- Most hydroxides are insoluble, with the exception of ammonium, potassium, and sodium hydroxides.
- Calcium hydroxide is only slightly soluble.

2 Most abundant compounds in seawater

- Seawater is a solution of many different salts. The main salt present in seawater is sodium chloride.
- The concentration of solids in seawater depends on the location. The saltiest water occurs in the Red Sea, where there is 40 g of dissolved solids per 1,000 g of water. The North Atlantic is the saltiest of the major oceans, with an average of 37.9 g of dissolved solids per 1,000 g of water. The least salty waters are found in polar seas and the Baltic Sea, which contains only 5–15 g of dissolved solids per 1,000g of water.

Key words

solubility curve

Expressing solubility

- Solubility is normally expressed in g / 100 g of water. The solubility of a compound varies (normally increases) with temperature, so when quoting solubility, it is necessary to state the temperature for which it is given.
- A *solubility curve* is a graph that shows how the solubility of a salt varies between 0°C (the freezing point of water) and 100°C (the boiling point of water).
- The solubility curve of a compound is plotted using data about the solubility of the compound over the whole temperature range. Solubility curves are generally not straight lines.
- Over the temperature range 0–100°C, the solubility of some salts remains nearly constant (sodium chloride), while the solubility of others either increases gradually (potassium sulfate) or increases very rapidly (potassium nitrate).

Solubility curves

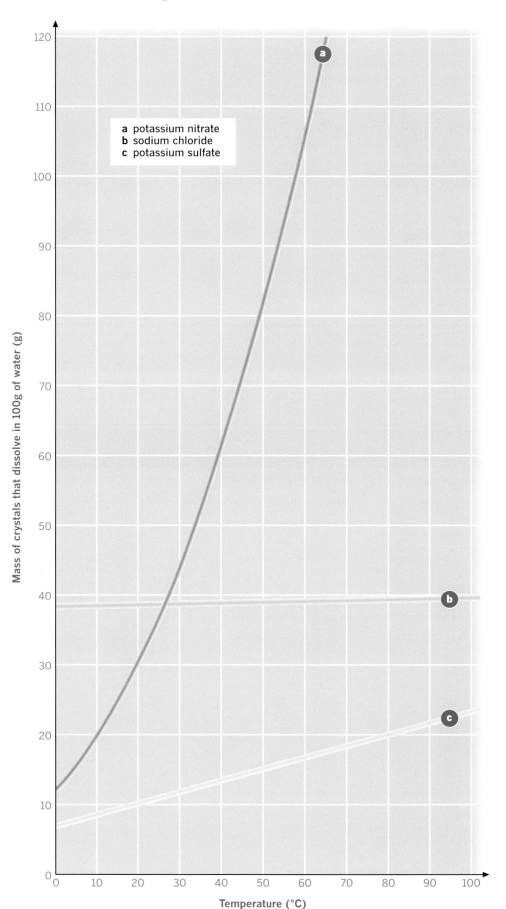

a potassium nitrate
b sodium chloride
c potassium sulfate

Solubility of copper(II) sulfate

Key words

saturated
solute
solution
solubility curve

1 Table of solubility of copper(II) sulfate at different temperatures

Temperature °C	Solubility g/100g water	Temperature °C	Solubility g/100g water
0	14.3	60	40.0
10	17.4	70	47.1
20	20.7	80	55.0
30	24.3	90	64.8
40	28.5	100	75.4
50	34.0		

2 Solubility curve for copper(II) sulfate

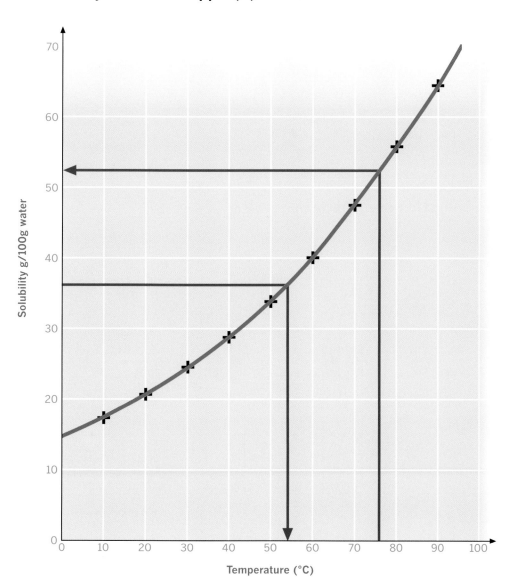

1 Solubility of copper(II) sulfate at different temperatures

- When no more solid will dissolve in a *solution* at a given temperature, the solution is said to be *saturated*.
- Normally when a solution is cooled below the saturation temperature for the quantity of *solute* present, some solute crystallizes out. Under certain conditions a solution may be cooled below this temperature without crystallization occurring. Such a solution is said to be supersaturated.
- A *solubility curve* is plotted by finding the amount of solid needed to make a saturated solution at a number of different temperatures over the range 0–100°C.

2 Solubility curve for copper(II) sulfate

- The solubility of copper(II) sulfate at 76°C is found by drawing a vertical line from 76°C to the solubility curve and then a horizontal line to the solubility axis. The value is 52 g of copper(II) sulfate per 100 g of water.
- The temperature at which the solubility of copper(II) sulfate is exactly 36 g per 100 g of water is found by drawing a horizontal line from 36 g / 100 g water to the solubility curve and then a vertical line to the temperature axis. The temperature is 54°C.
- The solubility of copper(II) sulfate at 90°C is 64.8 g / 100 g water and at 20°C is 20.7 g / 100 g water. If 100 g of saturated copper(II) sulfate solution was allowed to cool from 90°C to 20°C the mass of copper(II) sulfate crystals formed would be 64.8 – 20.7 = 44.1 g.
- The size of crystals formed is related to how quickly the solution is cooled. If cooling is rapid many small crystals are formed but if cooling is slow a smaller number of large crystals are formed.

Key words

anhydrous
dry gas
hydrochloric acid
hydrogen

Hydrogen: preparation

1 Obtaining hydrogen using Kipps apparatus

- Traditionally, *hydrogen* is generated using a Kipps apparatus. When the tap is opened, dilute *hydrochloric acid* floods the bottom compartment and the level rises until it reacts with granulated zinc in the middle compartment. Zinc reacts with dilute hydrochloric acid to produce hydrogen:

$$Zn(s) + 2HCl(aq) \rightarrow ZnCl_2(aq) + H_2(g)$$

- If the tap is closed, hydrogen continues to be produced for a short time, and the pressure of the gas in the middle compartment gradually increases. Eventually the pressure is sufficient to force the dilute hydrochloric acid back down and out of the middle compartment, and the reaction stops.

- In a modern laboratory, hydrogen is often obtained directly from a cylinder of the gas.

2 Collecting dry hydrogen

- A *dry gas* is a natural gas from which all water vapor has been reduced.

- Hydrogen is dried by passing through *anhydrous* calcium chloride. The gas is collected by upward delivery (downward displacement of air) because it is less dense than air.

1 Obtaining hydrogen using Kipps apparatus

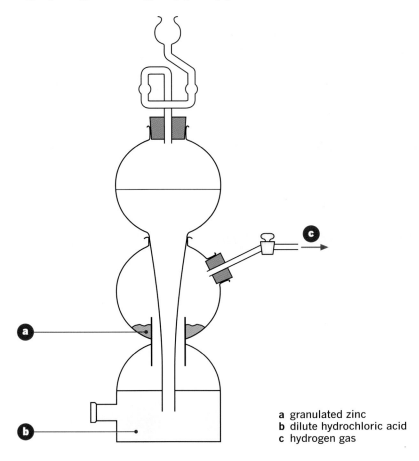

a granulated zinc
b dilute hydrochloric acid
c hydrogen gas

2 Collecting dry hydrogen

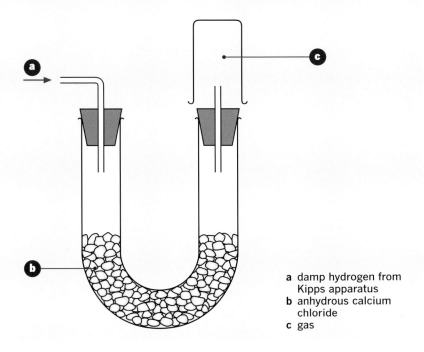

a damp hydrogen from Kipps apparatus
b anhydrous calcium chloride
c gas

Hydrogen: comparative density

Key words

carbon dioxide
diffusion
Graham's law
hydrogen

1 Gaseous diffusion of hydrogen in air

1A   1B

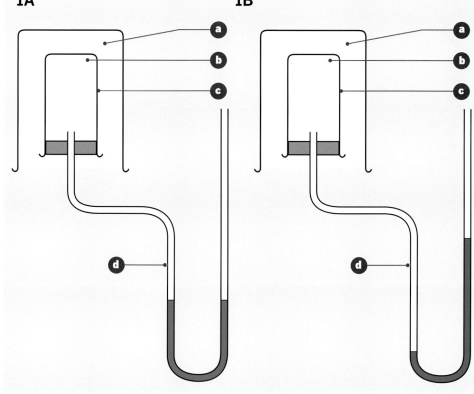

2 Gaseous diffusion of carbon dioxide in air

2A   2B

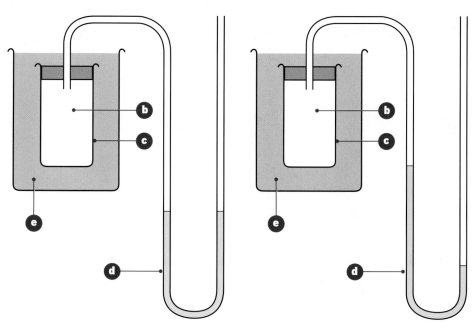

a hydrogen   c porous vessel   e carbon dioxide
b air   d manometer

1 Gaseous diffusion of hydrogen

- Gases are able to pass into and out of a porous vessel.
- *Hydrogen* is less dense than air, so it is contained in an inverted beaker (1A).
- Hydrogen diffuses into the porous vessel more quickly than air diffuses out of it.
- The gas pressure inside the porous vessel increases and becomes greater than atmospheric pressure (1B). Liquid is forced up the right side of the manometer (an instrument used to measure the pressure of a fluid).

2 Gaseous diffusion of carbon dioxide

- *Carbon dioxide* is more dense than air, so it is contained in an upright beaker (2A).
- Carbon dioxide diffuses into the porous vessel more slowly than air diffuses out of it.
- The gas pressure inside the porous vessel decreases and becomes less than atmospheric pressure. Liquid is forced up the left side of the manometer (2B).

Comparative density

- *Graham's law* of *diffusion* states that the rate at which a gas diffuses (r) is proportional to the square root of 1 over its density (d):
  $$r \propto \sqrt{1/d}$$
- The density of hydrogen is lower that air. Therefore, it diffuses more quickly.
- The density of carbon dioxide is higher that air. Therefore it diffuses more slowly.

Key words

anhydrous	hydrogen sulfide
anode	lead sulfide
calcium	photochemical
carbonate	reaction
cathode	sulfuric acid
electrolysis	

1 Hydrogen and oxygen

- *Electrolysis* of dilute *sulfuric acid* produces oxygen at the *anode* (positive electrode) and hydrogen at the *cathode* (negative electrode).
- At the anode:
  $$4OH^-(aq) \rightarrow O_2(g) + 2H_2O(l) + 4e^-$$
- At the cathode:
  $$4H^+(aq) + 4e^- \rightarrow 2H_2(g)$$
- A mixture of hydrogen and oxygen explodes when ignited:
  $$2H_2(g) + O_2(g) \rightarrow 2H_2O(g)$$

2 Hydrogen and air

- Hydrogen burns in air to produce water.
- The hydrogen gas is dried by passing it through *anhydrous calcium carbonate* so any water produced must be the result of combustion.
- Water vapor condenses on the outer surface of the beaker of cold water and collects in the water glass.
- The liquid turns anhydrous blue cobalt chloride paper pink, showing it is water.

3 Hydrogen and sulfur

- Hydrogen reacts with sulfur to produce *hydrogen sulfide*:
  $$H_2(g) + S(l) \rightarrow H_2S$$
- Hydrogen sulfide turns damp lead acetate paper black due to the formation of *lead sulfide*:
  $$Pb^{2+}(aq) + H_2S(g) \rightarrow PbS(s) + 2H^+(aq)$$

4 hydrogen and chlorine

- A mixture of hydrogen and chlorine react in bright light.
- This is an example of a *photochemical reaction*. Light provides the energy needed for the reaction to start:
  $$H_2(g) + Cl_2(g) \rightarrow 2HCl(g)$$

Hydrogen: reaction with other gases

1 Explosion of hydrogen/oxygen mixture

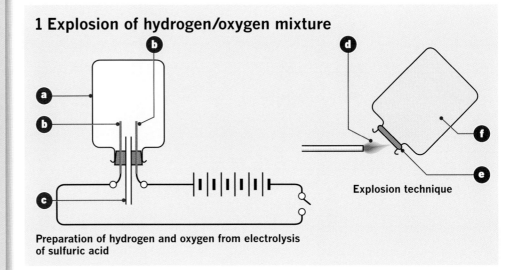

Preparation of hydrogen and oxygen from electrolysis of sulfuric acid

Explosion technique

2 Hydrogen and air

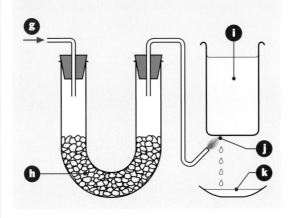

3 Reaction of hydrogen with sulfur

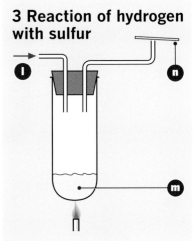

4 Photocatalytic explosion of hydrogen with chlorine

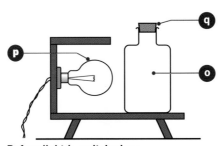

Before light is switched on

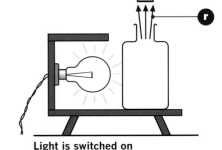

Light is switched on

a polyethylene bottle containing dilute H_2SO_4
b platinum electrodes
c polyethelene tubing
d bunsen flame
e loose support
f hydrogen/oxygen mixture
g hydrogen from Kipps apparatus
h anhydrous calcium chloride
i beaker containg cold water
j hydrogen burning
k water collected
l dry hydrogen
m boiling sulfur
n filter paper soaked in lead acetate
o polyethylene bottle containing mixture of chlorine and hydrogen
p powerful light source
q rubber bung
r white fumes of hydrogen chloride

Hydrogen: anomalies in ammonia and water

Key words

ammonia   group 8
boiling point   hydride
dipole   lone pair
group 5   orbital
group 6

1 Anomalous boiling points of ammonia and water

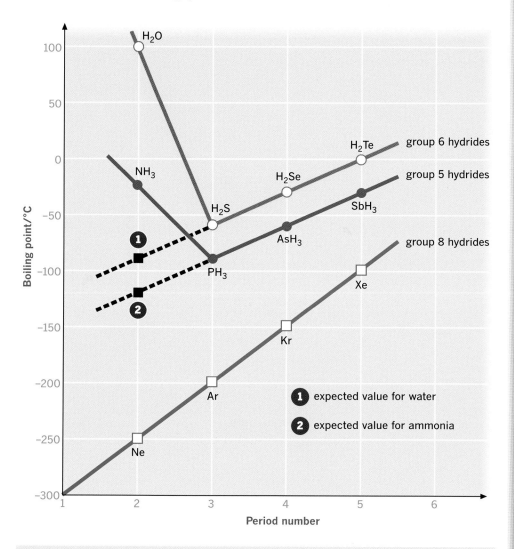

2 Strong bonding between water molecules

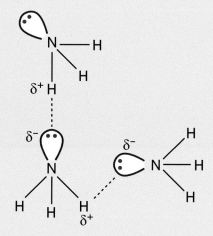

1 Anomalous boiling points of ammonia and water

- Atoms of the *group 8* elements have a full outer *orbital* of electrons. They exist as single atoms, and there are very weak forces of attraction between them. The *boiling point* of these elements increases in proportion to the size of the atom.
- The boiling points of the *group 5* and *group 6 hydrides* also increases with molecular size. However, the boiling point of water and *ammonia* are significantly higher than might be expected when compared to the other hydrides in their groups. This is the result of strong forces of attraction, called hydrogen bonding, between water molecules and between ammonia molecules.

2 Strong bonding between water molecules

- There are five electrons in the outer orbital of a nitrogen atom. In ammonia, three of the electrons are used in nitrogen–hydrogen bonds, while the remaining two form a non-bonding or *lone pair*.
- The nitrogen atom in ammonia is more electronegative than the hydrogen atoms. The result is that a pair of bonding electrons lies nearer to the nitrogen atom than the hydrogen atom in each nitrogen–hydrogen bond.
- This forms a *dipole*, a chemical compound with an unequally distributed electric charge. The nitrogen–hydrogen bond is polarized, leaving the nitrogen slightly negative (sometimes shown as δ-) and the hydrogen slightly positive (sometimes shown as δ+).
- The slightly positive hydrogen atom is attracted to the slightly negative nitrogen atom and the non-bonding pair of electrons on neighboring ammonia molecules.

Key words	
alkali	hydrocarbon
base	hydroxide
catalyst	oxide
hydride	peroxide
hydrogen	

1 Preparation

- Water, in the form of steam, can be reduced by either carbon or *hydrocarbons* to give *hydrogen*.
- This reaction is used to provide hydrogen for the Haber process in the industrial manufacture of ammonia (See page 74):

$CH_4(g) + H_2O(g) \rightleftharpoons CO(g) + 3H_2(g)$

2 Reactions of hydrogen

- Hydrogen forms hydrides with both metals and non-metals.
- Hydrogen can be used to reduce the *oxides* of metals that are low in the reactivity series, such as copper(II) oxide.

3 The oxides

- Hydrogen reacts with oxygen to form both an oxide (water) and a *peroxide* (hydrogen peroxide).
- Hydrogen peroxide contains an unstable peroxide –O-O- bond.
- A variety of substances, including manganese(IV) oxide, act as *catalysts* to break this bond, forming water and oxygen.

4 The hydroxy compounds

- All metal *hydroxides* are *bases*.
- Metal hydroxides that dissolve in water are *alkalis*.
- Sodium hydroxide solution can be used to form precipitates of insoluble metal hydroxides like copper(II) hydroxide.

5 Acids

- All acids produce solutions containing hydrogen ions, H^+.

Basic reactions of hydrogen

1 Preparation

A $\quad C + H_2O \longrightarrow CO + H_2$

B $\quad C_7H_{16} + 7H_2O \longrightarrow 7CO + 15H_2$

C $\quad 2H_2O + 2e^- \longrightarrow 2OH^- + H_2$

D $\quad Zn + 2HCl \longrightarrow ZnCl_2 + H_2$

2 Reactions of hydrogen

A $\quad 2Na + H_2 \longrightarrow 2NaH$

$\quad N_2 + 3H_2 \longrightarrow 2NH_3$

$\quad O_2 + 2H_2 \longrightarrow 2H_2O$

$\quad Cl_2 + H_2 \longrightarrow 2HCl$

B $\quad CuO + H_2 \longrightarrow Cu + H_2O$

3 The oxides

A $\quad 2Na + 2H_2O \longrightarrow 2NaOH + H_2$

B $\quad 2H_2O_2 \xrightarrow{MnO_2} 2H_2O + O_2$

4 The hydroxy compounds

$\quad NaOH + HCl \longrightarrow NaCl + H_2O$

$\quad 2NaOH + CuCl_2 \longrightarrow Cu(OH)_2\downarrow + 2NaCl$

5 Acids

$\quad HCl \longrightarrow H^+ + Cl^-$

$\quad HNO_3 \longrightarrow H^+ + NO_3^-$

$\quad H_2SO_4 \longrightarrow 2H^+ + SO_4^{2-}$

1A from coal
1B from oil
1C electrolysis of brine
1D laboratory preparation
2A it reduces other elements
2B it reduces compound

3A water
3B hydrogen peroxide
4 metallic hydroxides are bases

The gases in air

Key words

argon	methane
carbon dioxide	ozone
carbon monoxide	pollutant
compound	sulfur dioxide
element	

1 Composition of air

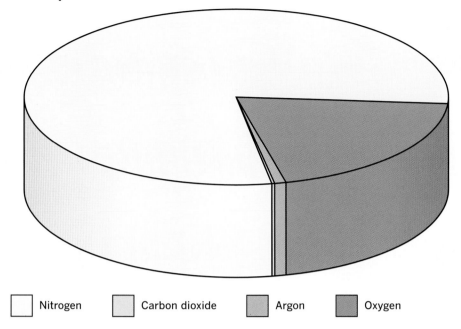

Nitrogen   Carbon dioxide   Argon   Oxygen

2 Gases present in clean dry air

Gases	Symbol or formula	Percentage of volume
Nitrogen	N	78.08
Oxygen	O	20.95
Argon	Ar	0.93
Carbon dioxide	CO_2	0.04
Neon	Ne	
Helium	He	traces
Krpton	Kr	
Xenon	Xe	

3 Gases that may be found in polluted air

Gases	Symbol or formula	Example of source
Ammonia	NH_3	Industrial processes
Carbon monoxide	CO	Motor vehicle exhaust
Methane	CH_4	Decay of organic material, passed in wind by herbivorous animals
Nitrogen oxides	NO_x	Motor vehicle and furnace exhaust
Ozone	O_3	Motor vehicle exhaust
Sulphur dioxide	SO_2	Coal-fired power stations

1 Composition of air

- Air is not a chemical *compound* but a mixture of *elements* and compounds. The exact composition of air varies slightly from place to place depending on conditions. For example, the proportion of *carbon dioxide* in the air above a forest will be less than in the air above a city. Trees remove carbon dioxide for photosynthesis, while burning fossil fuels releases carbon dioxide.

2 Gases present in clean dry air

- Clean dry air is approximately 80 percent nitrogen and 20 percent oxygen.
- *Argon* makes up the largest portion of the remaining 10 percent.
- Air usually contains water vapor, with the amount depending on local conditions.

3 Gases in polluted air

- Air may contain *pollutants* released from a variety of sources.
- *Sulfur dioxide* and nitrogen oxides dissolve in water in the atmosphere and increase the acidity of rainwater.
- *Carbon monoxide* is a poisonous gas. If it is inhaled, it bonds onto the hemoglobin in red blood cells and prevents them from transporting oxygen.
- *Ozone* is essential in the upper atmosphere (ozone layer), where it prevents harmful ultraviolet radiation from reaching Earth. At ground level, however, it is responsible for the formation of smog.
- *Methane* and carbon dioxide are greenhouse gases. In the upper atmosphere, they prevent heat radiation from passing out into space, thus causing the global temperature to rise.

Key words

group 5
nitrogen
solubility
triple bond

1 Nitrogen atom and molecule

- *Nitrogen* is in *group 5* of the periodic table. Nitrogen atoms have five electrons in the outer orbital and require an additional three electrons in order to fill the shell.
- Nitrogen exists as nitrogen molecules, N_2, in which each nitrogen atom provides three electrons. The nitrogen atoms are held together by a *triple bond*. A large amount of energy is needed to break the $N\equiv N$ triple bond (945.4 kJ mol^{-1}), which accounts for the unreactive nature of nitrogen.

2 Physical properties of nitrogen

- The melting point and boiling point of nitrogen are both very low, and nitrogen is only a liquid over a small range of temperature. This indicates that the intermolecular forces in nitrogen are weak.
- The *solubility* of gases decreases with increasing temperature. The solubility of nitrogen falls from 2.3 cm^3 per 100 g water at 0°C to 1.0 cm^3 per 100 g water at 100°C.

3 Laboratory preparation of nitrogen

- Nitrogen is formed by the thermal decomposition of ammonium nitrite:
  $$NH_4NO_2(s) \rightarrow 2H_2O(g) + N_2(g)$$
- Ammonium nitrite is difficult to store because it decomposes over time. It is best made when it is needed by mixing ammonium chloride and sodium nitrite:
  $$NH_4Cl(s) + NaNO_2(s) \rightarrow$$
  $$NH_4NO_2(s) + NaCl(s)$$

Nitrogen

1 Nitrogen atom and molecule

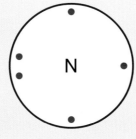
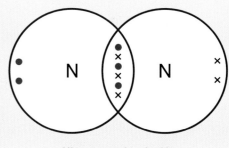

Nitrogen atom, $^{14}_{7}N$

Nitrogen molecule, N_2

2 Physical properties of nitrogen

Physical properties	m.p./°C	b.p./°C	density (relative to air)	color	smell	solubility at STP
Nitrogen	–120	–196	0.97	none	none	1.52 cm^3 in 100g of water

3 Laboratory preparation of nitrogen from ammonium chloride and sodium nitrate

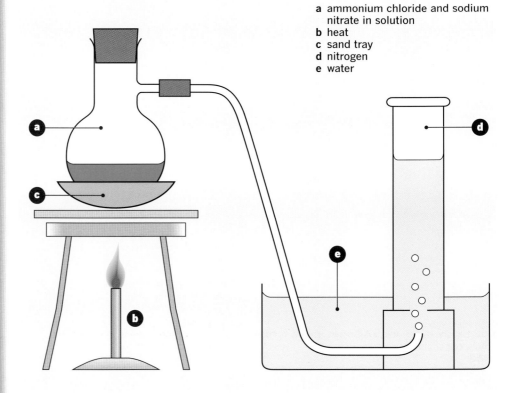

a ammonium chloride and sodium nitrate in solution
b heat
c sand tray
d nitrogen
e water

Other methods of preparing nitrogen

Key words

ammonia
group 8
inert
nitrogen
soluble

1 Extraction of nitrogen from the atmosphere

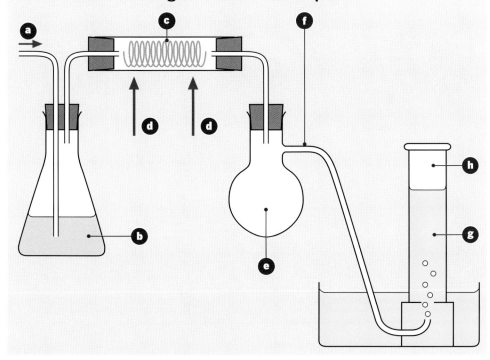

2 Preparation of nitrogen from ammonia

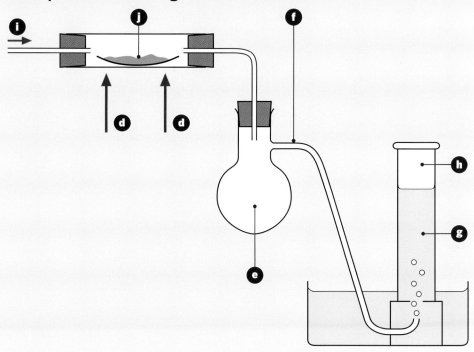

Other methods

- In addition to preparing *nitrogen* from ammonium chloride and sodium nitrate, it can be extracted from the air or from the reduction of copper(II) oxide by *ammonia*.

1 Extraction of nitrogen from the atmosphere

- Air is approximately 80 percent nitrogen and 20 percent oxygen. Impure nitrogen can be obtained by removing carbon dioxide and oxygen from air.
- Potassium hydroxide solution reacts with carbon dioxide:

$$KOH(aq) + CO_2(g) \rightarrow KHCO_3(aq)$$

- A hot copper pile reacts with oxygen:

$$2Cu(s) + O_2(g) \rightarrow 2CuO(s)$$

- Nitrogen prepared in this way contains argon and other *group 8* gases. However, because these are chemically *inert*, they would not interfere with any subsequent reactions.

2 Preparation of nitrogen from ammonia

- Ammonia can be used to reduce copper(II) oxide to copper. Nitrogen is one of the other products of this reaction:

$$3CuO(s) + 2NH_3(g) \rightarrow$$
$$3Cu(s) + 3H_2O(g) + N_2(g)$$

- Nitrogen is not very *soluble* and is readily collected over water.
- Water vapor condenses in the water trough. Ammonia is very soluble, and unreacted ammonia dissolves in the water.

---

a air intake
b potassium hydroxide solution to absorb carbon
c hot copper coil to remove oxygen
d heat
e safety trap
f delivery tube
g water
h nitrogen collected over water
i dry ammonia gas
j dry copper(II) oxide

Key words

ammonia
nitrate
nitrite
nitrogen
nitrogen cycle

Nitrogen cycle

- *Nitrogen* is continually being recycled between the soil and the air by natural processes.

- Lightning provides the energy for atmospheric nitrogen and oxygen to react, forming nitrogen oxides. For example:

$$N_2(g) + O_2(g) \rightarrow 2NO(g)$$
$$N_2(g) + 2O_2(g) \rightarrow 2NO_2(g)$$

- These oxides dissolve in water vapor in the atmosphere and eventually fall to the ground as rain.

- Atmospheric nitrogen is also converted into nitrogen compounds by nitrogen-fixing bacteria found in the root nodules of some plants.

- Nitrogen compounds are released into the soil as a result of the decay of animal waste products and by the decay of dead plants and animals. In the soil, the *ammonia* formed during decay processes is converted into *nitrates* by the action of nitrifying bacteria:

Ammonia → Ammonium compounds
→ *Nitrites* → Nitrates

- Nitrogen compounds may also be added to soil as artificial fertilizers. Ammonium nitrate is widely used by farmers and gardeners to provide growing plants with essential nitrogen.

- Nitrogen compounds are taken out of the soil by plants, which use them to make proteins and other essential chemicals. Animals subsequently eat the plants.

- Nitrogen compounds in the soil are converted to nitrogen gas by denitrifying bacteria.

The nitrogen cycle

Nitrogen cycle schematic

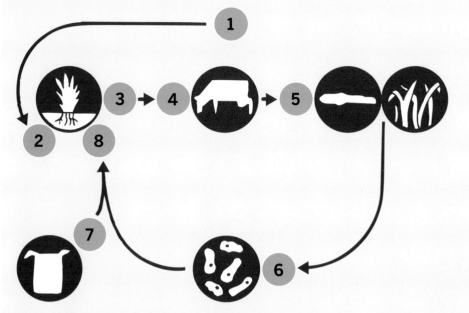

All plants and animals need nitrogen, present in proteins and nucleic acids. Most living things, however, cannot use nitrogen directly from the atmosphere.

1 Nitrogen in the air.
2 Nitrogen in the atmosphere is trapped by some plant roots.
3 Plants use nitrogen for making proteins.
4 Animals eat plant proteins.
5 The proteins in dead organisms and in body wastes are converted to ammonia by bacteria and fungi.
6 Other bacteria convert the ammonia to nitrates.
7 Artificial nitrates are added to the soil as fertilizer.
8 Plants absorb the nitrates.

Nitrogen cycle

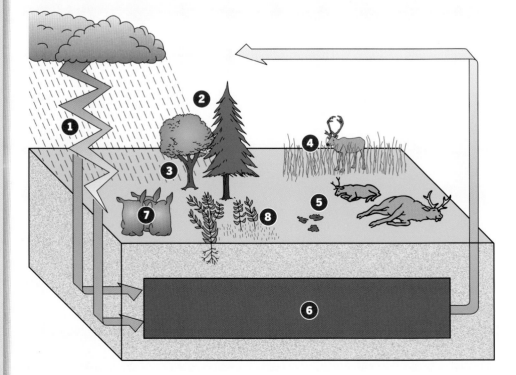

Preparation and properties of ammonia

Key words

alkali
ammonia
ammonium
  hydroxide
bond angle

lone pair
shell

1 Laboratory preparation of ammonia

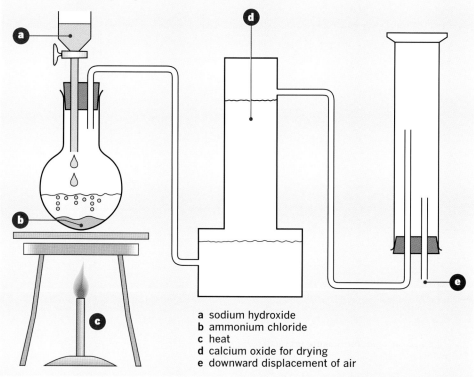

a sodium hydroxide
b ammonium chloride
c heat
d calcium oxide for drying
e downward displacement of air

1 Laboratory preparation of ammonia

- *Ammonia* is formed by the reaction of an ammonium compound, such as ammonium chloride, with an *alkali*, such as sodium hydroxide:

$NH_4Cl(s) + NaOH(aq) \rightarrow$
$\quad NH_3(g) + NaCl(aq) + H_2O(l)$

- Ammonia gas is dried by passing it through a column of calcium oxide.

2 Bonding angle

- The five electrons in the outer electron *shell* of nitrogen plus three shared electrons from the hydrogen atoms form three pairs of bonding electrons and one pair of non-bonding electrons (*lone pair*).
- The four pairs of electrons are directed toward the corners of a tetrahedron. However, repulsion between the non-bonding pair of electrons and the bonding pairs of electrons forces the nitrogen–hydrogen bonds slightly closer to each other, resulting in a *bond angle* of 107°. By comparison, the bond angle in methane is 109.5°.

3 Physical properties of ammonia

- Ammonia is less dense than air and is collected by upward delivery (downward displacement of air).
- Ammonia is exceptionally soluble and cannot be collected over water. 680 cm³ of ammonia will dissolve in 1 g of water at 20°C.
- Ammonia dissolves in water to form a solution that is a weak alkali:

$NH_3(g) + H_2O(l) \rightleftharpoons$
$\quad NH_4^+(aq) + OH^-(aq)$

- Ammonia solution is sometimes referred to as *ammonium hydroxide*.

2 Bonding angle

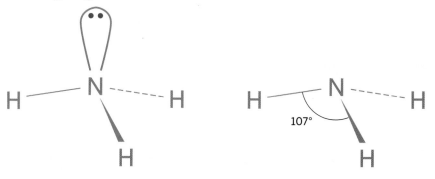

107°

3 Physical properties of ammonia

Physical property	Ammonia
Ammonia	−77.7
Carbon monoxide	−33.5
Methane	0.59
Nitrogen oxides	colorless
Ozone	characteristic unpleasant odour
Sulphur dioxide	68 000 cm³ in 100 g of water

© Diagram Visual Information Ltd.

Key words

ammonia	product
equilibrium	reactant
Le Chatelier's principle	

1 Reversible reaction

- *Ammonia* is made industrially by the reaction of nitrogen and hydrogen.
- The reaction is reversible.
  Forward reaction:
  $N_2(g) + 3H_2(g) \rightarrow 2NH_3(g)$
  Backward reaction:
  $N_2(g) + 3H_2(g) \leftarrow 2NH_3(g)$
- The concentration of ammonia in the equilibrium mixture depends on the pressure and temperature at which the reaction is carried out.
- According to *Le Chatelier's principle*, if any change is made to the external conditions (such as temperature, concentration and pressure) of a system at *equilibrium*, the equilibrium position will alter so as to oppose the change.

2 Variation of percent ammonia with pressure

- In the forward reaction, four moles of *reactants* are converted into two moles of *product* so there is a drop in pressure.
- According to Le Chatelier's principle, an increase in pressure will favor the forward reaction. The equilibrium position will move to the right in order to oppose the increase in pressure, so the equilibrium mixture will contain more ammonia.

3 Variation of percent ammonia with temperature

- The reaction is exothermic; heat is given out.
- According to Le Chatelier's principle, a decrease in temperature will favor the forward reaction. The equilibrium position will move to the right in order to oppose the decrease in temperature, so the equilibrium mixture will contain more ammonia.

Industrial preparation of ammonia (the Haber process): theory

1 Reversible reaction

$$N_2(g) + 3H_2(g) \rightleftharpoons 2NH_3(g) \qquad \Delta H = -92 \text{ kJ mol}^{-1}$$

4 moles → 2 moles

2 Variation of percent ammonia with pressure

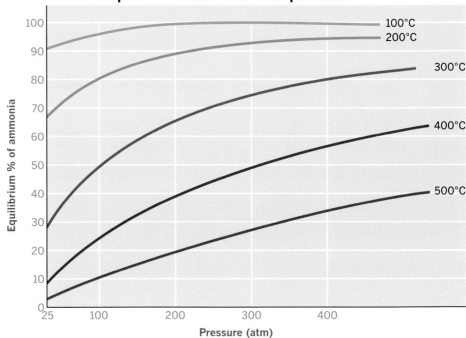

3 Variation of percent ammonia with temperature

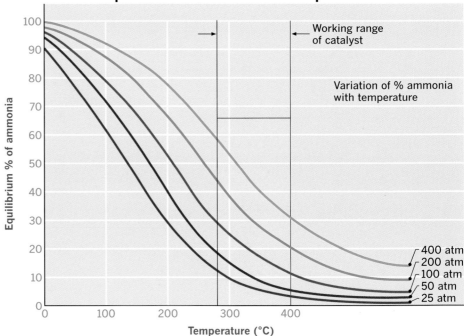

Industrial preparation of ammonia (the Haber process): schematic

Key words

ammonia
catalyst
equilibrium
fractional
 distillation

hydrocarbon
hydrogen
nitrogen

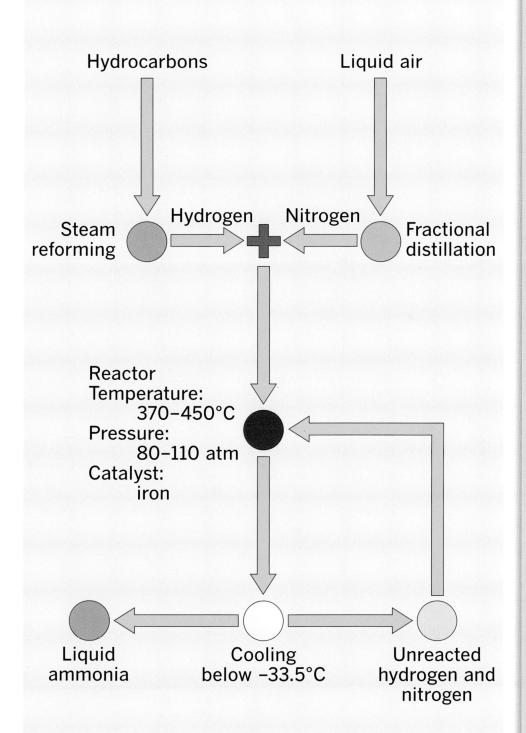

The process

- The raw materials for the Haber process are *hydrogen* and *nitrogen*.
- Hydrogen is obtained by the steam reforming of *hydrocarbons*, such as methane, or the reaction of steam with coke.

$$CH_4(g) + H_2O(g) \rightleftharpoons CO(g) + 3H_2(g)$$
$$C(s) + H_2O(g) \rightleftharpoons CO(g) + H_2(g)$$

- Nitrogen is obtained from the *fractional distillation* of liquid air.
- The formation of *ammonia* is favored by high pressure, and the reaction is normally carried out at 80–110 atm. It is also favored by low temperature, but this also lowers the rate of reaction, so a *catalyst* is used. The reaction is normally carried out at 370–450°C in the presence of a finely divided iron catalyst.
- In reality, the reaction is not allowed to reach *equilibrium*. A single pass through the reactor results in about 15 percent conversion to ammonia.
- The reaction mixture is cooled to below the boiling point of ammonia, at which point liquid ammonia condenses out and is removed. The mixture of unreacted hydrogen and nitrogen is recycled back into the reactor.
- Around 80 percent of the ammonia produced each year is used to make fertilizers, including ammonia solution, ammonium nitrate, ammonium sulfate, and urea.

Key words

ammonia
azeotropic
 mixture
exothermic
nitric acid

oxidation

Industrial preparation of nitric acid

1 Preparation

- The industrial production of *nitric acid* involves two stages: the *oxidation* of *ammonia* and the absorption of the resulting nitrogen oxides.
- In the converter, a mixture of ammonia and air is passed through a platinum–rhodium gauze and the ammonia is oxidized:

$$4NH_3(g) + 5O_2(g) \rightleftharpoons 4NO(g) + 6H_2O(g)$$
$$\Delta H = -909 \text{ kj mol}^{-1}$$

- The reaction is *exothermic*, and a large quantity of heat is produced.
- Conditions are carefully controlled to minimize a competing reaction in which ammonia is oxidized to nitrogen:

$$4NH_3(g) + 3O_2(g) \rightleftharpoons 2N_2(g) + 6H_2O(g)$$

- Air is added to the nitrogen oxides in order to make nitrogen dioxide and, subsequently, dinitrogen tetroxide.

$$2NO(g) + O_2(g) \rightleftharpoons 2NO_2(g)$$
$$2NO_2(g) \rightleftharpoons N_2O_4(g)$$

- Dinitrogen tetroxide reacts with water to produce nitric acid.

$$3N_2O_4(g) + 2H_2O(l) \rightleftharpoons$$
$$4HNO_3(aq) + 2NO(g)$$

- The acid from the absorption towers typically contains 55–60 percent nitric acid by mass. Most of the modern demand is for acid of this concentration.
- Nitric acid and water form an *azeotropic mixture* (a mixture that boils without a change in composition) containing 68.5 percent nitric acid by mass. Thus, concentrated nitric cannot be obtained by distillation. Concentrated sulfuric acid is used to reduce the water content and give concentrated nitric acid.

2 Uses of nitric acid

- Over two thirds of nitric acid production is directed to making ammonium nitrate, which is used as a fertilizer and in explosives.

1 Industrial manufacture of nitric acid

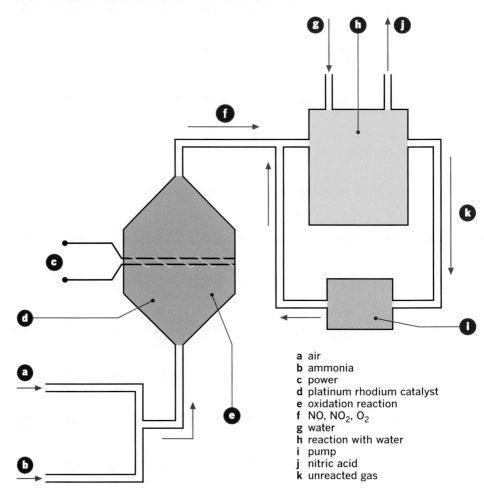

a air
b ammonia
c power
d platinum rhodium catalyst
e oxidation reaction
f NO, NO$_2$, O$_2$
g water
h reaction with water
i pump
j nitric acid
k unreacted gas

2 Summary of uses

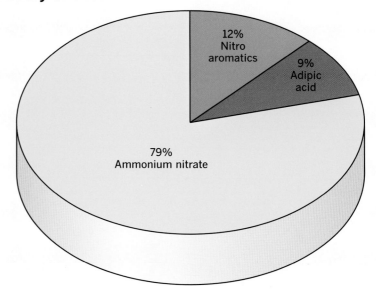

12% Nitro aromatics

9% Adipic acid

79% Ammonium nitrate

Nitrogen: reactions in ammonia and nitric acid

Key words

ammonia
nitric acid
oxide
oxidizing agent
reducing agent

1 Redox chemistry (ammonia)

$$2NH_3 + 3Cl_2 \longrightarrow N_2 + 6HCl$$

Ammonia reduces chlorine to hydrogen chloride and nitrogen

$$2NH_3 + 3CuO \longrightarrow 3Cu + 3H_2O + N_2$$

Ammonia reduces copper oxide to copper, water, and nitrogen

2 Redox chemistry (nitric acid)

$$C + 4HNO_3 \longrightarrow CO_2 + 4NO_2 + 2H_2O$$

Concentrated nitric acid oxidizes carbon to carbon dioxide

$$3Cu + 8HNO_3(dilute) \longrightarrow 3Cu(NO_3)_2 + 4H_2O + 2NO\uparrow$$

Dilute nitric acid oxidizes copper to produce copper nitrate, water, and nitrogen oxide

$$Cu + 4HNO_3(conc) \longrightarrow Cu(NO_3)_2 + 2H_2O + 2NO_2\uparrow$$

Concentrayed nitric acid oxidizes copper to produce copper nitrate, water, and nitrogen dioxide

3 Complex ammonia salts

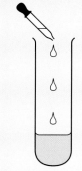

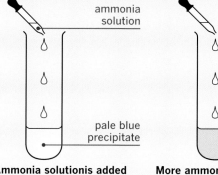

ammonia
solution

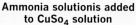
pale blue
precipitate

Ammonia solutionis added to CuSo$_4$ solution

More ammonia solution is added

The precipitate diasppears, leaving a deep royal blue solution (a complex salt)

4 Tetraamminecopper(II) ion

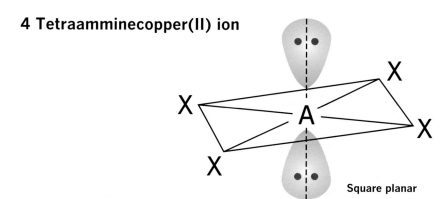

Square planar

1 Redox chemistry (ammonia)

- *Ammonia* is a *reducing agent* and will reduce chlorine and heated metal *oxides* such as copper oxide. During the reactions, the ammonia is oxidized to nitrogen.

2 Redox chemistry (nitric acid)

- In addition to its properties as an acid, *nitric acid* is also a powerful *oxidizing agent*. It is able to oxidize both non-metals and metals.

3 Complex ammonia salts

- When ammonia solution is added drop by drop to copper(II) sulfate solution, a pale blue precipitate of copper(II) hydroxide is formed:
  $$Cu^{2+}(aq) + 2OH^-(aq) \rightarrow Cu(OH)_2(s)$$
- When an excess of ammonia solution is added, the pale blue precipitate redissolves, forming a deep blue solution:
  $$Cu(OH)_2(s) + 4NH_3(aq) \rightarrow [Cu(NH_3)_4]^{2+}$$
- The deep blue solution contains the complex ion tetraamminecopper(II), $[Cu(NH_3)_4]^{2+}$.
- Ammonia also forms complex ions with other metals, such as diamminesilver(I), $[Ag(NH_3)_2]^+$ and hexaamminenickel(II), $[Ni(NH_3)_6]^{2+}$.

4 Tetraamminecopper(II)

- In the tetraamminecopper(II) ion, a copper ion is surrounded by four ammonia molecules in a square planar arrangement. The non-bonding pair of electrons on each nitrogen atom is attracted to the central positively charged copper ion.

acid	nitrogen
ammonia	oxide
nitrate	oxidizing agent
nitric acid	salt
nitrite	

1 With metals and non-metals

- *Nitrogen* combines directly with both metals, such as magnesium, and non-metals, such as sodium and hydrogen.

2 Basic reactions of ammonia

- *Ammonia* reacts with water to produce a soluble alkaline gas (2A).
- Ammonia reacts with an *acid* to produce a *salt* (2B).
- Ammonia reacts with an *oxide* to produce a metal and nitrogen (2C).
- Ammonia reacts with oxygen to produce *nitric acid* (2D).

3 Nitric acid

- Nitric acid is both a strong acid (3A) and a powerful *oxidizing agent* (3B).
- Cold, dilute nitric acid produces nitrogen oxide when reacting with a metal (3C).
- Hot, concentrated nitric acid produces nitrogen dioxide when reacting with a metal (3D).

4 Nitrates

- All *nitrates* are very soluble in water.
- Group 1 metal nitrates (apart form lithium nitrate) decompose on heating to form metal *nitrites* and oxygen.
- Other metal nitrates decompose on heating to form metal oxides, nitrogen dioxide, and oxygen.
- Ammonium nitrate decomposes on heating, forming water and dinitrogen oxide.

Basic reactions of nitrogen

1 With metals and non-metals

$$3Mg + N_2 \longrightarrow Mg_3N_2$$
$$6Na + N_2 \longrightarrow 2Na_3N$$
$$N_2 + 3H_2 \underset{}{\overset{Fe\ catalyst}{\rightleftharpoons}} 2NH_3$$

2 Basic reactions of ammonia

A $NH_3 + H_2O \rightleftharpoons NH_4^+ + OH_2^-$

$NH_3 + HCl \rightleftharpoons NH_4Cl$

B $2NH_3 + 3CuO \longrightarrow 3Cu + 3H_2O + N_2$

C $4NH_3 + 5O_2 \longrightarrow 4NO + 6H_2O$

then $2NO + O_2 \longrightarrow 2NO_2$

and $4NO_2 + O_2 + 2H_2O \longrightarrow 4HNO_3$

D $Cu(OH)_2 + 4NH_3 \rightleftharpoons Cu(NH_3)_4^{2+} + 2OH^-$

3 Nitric acid

A $HNO_3 + H_2O \longrightarrow H_3O^+ + NO_3^-$

B $C + 2HNO_3 \longrightarrow CO_2 + 2NO_2 + H_2O$

$Cu + 4HNO_3 \longrightarrow Cu(NO_3)_2 + 2H_2O + 2NO_2$

4 Nitrates

A $2NaNO_3 \longrightarrow 2NaNO_2 + O_2$

B $2Pb(NO_3)_2 \longrightarrow 2PbO + 4NO_2 + O_2$

C $NH_4NO_3 \longrightarrow 2H_2O + N_2O$

2A soluble alkaline gas
2B reducing agent
2C ammonia with oxygen to make nitric acid
2D complexing agent
3A strong acid
3B oxidizing agent

4A group 1 (excluding $LiNO_3$)
4B others
4C ammonium nitrate

Nitrate fertilizers

1 Atmospheric nitrogen

Nitrogen → Ammonia → Nitric acid

Ammonium nitrate

$$NH_3(aq) + HNO_3(aq) \rightarrow NH_4NO_3(aq)$$

2 Ammonia nitrate

Formula mass of ammonium nitrate = $14 + 4 + 14 + 3 \times 16 = 80$

Percentage of nitrogen in ammonium nitrate $= \dfrac{2 \times 14 \times 100}{80} = 35\%$

3 Nitrogen in plants

$$H_2N — CH — COOH$$

amino acids

↓

proteins

Chlorophyll a
(In chlorophyll b, the methyl group
marked by an asterisk is replaced
by a —CHO group)

4 Table of nitrogen fertilizers

Compound	Formula	Percentage of nitrogen
Ammonium nitrate	NH_4NO_3	35.00
Ammonium sulphate	$(NH_4)_2SO_4$	21.21
Urea	H_2NCONH_2	46.67

1 Atmospheric nitrogen

- Atmospheric nitrogen is an important raw material in the manufacture of *ammonia* and *nitric acid*.
- Ammonia solution is *alkali*, while nitric acid is acidic.
- The two solutions undergo a *neutralization* reaction to form the salt ammonium nitrate.

2 Ammonia nitrate

- The percentage of nitrogen in a nitrogenous fertilizer is an important factor in determining how much fertilizer should be used on an area of crops.
- Ammonium nitrate is very soluble in water. Any excess that is applied to soil is readily washed out into streams and rivers, where it causes environmental problems.

3 Nitrogen in plants

- Plants use nitrogen to make *amino acids* and, from these, to make *proteins*.
- Plants also use nitrogen to make other important chemicals, such as *chlorophyll*.

4 Nitrogen fertilizers

- Ammonium sulfate is formed by the neutralization reaction between ammonia solution and sulfuric acid:
$$2NH_3(aq) + H_2SO_4(aq) \rightarrow (NH_4)_2SO_4(aq)$$
- Urea is a waste product of animal metabolism and is excreted from the body in sweat and urine. It is made industrially by the reaction of ammonia with carbon dioxide. This reaction is carried out at 200 °C and 200 atmospheres:
$$CO_2(g) + 2NH_3(g) \rightarrow H_2NCONH_2(l) + H_2O(g)$$

1 Atoms and molecules

- *Oxygen* and *sulfur* are both in *group 6* of the periodic table. Atoms of each element have six electrons in the outer electron shell and require two electrons to fill the shell.
- Oxygen exists as oxygen molecules, O_2, in which each oxygen atom provides two electrons. The oxygen atoms are held together by a *double bond*, $O=O$.
- At room temperature, sulfur exists as a molecule composed of eight sulfur atoms, S_8, arranged in the shape of a crown.

2 Laboratory preparation of oxygen

- Oxygen is prepared in the laboratory by the decomposition of hydrogen peroxide using a suitable *catalyst*, such as manganese dioxide:
$$2H_2O_2(l) \rightarrow O_2(g) + 2H_2O(l)$$
- Hydrogen peroxide is rapidly decomposed by a variety of catalysts, including the *enzyme* catalase. In one second, one molecule of catalase can decompose up to 50,000 molecules of hydrogen peroxide.
- Oxygen is only slightly soluble and can be collected over water.
- Hydrogen peroxide is usually supplied in solutions designated by volume strength. For example, 20-volume hydrogen peroxide yields 20 volumes of oxygen gas per volume of solution.

3 Physical properties of oxygen and sulfur

- At room temperature, oxygen is a colorless, odorless gas, while sulfur is a yellow solid.

Oxygen and sulfur

1 Atoms and molecules

Oxygen atom $^{16}_{8}O$

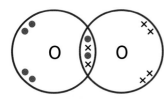

Oxygen molecule O_2

Sulfur atom $^{32}_{16}S$

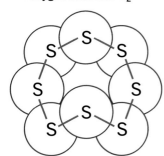

Sulfur molecule S_8
(crown-shaped)

2 Laboratory preparation of oxygen

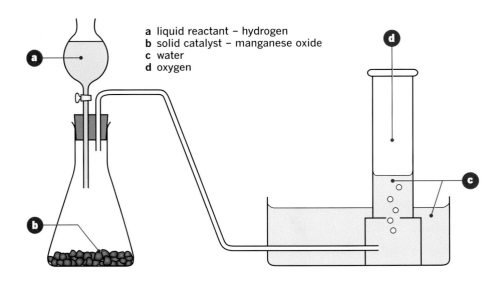

a liquid reactant – hydrogen
b solid catalyst – manganese oxide
c water
d oxygen

3 Physical properties of oxygen and sulfur

Physical properties	Oxygen	Sulfur
m.p./°C	−218	119
b.p./°C	−183	444
Density g/dm³	1.31	2070
Color	none	yellow
Smell	none	slight
Solubility	0.007g per 100g/H_2O	almost insoluble

Extraction of sulfur—the Frasch process

The Frasch process

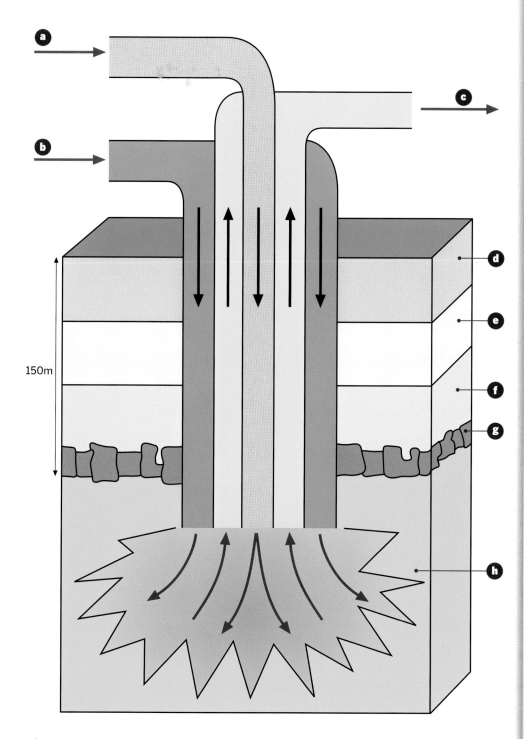

a hot compressed air
b superheated water (at 170°C)
c molten sulfur and water
d clay

e quicksand
f sand
g limestone
h sulfur

Processing and uses

- Hot compressed air and superheated steam are piped underground. This forces water and molten *sulfur* to the surface.

- The sulfur obtained is about 99.5 percent pure, and may be stored and transported molten or allowed to cool and solidify.

- A significant proportion of the elemental sulfur used in industry is obtained as a by-product of other industrial processes such as the refining of metal *sulfide ores* and petroleum refining.

- In petroleum refining, sulfur compounds like thiols (R-SH) and disulphides (R-S-S-R) are removed from some of the petroleum fractions because they would damage the catalysts used in refining processes and also because of their potential to cause environmental problems. For example, if they were not removed from fuels like gasoline, they would burn to form *sulfur dioxide*. This gas dissolves in water in the atmosphere, forming an acid, and would significantly increase the acidity of rain water.

- Sulfur compounds are converted to hydrogen sulfide by catalytic hydrogenation:
$$R\text{-}SH(g) + H_2(g) \rightarrow$$
$$R\text{-}H(g) + H_2S(g)$$
$$R\text{-}S\text{-}S\text{-}R(g) + 3H_2(g) \rightarrow$$
$$2R\text{-}H(g) + 2H_2S(g)$$

- Hydrogen sulfide can be converted to sulfur using the Claus process:
$$6H_2S(g) + 5O_2(g) \rightarrow$$
$$2SO_2(g) + 2S_2(g) + 6H_2O(g)$$
$$4H_2S(g) + 2SO_2(g) \rightarrow$$
$$3S_2(g) + 4H_2O(g)$$

Key words

allotrope	ozone
bond	sulfur
diatomic	viscosity
molecule	
oxygen	

Allotropes

- *Allotropes* are different forms of the same element in the same physical state. Many elements, including *oxygen* and *sulfur*, exist as more than one allotrope.

1 Oxygen

- The most common form of oxygen is a *diatomic molecule*, O_2. The gas also exists as a triatomic molecule, O_3, which is called *ozone*.
- Oxygen has two *bonds* between the atoms. Each atom donates one electron to each bond.
- In ozone, the central oxygen atom donates a pair of electrons to form a bond with the other two atoms. One of the other atoms also donates a pair of electrons, while the other does not.

2 Sulfur

- Sulfur has several allotropes in the solid form, including rhombic sulfur and monocline sulfur.
- Rhombic sulfur crystals have a lemon-yellow appearance.
- Monocline sulfur crystals are needle-like and have a deeper yellow color.
- Each allotrope is composed of S8 puckered molecular rings, but arranged in different ways.

3 Heating sulfur

- Sulfur melts when gently heated, and the sulfur molecules are able to move around, forming a low-*viscosity* liquid.
- On stronger heating, the sulfur rings break open, yielding sulfur molecules. These molecules join by cross-linking, causing a sharp increase in viscosity.
- On even stronger heating, the cross-linked structure breaks, yielding small sulfur molecules, which are free-moving, and the viscosity falls.

Oxygen and sulfur: allotropes

1 Allotrope of oxygen

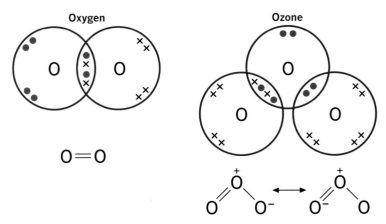

2 Allotropes of sulfur

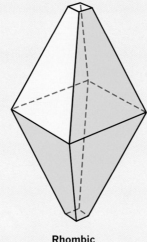

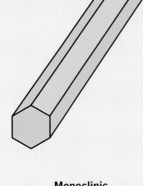

Rhombic sulfur

Monoclinic sulfur

3

Structure				
Color	yellow	yellow	red	black
State of matter	solid	liquid	liquid	liquid
Viscosity	–	low	high	low

Oxygen and sulfur: compound formation

Key words

hydrogen	oxide
hydrogen	oxygen
peroxide	peroxide
hydrogen sulfide	sulfide
magnesium	sulfur

1 Oxygen and magnesium

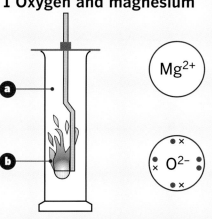

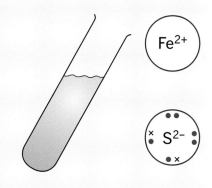

Oxygen reacts with magnesiun

Magnesium oxide is ionic

2 Reaction of sulfur and iron

Sulfur and iron glow

Iron sulfide is also ionic

3 Phosphorous reacts with atmospheric oxygen

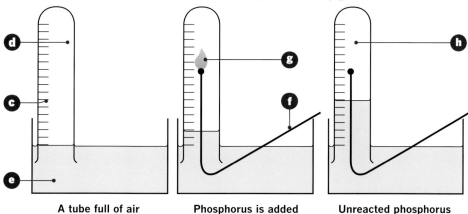

A tube full of air

Phosphorus is added

Unreacted phosphorus is left behind

a oxgen
b magnesium burning
c volume scale

d 100 cm³ of air
e water
f stiff wire

g phosphorus reacting
h 79 cm³ of air is left behind

4 Water, hydrogen peroxide, and hydrogen sulfide

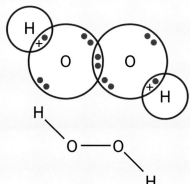

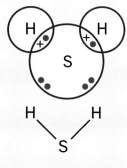

Water is formed when oxygen and hydrogen are exploded together

Hydrogen peroxide is made by reacting a metal peroxide with acid

Hydrogen sulfide is made by the reaction of a metal sulfide with dilute acid

1 Oxygen and magnesium

- *Oxygen* reacts with most metals to form metal *oxides*. Magnesium burns in air with a bright flame, producing a white smoke of magnesium oxide. The reaction is even more vigorous in pure oxygen:
  $$2Mg(s) + O_2(g) \rightarrow 2MgO$$
- Soluble metal oxides dissolve in water to form alkaline solutions:
  $$MgO(s) + H_2O(l) \rightarrow Mg(OH)_2(aq)$$

2 Sulfur and iron

- *Sulfur* forms *sulfides* with many metals. When iron and sulfur are heated together, iron sulfide is formed:
  $$8Fe + S_8 = 8FeS$$

3 Oxygen and phosphorous

- Oxygen also reacts with non-metals to form oxides. Phosphorus burns in air to form phosphorus(V) oxide. Approximately 20 percent of the air is used:
  $$P_4(s) + 5O_2(g) \rightarrow P_4O_{10}(s)$$
- Non-metal oxides dissolve in water to form acids:
  $$P_4O_{10}(s) + H_2O(l) \rightarrow 4H_3PO_4(aq)$$

4 Other common reactions

- *Hydrogen* burns in oxygen to form water:
  $$2H_2(g) + O_2(g) \rightarrow 2H_2O(l)$$
- *Hydrogen peroxide* is formed by the reaction of metal *peroxides*, such as barium peroxide, with dilute acids:
  $$BaO_2(s) + H_2SO_4(aq) \rightarrow$$
  $$H_2O_2(aq) + BaSO_4(s)$$
- *Hydrogen sulfide* is formed by the reaction of a metal sulfide with a dilute acid:
  $$FeS(s) + 2HCl(aq) \rightarrow$$
  $$FeCl_2(aq) + H_2S(g)$$

Key words

catalyst	sulfur dioxide
lone pair	sulfurous acid
oxide	sulfur trioxide
sulfite	
sulfur	

Sulfur oxides

- *Sulfur* combines with oxygen to form two *oxides*: *sulfur dioxide* (sulfur(IV) oxide) and *sulfur trioxide* (sulfur(VI) oxide.

1 Laboratory preparation of sulfur dioxide

- Metal *sulfites*, such as sodium sulfite, react with dilute acids to from sulfur dioxide:

$$Na_2SO_3(s) + 2HCl(aq) \rightarrow$$
$$2NaCl(aq) + H_2O(l) + SO_2(g)$$

- Sulfur dioxide is dried by passing it through anhydrous calcium chloride and collected by downward delivery.
- Sulfur dioxide dissolves in water to form *sulfurous acid*:

$$H_2O(l) + SO_2(g) \rightarrow H_2SO_3(aq)$$

2 Laboratory preparation of sulfur trioxide

- Sulfur trioxide is formed when dry sulfur dioxide and oxygen are heated in the presence of a platinized asbestos *catalyst*:

$$2SO_2(g) + O_2(g) \rightleftharpoons 2SO_3(g)$$

- Sulfur trioxide forms needle-like crystals when cooled.
- Sulfur trioxide dissolves in water to form sulfuric acid:

$$H_2O(l) + SO_3(g) \rightarrow H_2SO_4(aq)$$

3 SO₂ and SO₃ molecules

- In sulfur dioxide, there are four pairs of bonding electrons and a non-bonding or *lone pair* of electrons around the sulfur atom. The pairs of electrons are kept as far from each other as possible by adopting a bent shape in which the double bonds between the sulfur and oxygen atoms are at an angle of 120°.
- In sulfur trioxide, the three double bonds form a trigonal planar structure around the sulfur atom in which the bond angle is also 120°.

The oxides of sulfur

1 Laboratory preparation of sulfur dioxide

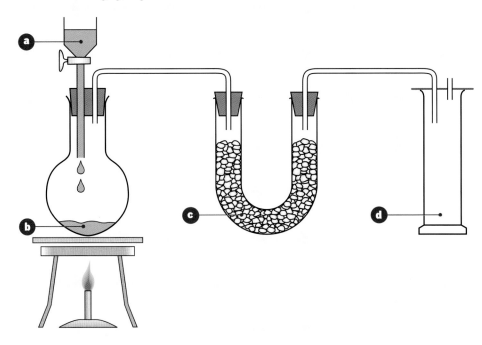

2 Laboratory preparation of sulfur trioxide

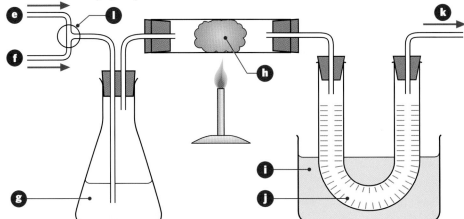

a dilute	f sulfur dioxide	i freezing mixture of ice and
b sodium sulfite	g concentrated sulfuric acid	salt
c anhydrous CaCl₂	for drying	j needles of sulfur oxide
d upward displacement	h plantinized asbestos	k to the fume cupboard
e oxygen		l 3-way tap

3 SO₂ and SO₃ molecules

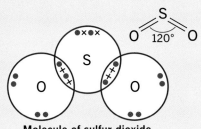

Molecule of sulfur dioxide

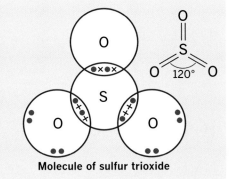

Molecule of sulfur trioxide

Industrial preparation of sulfuric acid (the contact process): theory

Key words

catalyst	sulfuric acid
exothermic	sulfur trioxide
equilibrium	
sulfur	
sulfur dioxide	

1 Sulfur burning

$$S(1) + O_2(g) \rightarrow SO_2(g) \qquad \Delta H = -297 \text{ kJ mol}^{-1}$$

2 Conversion

$$2SO_2(g) + O_2(g) \rightleftharpoons 2SO_3(g) \qquad \Delta H = -192 \text{ kJ mol}^{-1}$$

4 moles   2 moles

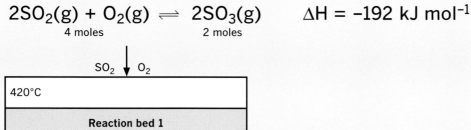

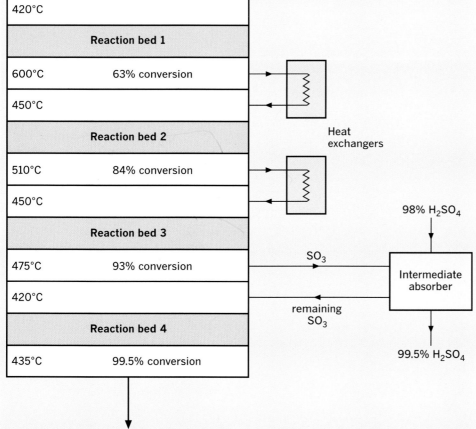

$SO_3(g)$
to final absorber

3 Absorption

$$H_2SO_4(1) + SO_3(g) \rightleftharpoons H_2S_2O_7(1)$$

$$H_2S_2O_7(1) + H_2O(1) \rightarrow 2H_2SO_4(1)$$

Preparation of sulfuric acid
- The industrial preparation of *sulfuric acid* is a three stage process:
  1. *Sulfur* burning
  2. Conversion of *sulfur dioxide* to *sulfur trioxide*
  3. Absorption of sulfur trioxide to form sulfuric acid.

1 Sulfur burning
- Molten sulfur is sprayed into a furnace and burned in a blast of dry air. The reaction is very *exothermic*, and the reaction temperature rises to over 1,000°C. The mixture of gases, containing sulfur dioxide and oxygen, is cooled before conversion.

2 Conversion
- The conversion of sulfur dioxide into sulfur trioxide is an exothermic reaction. The forward reaction is favored by a low temperature. However, this would also reduce the rate of reaction, so it would take longer for the reaction mixture to reach *equilibrium*.
- The reaction is carried out at temperatures between 420–620°C in the presence of a vanadium(V) oxide *catalyst*.
- Modern converters consist of four reaction beds. The reaction mixture is cooled after passing through each of the first two beds in order to maximize conversion in subsequent beds.

3 Absorption
- Sulfur trioxide is removed and absorbed after the reaction mixture has passed through both the third and fourth beds.
- Sulfur trioxide is absorbed into 98 percent sulfuric acid to form 99.5 percent sulfuric acid, which is sometimes referred to as oleum and given the chemical formula $H_2S_2O_7$.
- Oleum is then diluted to give 98 percent sulfuric acid.

Key words

catalyst	sulfuric acid
ore	sulfur trioxide
sulfide	
sulfur	
sulfur dioxide	

Preparing sulfuric acid

- The *sulfur* needed for the manufacture of *sulfuric acid* is obtained either directly from the ground or as a by-product of other industrial processes, such as the refining of metal *sulfide ores* and the refining of crude oil.

- An excess of dry air is used to ensure there is sufficient oxygen remaining in the reaction mixture for the conversion of *sulfur dioxide* to *sulfur trioxide*.

- The vanadium(V) oxide (vanadium pentoxide) *catalyst* is activated by potassium sulfate on a silica support. It is generally in the form of small cylindrical pellets that ensure a large surface area for reaction. The catalyst is inactive below about 380°C and has an optimum working temperature between 420–620°C.

- The catalyst pellets are packed onto perforated plate supports to form reaction beds. In a modern converter, there four reaction beds, each consisting of a layer of catalyst pellets about 0.6 m deep.

- A conversion of 99.5 percent of sulfur dioxide to sulfur trioxide is essential for both economic and environmental reasons. This can only be attained by removing heat between reaction beds and by removing the sulfur trioxide produced between the third and fourth beds.

- The mixture of gases that remain after absorption consists mostly of nitrogen, together with a small proportion of oxygen and traces of sulfur dioxide. The gases are filtered to remove any sulfuric acid before being released into the atmosphere at high level via a stack.

- Sulfuric acid is used in a wide variety of industries. Important uses include the manufacture of general chemicals, paints and pigments, detergents and soaps, and phosphatic fertilizers.

Industrial preparation of sulfuric acid (the contact process): schematic

Industrial preparation of sulfuric acid

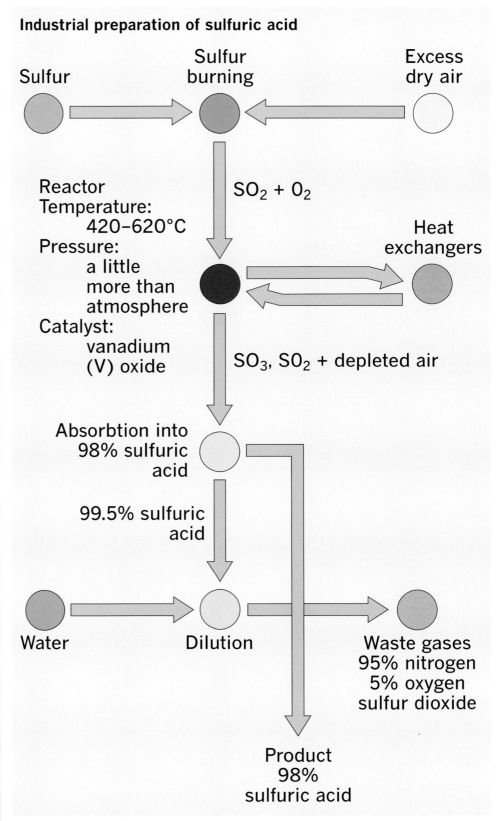

Affinity of concentrated sulfuric acid for water

Key words

alcohol	sulfuric acid
alkene	
carboxylic acid	
catalyst	
ester	

1 Sulfuric acid and atmospheric water

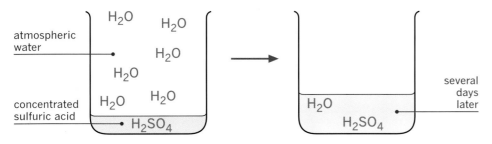

2 Illustrating sulfuric acid's affinity for water

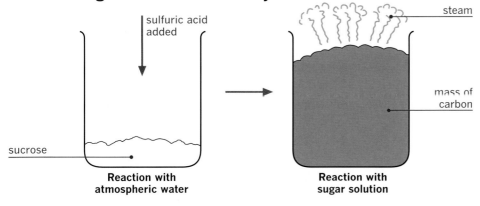

Reaction with atmospheric water

Reaction with sugar solution

3 Drying gases

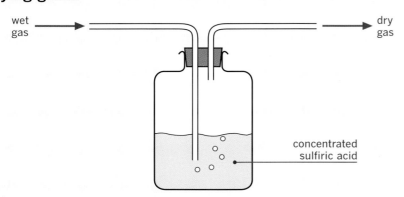

4 Forming esters and alkenes

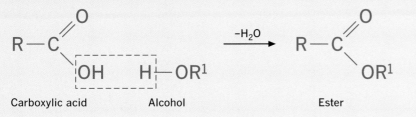

Carboxylic acid   Alcohol   Ester

---

1 Sulfuric acid and atmospheric water

- Concentrated *sulfuric acid* will absorb water from the air.
- The level of liquid in a beaker containing concentrated sulfuric acid rises as water is absorbed and the acid becomes more dilute.

2 Sulfuric acid's affinity for water

- Concentrated sulfuric acid will remove the elements of water from organic chemicals such as sucrose ($C_{12}H_{22}O_{11}$).
- When concentrated sulfuric acid is poured onto sucrose, the crystalline white sucrose turns into a black amorphous mass of carbon.

3 Drying gases

- Concentrated sulfuric acid can be used to dry gases, such as hydrogen. The gas is bubbled through the acid in a suitable container.
- Some gases, such as ammonia, react with concentrated sulfuric acid and cannot be dried in this way.

4 Forming esters and alkenes

- Concentrated sulfuric acid is used as a *catalyst* in the formation of *esters* from *carboxylic acids* and *alcohols*. Concentrated sulfuric acid removes the elements of water from alcohols to form *alkenes*:

$$R\text{-}CH_2\text{-}CH_2OH \xrightarrow{-H_2O} R\text{-}CH=CH_2$$

Key words	
hydrogen peroxide	oxygen
	redox reaction
hydrogen sulfide	reduction
	sulfur
oxidizing agent	sulfur dioxide

1 Common redox reactions

- *Oxidation* reactions and *reduction* reactions are more accurately described as *redox reactions* because they cannot occur in isolation. One substance is reduced and another is oxidized at the same time.
- *Hydrogen sulfide* reduces chlorine gas to chloride ions. The sulfide is oxidized to elemental *sulfur*:

  $Cl_2 + 2e^- \rightarrow 2Cl^-$ reduction

  $S^{2-} \rightarrow S + 2e^-$ oxidation
- *Hydrogen peroxide* is an oxidizing agent but is itself oxidized by a more powerful oxidizing agent such as potassium manganate(VII).
- *Sulfur dioxide* is a reducing agent both in the gaseous form and in aqueous solution. It reduces iron(III) to iron(II) while being itself oxidized to a sulfate:

  $Fe^{3+} + e^- \rightarrow Fe^{2+}$ reduction
- Sulfur dioxide can be oxidized to sulfur trioxide by reaction with *oxygen*.
- Copper reacts with concentrated sulfuric acid. In this reaction, the concentrated sulfuric acid acts as an oxidizing agent, oxidizing copper metal to copper(II). The sulfuric acid is itself reduced to sulfur dioxide:

  $Cu \rightarrow Cu^{2+} + 2e^-$ oxidation

2 Sulfuric acid and sulfate reactions

- Sulfuric acid reacts with metal oxides to form sulfates and water.
- Sulfuric acid reacts with metal hydroxides to form sulfates and water
- Sulfuric acid reacts with metal carbonates to form salts, carbon dioxide, and water
- In all of these reactions, no oxidation or reduction takes place. The charge on the metal ion in the oxide, hydroxide, and carbonate is the same as it is in the sulfate.

Oxygen and sulfur: oxidation and reduction

1 Common redox reactions

$$8H_2S + 8Cl_2 \longrightarrow S_8 + 16HCl$$

Hydrogen sulfide reduces chlorine gas

$$H_2O_2 + 3KMnO_4 \longrightarrow 2KOH + 2MnO_2 + 2O_2$$

Hydrogen peroxide reduces potassium manganate(VII) solution

$$SO_2 + 2FeCl_3 + 2H_2O \longrightarrow 2FeCl_2 + 2HCl + H_2SO_4$$

Sulfur oxide reduces iron chloride solution

$$O_2 + 2SO_2 \longrightarrow 2SO_3$$

Oxygen oxidizes sulfur dioxide

$$Cu + 2H_2SO_4 \longrightarrow CUSO_4 + H_2O + SO_2\uparrow$$

Concentrated sulfuric acid oxidizes copper

2 Sulfuric acid and sulfate reactions

Acid + metal oxide	=	Salt + water

$$H_2SO_4 + MgO \longrightarrow MgSO_4 + H_2O$$

Acid + metal hydroxide	=	Salt + water

$$H_2SO_4 + Cu(OH)_2 \longrightarrow CuSO_4 + 2H_2O$$

Acid + metal carbonate	=	Salt + carbon dioxide + water

$$H_2SO_4 + ZnCO_3 \longrightarrow ZnSO_4 + CO_2 + H_2O$$

Basic reactions of oxygen

1 Reactions

Oxidizes other elements

$$2H_2 + O_2 \longrightarrow 2H_2O$$
$$4Na + O_2 \longrightarrow 2Na_2O$$
$$2Na + O_2 \longrightarrow Na_2O_2$$
$$S_8 + 8O_2 \longrightarrow 8SO_2$$
$$P_4 + 5O_2 \longrightarrow P_4O_{10}$$
$$2Cu + O_2 \longrightarrow 2CuO$$

Oxidizes other elements

$$2CO + O_2 \longrightarrow 2CO_2$$
$$2SO_2 + O_2 \rightleftharpoons 2SO_3$$
$$4NH_3 + 5O_2 \longrightarrow 4NO + 6H_2O$$

2 The hydrides

Water

a $\quad 2Na + 2H_2O \longrightarrow 2NaOH + H_2\uparrow$

b $\quad H_2O + HCl \longrightarrow H_3O^+ + Cl^-$

c $\quad H_2O + NH_3 \rightleftharpoons NH_4^+ + OH^-$

d $\quad H_2O + CO_2 \rightleftharpoons H_2CO_3$

$\quad\quad H_2O + SO_2 \rightleftharpoons H_2SO_3$

Oxidizes other elements

e $\quad BaO_2 + H_2SO_4 \longrightarrow H_2O_2 + BaO_4\downarrow$

f $\quad H_2O_4 + 2FeCl_2 + 2HCl \longrightarrow 2FeCl_3 + 2H_2O$

g $\quad H_2O_2 + 2KMnO_4 \longrightarrow 2KOH + 2MnO_2 + 2O_2$

3 The oxides

Oxidizes other elements

h $\quad CuO + H_2SO_4 \longrightarrow CuSO_4 + H_2O$

i $\quad ZnO + H_2SO_4 \longrightarrow ZnSO_4 + H_2O$

$\quad\quad ZnO + 2NaOH \longrightarrow Na_2Zn(CH)_4 + H_2O$

Oxidizes other elements

j $\quad SO_2, CO_2$

k $\quad H_2O, CO$

a oxidizes reactive metals
b accepts protons from acids
c gives protons to bases
d reacts with non-metal oxides

e preparation
f an oxiding agent
g a reducing agent
h basic

i amphoteric
j acidic
k neutral

1 Reactions

- *Oxygen* reacts with both metals and non-metals to form *oxides*.
- Group 1 and group 2 metals often form more than one oxide:
  Na_2O sodium monoxide
  Na_2O_2 sodium peroxide
  NaO_2 sodium dioxide
- *Transition metals* form oxides in which the metal exhibits different *valency* states:
  Cu_2O copper(I) oxide
  CuO copper(II) oxide
- Non-metallic elements also form more than one oxide:
  P_4O_6 phosphorus(III) oxide
  P_4O_{10} phosphorus(V) oxide

2 The hydrides

- Water reacts with group 1 and group 2 metals to give the metal *hydroxide* and hydrogen. In these reactions, the metal is oxidized to a metal *cation* and the water is reduced:
  $M \rightarrow M^+$ and $M \rightarrow M^{2+}$
- In the Brønsted-Lowry theory of acids and bases, an acid is defined as a substance that donates protons and a base as a substance that accepts protons. Water acts as both an acid and a base.
- Non-metallic oxides dissolve in water to form acids:
  $H_2CO_3 \rightleftharpoons H^+ + HCO_3^-$ carbonic acid
  $H_2SO_3 \rightleftharpoons H^+ + HSO_3$ sulfurous acid

3 The oxides

- Metal oxides are basic and react with acids to form salts and water.
- Non-metallic oxides are acidic or neutral.
- Some metal oxides are *amphoteric*: they react with both acids and *alkalis*.

Basic reactions of sulfur

Key words

dehydrating agent	sulfide
hydrogen sulfide	sulfur
oxidizing agent	sulfur dioxide
redox reaction	sulfuric acid

1 Reactions of sulfur

- *Sulfur* reacts with most metals and hydrogen to form *sulfides*. Metal sulfides react with acids to give *hydrogen sulfide*:
$FeS(s) + 2HCl(aq) \rightarrow$
$FeCl_2(aq) + H_2S(g)$
- Sulfur combines with non-metals such as oxygen and chlorine.
- *Sulfur dioxide* is formed by the reaction between concentrated *sulfuric acid* and sulfur.

2 The hydrides

- Hydrogen sulfide dissolves in water to form a weak acid.
- Group 1 metal sulfides are soluble in water, however, other metal sulfides are only sparingly soluble and form characteristically colored precipitates. Moist lead(II) ethanoate paper turns black in the presence of hydrogen sulfide due to the formation of lead sulfide:
$Pb^{2+} + S^{2-} \rightarrow PbS$
- Hydrogen sulfide and sulfur dioxide undergo a *redox reaction* to form elemental sulfur.

3 The oxides SO_2 and SO_3

- Sulfur dioxide dissolves in water to form sulfurous acid, a weak acid.
- Sulfur dioxide is oxidized to sulfur trioxide.
- Sulfur trioxide dissolves in water to form sulfuric acid, a strong acid.

4 The hydroxy compound

- Concentrated sulfuric acid is a strong *oxidizing agent* and will oxidize both metals and non-metals.
- Concentrated sulfuric acid is a strong *dehyrating agent* and will remove water or the elements of water.

---

1 Reactions of sulfur

Oxidizes some elements

$Fe + S \longrightarrow FeS$

$2Cu + S \longrightarrow Cu_2S$

$H_2 + S \longrightarrow H_2S$

Reduces other elements elements

$S + O_2 \longrightarrow SO_2$

$2S + Cl_2 \longrightarrow S_2Cl_2$

Reduces some compounds

$3S + 2H_2SO_4 \longrightarrow 3SO_2\uparrow + 2H_2O$

---

2 The hydrides

Is a sparingly soluble acidic gas

$H_2S + H_2O \rightleftharpoons H_3O^+ + HS^-$

Is a reducing agent

$2H_2S + SO_2 \longrightarrow 2H_2O + 3S\downarrow$

Causes precipitation of insoluble metel sulfides

$CuSO_4 + H_2S \longrightarrow CuS\downarrow + H_2SO_4$

---

3 The oxides SO_2 and SO_3

Is a sparingly soluble acidic gas

$SO_2 + H_2O \rightleftharpoons H_2SO_3$

Is reducing agent

$2SO_2 + O_2 \rightleftharpoons 2SO_3$

$SO_2 + 2H_2S \longrightarrow 3S\downarrow + 2H_2O$

SO_3 is very acidic

$SO_3 + H_2O \longrightarrow H_2SO_4$

---

4 The hydroxy compound

As a strong acid

$H_2SO_4 + H_2O \longrightarrow H_3O^+ + HSO_4^-$

As an oxidizing agent

$2H_2SO_4 + C \longrightarrow CO_2 + 2SO_2\uparrow + 2H_2O$

$Cu + 2H_2SO_4 \longrightarrow CuSO_4 + SO_2\uparrow + 2H_2O$

As a dehydrating agent

$CH_3CH_2OH \xrightarrow[170°C]{H_2SO_4} CH_2 = CH_2$

$C_{12}H_{22}O_{11} \xrightarrow[-11H_2O]{H_2SO_4} 12C$

$CuSO_4.5H_2O \xrightarrow[-5H_2O]{H_2SO_4} CuSO_4$

The halogens: group 7

1 Electron structure

F			2	7
Cl			8	7
Br		2	18	7
I	2	8	18	7

inner electrons   outer shell

2 Halogen atom and molecule

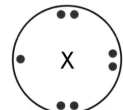

Halogen atom

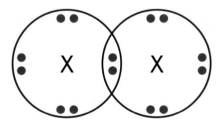

Halogen molecule

3 Physical properties

Element	Fluorine	Chlorine	Bromine	Iodine
Atomic number	9	17	35	53
Relative atomic mass	19.0	35.5	79.9	126.9
State at 20°C	gas	gas	liquid	solid
Color	pale yellow	pale green	red-brown	black
m.p./°C	−220	−101	−7	113
b.p./°C	−188	−35	59	183
Solubility/g per 100g of water at 20°C	reacts readily with water	0.59 (reacts slightly	3.6	0.018

Key words

astatine   fluorine
bromine   halogens
chlorine   iodine
covalent bond   ionic compound
covalent
  compound

Halogens

- The elements of group 7 are sometimes referred to as the *halogens*. They are *flourine*, *chlorine*, *bromine*, *iodine*, and *astatine*. The symbol 'X' is often used to denote a halogen atom and 'X⁻' a halogen ion.

1 Electron structure

- All halogen atoms have seven electrons in their outer shell. A halogen atom needs one more electron to fill the outer shell, and it can obtain this either by forming a single *covalent bond* or by forming an ion, X^-. Halogens form both *covalent compounds* and *ionic compounds*.

2 Halogen atom and molecule

- Halogens exist as diatomic molecules. Each atom in the molecule provides a single electron to form a covalent bond. The result is that each atom has control over eight electrons.

3 Physical properties

- There is a gradation of physical properties going down group 7.
  1. State changes from solid to liquid to gas. Bromine is one of only two elements that exist as liquids at room temperature.
  2. The color darkens from pale yellow to black.
  3. Melting point and boiling point increase.
- There is a gradual decrease in chemical reactivity going down group 7.
- Fluorine oxidizes water to give oxygen:
  $2F_2 + 2H_2O \rightarrow 4HF + O_2$
- Chlorine reacts less vigorously with water, forming an acidic solution:
  $C_2 + H_2O \rightleftharpoons HCl + HOCl$
- Bromine and iodine form solutions in water, although the latter is not very soluble.

Laboratory preparation of the halogens

1 Laboratory preparation of chlorine

- *Chlorine* is made in the laboratory by the *oxidation* of concentrated hydrochloric acid using a suitable *oxidizing agent* such as manganese dioxide (manganese(IV) oxide):

$$MnO_2(s) + 4HCl(aq) \rightarrow$$
$$MnCl_2(aq) + 2H_2O(l) + Cl_2(g)$$

- The gas is first passed through water to remove any hydrogen chloride gas, and then through concentrated sulfuric acid to dry the gas. Chlorine is more dense than air and is collected by downward delivery.

- Chlorine can also be conveniently made in the laboratory from bleaching powder, using dilute hydrochloric acid:

$$Ca(OCl)_2(s) + 4HCl(aq) \rightarrow$$
$$CaCl_2(aq) + 2H_2O(l) + 2Cl_2(g)$$

2 Laboratory preparation of bromine

- *Bromine* is made in a similar way to chlorine:

$$MnO_2(s) + 2NaBr(aq) + 2H_2SO_4(aq) \rightarrow$$
$$MnSO_4(aq) + Na_2SO_4(aq)$$
$$+ 2H_2O(l) + Br_2(g)$$

- Because it boils at 59°C, bromine is removed from the reaction mixture by *distillation*.

3 Laboratory preparation of iodine

- *Iodine* is made in a similar way to bromine. Hydrogen iodide is made *in situ* by reacting sodium iodide with concentrated sulfuric acid:

$$MnO_2(s) + 2KI(aq) + 2H_2SO_4(aq) \rightarrow$$
$$MnSO_4(aq) + K_2SO_4(aq) +$$
$$2H_2O(l) + I_2(g)$$

- Iodine is removed from the reaction mixture by sublimation. On heating, it changes directly from solid to vapor and then back to solid on cooling.

1 Laboratory preparation of chlorine

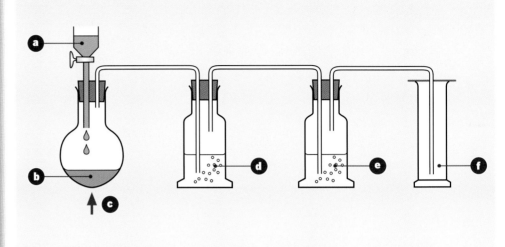

2 Laboratory preparation of bromine

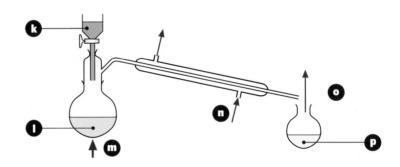

3 Laboratory preparation of iodine

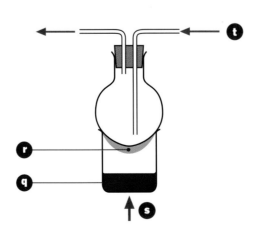

a concentrated hydrochloric acid
b manganese dioxide
c warm gently
d water to remove HCl fumes
e concentrated H_2SO_4 to dry Cl_2
f chlorine gas
g concentrated brine
h chlorine gas
i hydrogen gas
j water
k concentrated sulfuric acid
l manganese oxide + sodium bromide
m warm gently
p cold water
o fumes of HBr
p bromine
q manganese oxide + potassium iodine
   + concentrated H_2SO_4
s warm gently
t cold water

Compounds of chlorine

1 Chlorine and metals

Calcium burns in chlorine

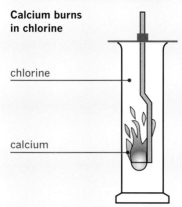

chlorine

calcium

Aluminum reacts when warmed in a stream of chloride

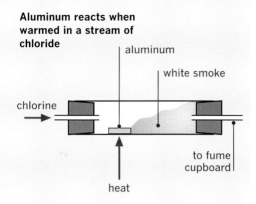

aluminum

white smoke

chlorine

heat

to fume cupboard

2 Laboratory preparation of hydrogen chloride

concentrated sulfuric acid

sodium chloride

hydrogen chloride

3 Compounds with non-metals

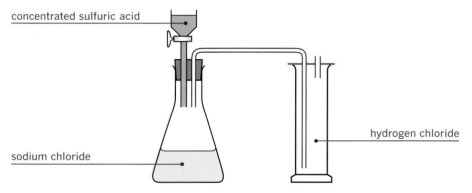

Carbon tetrachloride (CCl₄) CCl_4

Phosphorus trichloride (PCl₃) PCl_3

Sulfur monochloride (S₂Cl₂) S_2Cl_2

4 The structure of some chlorinated pesticides

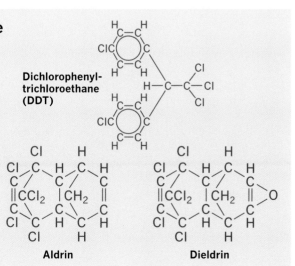

Dichlorophenyl-trichloroethane (DDT)

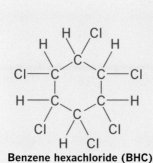

Benzene hexachloride (BHC)

Aldrin

Dieldrin

Key words

chloride	hydrogen
chlorine	chloride
covalent	sodium chloride
compound	sulfuric acid
halide	

1 Chlorine and metals

- Metals, such as calcium, burn in *chlorine* to produce the corresponding metal *chloride*:
$$Ca(s) + Cl_2(g) \rightarrow CaCl_2(s)$$
- Aluminum reacts with chlorine to form aluminum chloride:
$$2Al(s) + 3Cl_2(g) \rightarrow 2AlCl_3(s)$$
- Unlike many metal chlorides, aluminum chloride is hydrolyzed by water, giving off *hydrogen chloride* gas:
$$AlCl_3(s) + 3H_2O(l) \rightarrow$$
$$Al(OH)_3(s) + 3HCl(g)$$
It is for this reason that aluminum halides fume when they come into contact with moist air.

2 Laboratory preparation of hydrogen chloride

- Hydrogen chloride is made by the reaction of *sodium chloride* with concentrated *sulfuric acid*:
$$NaCl(s) + H_2SO_4(aq) \rightarrow$$
$$NaHSO_4(s) + HCl(g)$$

3 Compounds with non-metals

- Chlorine forms *covalent compounds* with non-metals such as carbon, phosphorus, and sulfur.

4 Pesticides

- Chlorinated compounds provide a range of pesticides.
- DDT, BHC, Aldrin, and Dieldrin have been the source of environmental concern, and their use is now prohibited or severely restricted.

Key words

carbonate	ion
covalent bond	ionic compound
covalent	
compound	
hydrogen	
chloride	

Hydrogen chloride

- *Hydrogen chloride* gas is a *covalent compound*. In solutions in organic solvents, it remains a covalent compound. It becomes an *ionic compound* in aqueous solutions.

1 In organic solvents

- In solution in organic solvents such as methylbenzene, hydrogen chloride remains a covalent compound. The hydrogen atom and the chlorine atom each donate one electron to form the *covalent bond*.
- The solution contains no ions and does not conduct electricity.
- The solution has no effect on blue litmus paper or on *carbonates*, thus showing that it is not an acid.

2 In aqueous solution

- In aqueous solution, hydrogen chloride becomes an ionic compound. The hydrogen atom loses an electron to become a hydrogen *ion*, **H⁺**, and the chlorine atom gains an electron to become a chloride ion, **Cl⁻**.
- The solution contains ions and conducts electricity. The ions are able to carry a charge through the solution.
- The solution turns blue litmus paper red and reacts with carbonates, showing that it is an acid:

$$Na_2CO_3(aq) + 2HCl(aq) \rightarrow$$
$$2NaCl(aq) + CO_2(g) + H_2O(l)$$

Hydrogen chloride in solution

1 In organic solvents

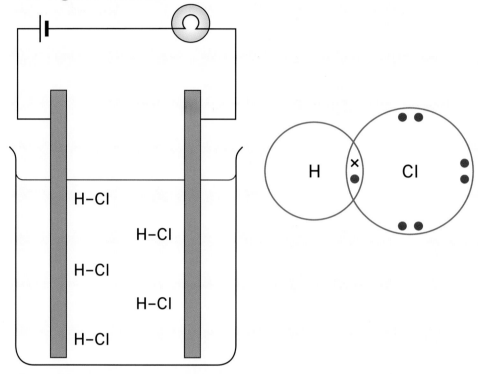

2 In aqueous solution

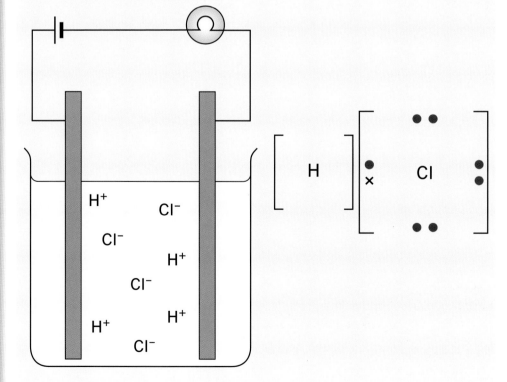

Acid/base chemistry of the halogens

Key words

halide	oxidizing agent
hydrochloric acid	reducing agent
hydrogen	silver nitrate
chloride	
nitric acid	

1 Laboratory preparation of hydrochloric acid

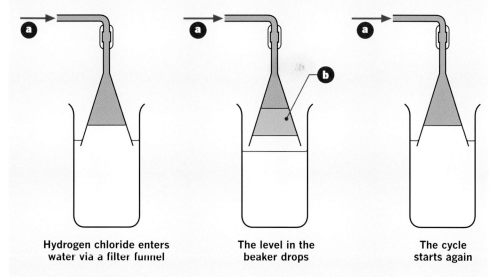

Hydrogen chloride enters water via a filter funnel	The level in the beaker drops	The cycle starts again

a hydrochloric acid (HCl)
b plug of liquid in funnel

2 Solubility of the halogens

$$2F_2 + 2H_2O \longrightarrow 4HF + O_2$$
Flourine is so reactive it decomposes water producing hydrofluoric acid and oxygen

$$Cl_2 + H_2O \rightleftharpoons HCl + HOCl$$
Chlorine is the next most reactive halogen after fluorine

3 Chloride test

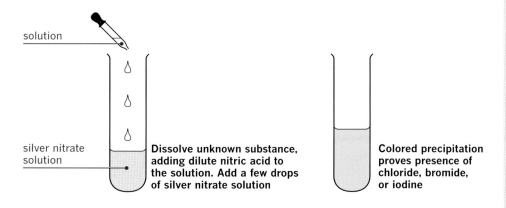

solution

silver nitrate solution

Dissolve unknown substance, adding dilute nitric acid to the solution. Add a few drops of silver nitrate solution

Colored precipitation proves presence of chloride, bromide, or iodine

1 Laboratory preparation of hydrochloric acid

- *Hydrochloric acid* is made in the laboratory by dissolving *hydrogen chloride* gas in water.
- Hydrogen chloride is very soluble in water. It is dissolved by passing through an inverted filter funnel, the rim of which sits just below the water level. When water is sucked into the funnel, the water level drops, and the funnel rim is no longer submerged. This prevents water being sucked back into the apparatus.

2 Solubility of the halogens

- All halogens are *oxidizing agents*. However, oxidizing power decreases down the group:
  fluorine > chlorine > bromine > iodine
- *Halide* ions are *reducing agents*. The reducing power increases down the group:
  fluorine < chlorine < bromine < iodine

3 Chloride test

- The presence of halide ions in solution can be detected by adding a few drops of dilute *nitric acid* followed by several drops of *silver nitrate* solution.
  1. Chloride ions form a white precipitate of insoluble silver chloride:
  $Ag^+(aq) + Cl^-(aq) \rightarrow AgCl(s)$
  2. Bromide ions form a cream precipitate of insoluble silver bromide:
  $Ag^+(aq) + Br^-(aq) \rightarrow AgBr(s)$
  3. Iodide ions form a yellow precipitate of insoluble silver iodide:
  $Ag^+(aq) + I^-(aq) \rightarrow AgI(s)$

Key words

chloride	redox reaction
chlorine	sulfur
noble gases	
oxidizing agent	
reactivity series	

1 Calcium and chlorine

- When hydrogen sulfide and chlorine are mixed, elemental *sulfur* is formed. *Chlorine* acts as an *oxidizing agent* and oxidizes the hydrogen sulfide by removing hydrogen. In turn, the chlorine gains hydrogen and is reduced to hydrogen chloride:

$8H_2S(g) + 8Cl_2(g) \rightarrow S_8(s) + 16HCl(g)$

2 Chlorine and ferrous chloride

- Chlorine can also be used to oxidize iron(II) to iron(III). When chlorine is bubbled into iron(II) chloride solution, the color changes from green to yellow-brown, showing the formation of iron(III). The chlorine atoms are reduced to *chloride* ions:

$2FeCl_2(aq) + Cl_2(g) \rightarrow 2FeCl_3(aq)$

3 Halogens and metals

- Halogens readily oxidize metals. Fluorine oxidizes all metals, including gold and silver, easily.
- Chlorine oxidizes all but the least reactive metals. When iron is heated in a stream of dry chlorine, iron(III) chloride is produced:

$2Fe(s) + 3Cl_2(g) \rightarrow 2FeCl_3(s)$

- The ease with which halogens oxidize metals decreases down the group, but even iodine will slowly oxidize metals low in the *reactivity series*.

4 Halogens and non-metals

- Fluorine oxidizes most non-metals except nitrogen and most of the *noble gases*.
- Chlorine reacts directly with phosphorus and sulfur, but carbon, nitrogen, and oxygen do not react directly with chlorine, bromine, or iodine.
- The relative reactivities of the halogens in *redox reactions* with non-metals is illustrated at right by their reaction with hydrogen.

Redox reactions of the halogens

1 Calcium burns in chlorine

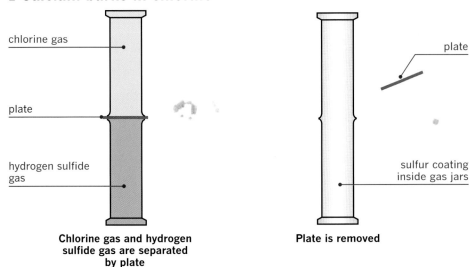

Chlorine gas and hydrogen sulfide gas are separated by plate

Plate is removed

2 Reaction of chlorine with ferrous chloride

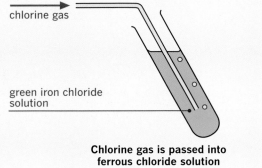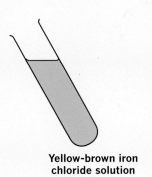

Chlorine gas is passed into ferrous chloride solution

Yellow-brown iron chloride solution

3 Halogens and metals

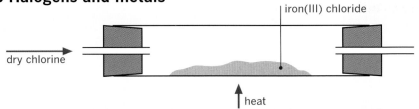

4 Halogens and non-metals

Reaction	Observations
$H_2(g) + F_2(g) \rightarrow 2HF(g)$	explosive
$H_2(g) + Cl_2(g) \rightarrow 2HCl(g)$	explosive in sunlight but slow in the dark
$H_2(g) + Br_2(g) \rightarrow 2HBr(g)$	needs heat and a catalyst
$H_2(g) + I_2(g) \rightarrow 2HI(g)$	slow even when heated

Reactivity of the halogens

1 Chemical reactivity of halogens with each other

	Chlorine	Bromine	Iodine
Chloride		✗	✗
Bromide	✓		✗
Iodide	✓	✓	

2 Reaction of chlorine and bromine

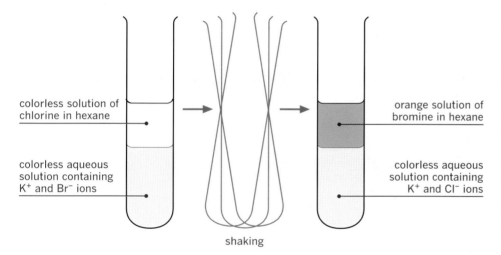

colorless solution of chlorine in hexane

colorless aqueous solution containing K^+ and Br^- ions

orange solution of bromine in hexane

colorless aqueous solution containing K^+ and Cl^- ions

shaking

3 Reaction of chlorine and iodine

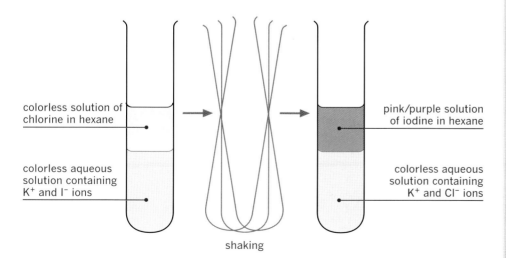

colorless solution of chlorine in hexane

colorless aqueous solution containing K^+ and I^- ions

pink/purple solution of iodine in hexane

colorless aqueous solution containing K^+ and Cl^- ions

shaking

1 Reactivity of halogens

- The chemical reactivity of the *halogens* decreases down group 7: fluorine > chlorine > bromine > iodine
- A more reactive halogen will displace the ions of a less reactive halogen from a metal *halide* solution. This is called a *displacement reaction*.
- Chlorine will displace bromide ions and iodide ions from solution.
- Bromine will displace iodide ions from solution.
- In a displacement reaction, the halogen acts as an oxidizing agent and is reduced while the halide ion is oxidized.

2 Chlorine and bromine

- Chlorine dissolves in the organic solvent hexane to give a colorless or slightly green solution, depending on concentration.
- Hexane is *immiscible* with water. When the two liquids are mixed, hexane forms a layer above water.
- When solutions of chlorine in hexane and potassium bromide in water are shaken together, chlorine displaces bromide ions from the aqueous solution. Bromine is more soluble in hexane than in water, and an orange layer of bromine in hexane forms:
$$2KBr + Cl_2 \rightarrow 2KCl + Br_2$$
$$2Br^- + Cl_2 \rightarrow 2Cl^- + Br_2$$

3 Chlorine and iodine

- When solutions of chlorine in hexane and potassium iodide in water are shaken together, chlorine displaces iodide ions from the aqueous solution. Iodine is more soluble in hexane than in water, and a pink-purple layer of iodine in hexane forms:
$$2KI + Cl_2 \rightarrow 2KCl + I_2$$
$$2I^- + Cl_2 \rightarrow 2Cl^- + I_2$$

Key words

aluminum	platinum
copper	silver
gold	uranium
iron	zinc
lead	

1 Gold, sliver, platinum, and uranium

- **Gold**: South Africa, USA, Canada, Russia
- **Silver**: USA, South America
- **Platinum**: South Africa, USA, South America
- **Uranium**: North America, Europe, Central and South Africa, Australia

2 Aluminum and copper

- **Aluminum**: South America, Jamaica, West Africa, Russia, India, Australia
- **Copper**: North America, Central and South Africa, Europe, Russia

3 Iron, zinc, and lead

- **Iron**: North and South America, Russia, Europe, Angola, Australia
- **Zinc** and **lead**: USA, Europe, Australia, Russia

World distribution of metals

1 Gold, sliver, platinum, and uranium

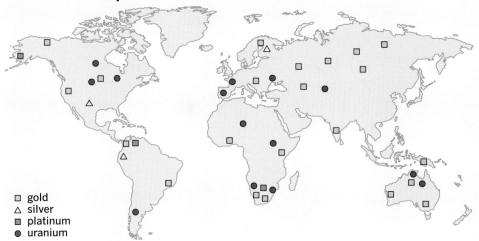

- □ gold
- △ silver
- ▢ platinum
- ● uranium

2 Aluminum and copper

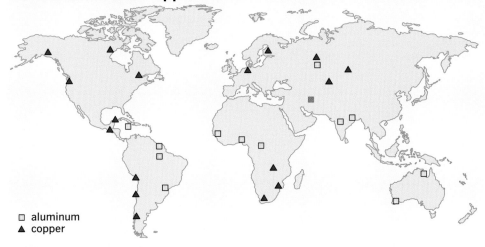

- □ aluminum
- ▲ copper

3 Iron, zinc, and lead

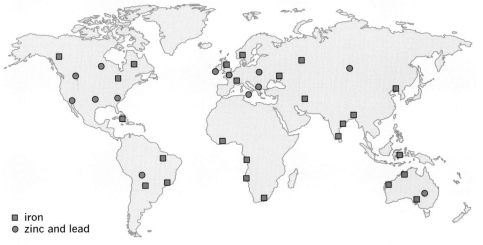

- ▢ iron
- ● zinc and lead

Main ores of metals

Metal Common name for ore(s)	Chemical name for ore(s)	Formula of ore(s)
aluminum bauxite	aluminum oxide	$Al_2O_3.2H_2O$
chromium chromite	iron chromium oxide	$FeCr_2O_4$
copper chalcopyrite bornite chalcocite	copper iron sulfide copper iron sulfide copper(I) sulfide	$CuFeS_2$ Cu_5FeS_4 Cu_2S
iron haematite magnetite	iron(III) oxide iron(II)iron(III) oxide	Fe_2O_3 Fe_3O_4
lead galena cerussite anglesite	lead(II) sulfide lead(II) carbonate lead(II) sulfate	PbS $PbCO_3$ $PbSO_4$
magnesium magnesite	magnesium carbonate	$MgCO_3$
mercury cinnabar	mercury sulfide	HgS
silver argentite	silver sulfide	Ag_2S
sodium salt	sodium chloride	$NaCl$
tin cassiterite	tin oxide	SnO_2
titanium rutile ilmenite	titanium oxide iron titanium oxide	TiO_2 $FeTiO_3$
uranium uraninite	uranium oxide	UO_2
zinc zinc blende calamine	zinc sulfide zinc carbonate	ZnS $ZnCO_3$

Key words

grade
mineral
ore
oxide
sulfide

Ores

- An *ore* is a *mineral* from which a metal (or non-metal) can be extracted.
- Metal ores are often metal *oxides* or metal *sulfides*.
- A metal may be present in a range of different minerals, but not all minerals will be suitable sources of that metal.

Recovering ores

- To be appropriate for mining, an ore must contain minerals that are valuable and that are concentrated enough to be mined profitably. It must also be economically viable to extract the ore from waste rock.
- Mineral deposits that are economically recoverable are called ore deposits. Not all mineral deposits are suitable for recovery. Some may be too low in *grade* (the concentration of the ore in the rock) or technically impossible to extract.

Formation

- The process of ore formation is called ore genesis.
- Ore genesis involves a variety of geological, internal, hydrothermal, metamorphic, and surficial processes.

Key words

alkali metals	radioactive
boiling point	shell
group 1	
melting point	
orbital	

1 Position in periodic table

- The *group 1* metals occupy the first column of the periodic table. Historically, they were known as the *alkali metals* because they all react with water to give alkaline solutions.
- The elements include lithium, sodium, potassium, rubidium, and cesium. Francium lies below cesium in the periodic table. However, it is not considered when discussing the group because it is *radioactive*, and little is known of its chemistry.

2 Electron-shell structure

- The electrons surrounding the nucleus of an atom are arranged in a series of *orbitals*, areas around the atom where there is a high probability of finding an electron. Orbitals are grouped in a series of *shells* (energy levels) at a gradually increasing distance from the nucleus. Different orbitals have different shapes: s orbitals are spherically symmetric; p orbitals point in a particular direction; and d orbitals have complicated shapes. Scientists describe an atom by describing the orbital structure. Thus, as the table indicates, sodium has 2s orbitals in the first shell, 2s and 6p orbitals in the second shell, and 1s orbital in the third shell.

3 Physical properties

- Reading down the group, the *melting point* decreases, the *boiling point* increases, the density increases, and the hardness decreases.

The group 1 metals

1 Position in the periodic table

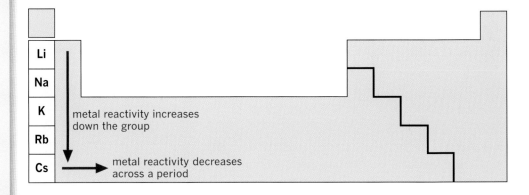

2 Electron-shell structure

Li	$1s^2 2s^1$
Na	$1s^2\ 2s^2\ 2p^6\ 3s^1$
K	$1s^2\ 2s^2\ 2p^6\ 3s^2\ 3p^6\ 4s^1$
Rb	$1s^2\ 2s^2\ 2p^6\ 3s^2\ 3p^6\ 4s^2\ 3d^{10}\ 4p^6\ 5s^1$
Cs	$1s^2\ 2s^2\ 2p^6\ 3s^2\ 3p^6\ 4s^2\ 3d^{10}\ 4p^6\ 5s^2\ 4d^{10}\ 5p^6\ 6s^1$

3 Physical properties of group I elements compared with a typical metal

Group 1 element		m.p./°C	b.p./°C	Density /g cm^{-3}	Hardness /Moh	Conductivity Ω^{-1}cm^{-1}
Lithium	Li	180	1336	0.53	0.6	11700
Sodium	Na	98	883	0.97	0.4	23800
Potassium	K	64	759	0.86	0.5	16400
Rubidium	Rb	39	700	1.53	0.3	9100
Cesium	Cs	29	669	1.88	0.2	2000
Typical metal						
Iron	Fe	1530	3000	7860	4–5	11300

The group 1 metals: sodium

Key words

acid
acid-base
 indicator
alkali
anode

cathode
electrolysis
salt
titration

1 Reaction of sodium hydroxide (NaOH) with hydrochloric acid (HCl)

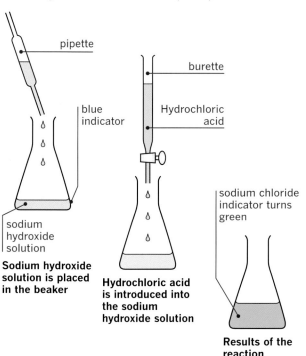

pipette

blue indicator

burette

Hydrochloric acid

sodium hydroxide solution

Sodium hydroxide solution is placed in the beaker

Hydrochloric acid is introduced into the sodium hydroxide solution

sodium chloride indicator turns green

Results of the reaction

2 Sodium burns readily in chlorine or oxygen

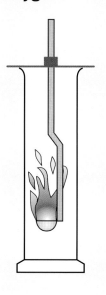

3 Sodium reacts with nitrogen gas

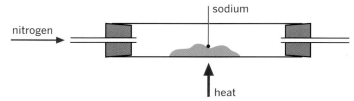

nitrogen

sodium

heat

4 Commercial preparation of sodium

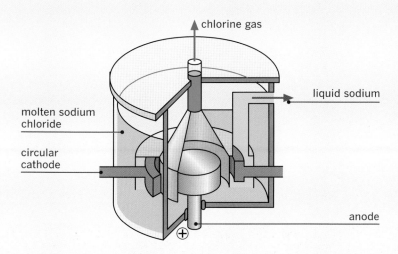

chlorine gas

liquid sodium

molten sodium chloride

circular cathode

anode

1 Reaction of NaOH with HCl

- Group 1 hydroxides are *alkalis*. They can be used to form *salts* by neutralizing them with *acids* in a process call *titration*. Sodium chloride is made by neutralizing sodium hydroxide with hydrochloric acid.
$$NaOH + HCl \rightarrow NaCl + H_2O$$
- A given volume of sodium hydroxide solution is put into a conical flask.
- A few drops of an *acid–base indicator* are added to the sodium hydroxide solution. The indicator is a different color in acids and alkalis.
- Hydrochloric acid is run into the sodium hydroxide solution burette until the indicator just changes color.

2 Burning sodium

- Sodium burns vigorously in chlorine to form sodium chloride:
$$2Na + Cl_2 \rightarrow 2NaCl$$
- Sodium also burns vigorously in oxygen to form sodium oxide:
$$4Na + O_2 \rightarrow 2Na_2O$$

3 Sodium and nitrogen

- When heated in a stream of nitrogen, sodium reacts to form sodium nitride:
$$6Na + N_2 \rightarrow 2Na_3N$$

4 Preparation of sodium

- Sodium is obtained by the *electrolysis* of molten sodium chloride in a Downs cell. Sodium is discharged at the negative electrode (*cathode*):
$$Na^+ + e^- \rightarrow Na$$
The product at the positive electrode (*anode*) is chlorine gas:
$$2Cl^- \rightarrow Cl_2 + 2e^-$$

Key words

alkaline earth metals	ionization energy
	orbital
group 2	radioactive
ion	reactivity

1 Position in periodic table

- The *group 2* metals occupy the second column of the periodic table. They include beryllium, magnesium, calcium, strontium, and barium. Radium, which lies below barium, is not usually considered when discussing the group because it is *radioactive*. Historically, group 2 metals were known as the *alkaline earth metals* because all but beryllium react with water to give alkaline solutions.
- The atomic radius and, therefore, the size of the atoms increases going down the group.

2 Electron-shell structure

- Scientists can describe an atom by describing its electron-shell structure (see page 150).
- All group 2 elements form *ions* by losing two outer electrons. The energy needed to do this is the sum of the first and second *ionization energies*, i.e., the energy needed to remove the first electron and the second electron.
- Going down the group, there is an increase in the number of *orbitals* of electrons. This affects the value of the ionization energy in two ways: 1) the two outer electrons are further from the positively charged nucleus, and 2) there are more layers of electrons between the nucleus and the outer electrons, which partially shields the outer electrons from the nucleus. Consequently, going down the group, less energy is needed to remove the outer two electrons, and the metals become progressively more reactive.

3 Reactivity

- As with the group 1 metals, the *reactivity* of the group 2 metals increases going down the group.
- The group 2 metals have similar chemical properties as group 1 metals; however, the reactivity of group 2 metals in the same period is less.

The group 2 metals

1 Position in the periodic table

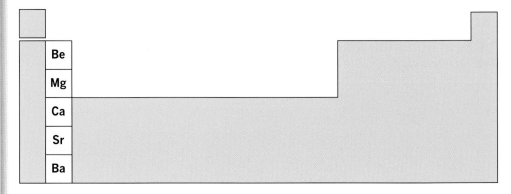

2 Electron-shell structure

energy level → **1s²** ← number of electrons in orbital
← type of orbital

Be	$1s^2 2s^2$
Mg	$1s^2\ 2s^2\ 2p^6\ 3s^2$
Ca	$1s^2\ 2s^2\ 2p^6\ 3s^2\ 3p^6\ 4s^2$
Sr	$1s^2\ 2s^2\ 2p^6\ 3s^2\ 3p^6\ 4s^2\ 3d^{10}\ 4p^6\ 5s^2$
Ba	$1s^2\ 2s^2\ 2p^6\ 3s^2\ 3p^6\ 4s^2\ 3d^{10}\ 4p^6\ 5s^2\ 4d^{10}\ 5p^6\ 6s^2$

3 Reactivity comparison with group I

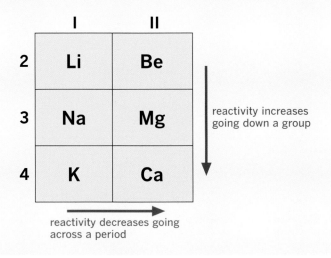

	I	II
2	Li	Be
3	Na	Mg
4	K	Ca

reactivity increases going down a group

reactivity decreases going across a period

The group 2 metals: general reactions

Key words

alkali	limewater
carbonic acid	soluble
group 2	
hydrochloric acid	
insoluble	

1 Sodium and water

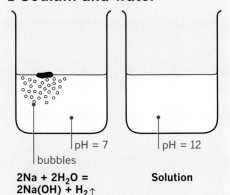

pH = 7
bubbles

2Na + 2H₂O = 2Na(OH) + H₂↑

$$2Na + 2H_2O = 2Na(OH) + H_2\uparrow$$

pH = 12

Solution

2 Calcium and water

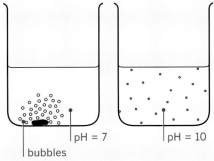

pH = 7
bubbles

pH = 10

$$Ca + 2H_2O = Ca(OH)_2 + H_2\uparrow$$

Suspension

3 Production of "rainwater"

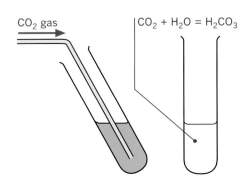

CO₂ gas

$$CO_2 + H_2O = H_2CO_3$$

Bubble unknown gas into limewater Ca(OH₂)

Result if the gas is CO₂

4 Effect of rainfall on fresh water

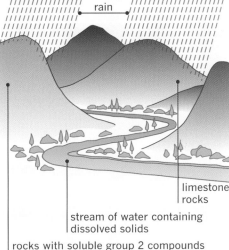

rain

limestone rocks

stream of water containing dissolved solids

rocks with soluble group 2 compounds (e.g., CaCl₂, CaSO)

5 Calcium hydroxide [Ca(OH)₂] test for carbon dioxide gas

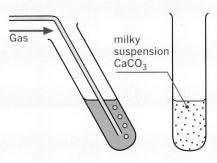

Gas

milky suspension CaCO₃

Bubble unknown gas into limewater Ca(OH₂)

Result if the gas is CO₂

6 Barium chloride (BaCl₂) test for metal sulfates

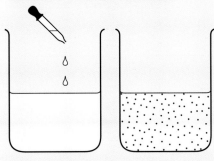

Add barium chloride dissolved in hydrochloric acid to the known solution

A white suspension is produced if the solution contains a sulfate

1 Sodium and water
- Sodium reacts vigorously with water to form sodium hydroxide solution (a strong alkali) and hydrogen gas.

2 Calcium and water
- Calcium reacts less vigorously with water than sodium to form calcium hydroxide solution and hydrogen gas.
- Calcium hydroxide is less *soluble* than sodium hydroxide and forms a weak *alkali* solution containing suspended particles of undissolved solid.

3 Rainwater
- Naturally occurring rainwater is always weakly acidic because carbon dioxide from the air dissolves in it, forming weak *carbonic acid*, H_2CO_3.

4 Effect of rainfall
- What rain flows over rocks, *group 2* metal compounds dissolve in it, resulting in water that contains dissolved solids.
- Magnesium and calcium carbonates are effectively *insoluble* in water, but they react with rainwater, because it is acidic, to form soluble hydrogencarbonates.

5 Ca(OH)₂ test
- *Limewater*, an aqueous solution of calcium hydroxide, is used to test for carbon dioxide.
- When carbon dioxide is bubbled into limewater, it turns milky due to the formation of insoluble calcium carbonate, $CaCo_3$.

6 BaCl₂ test
- The test solution is first acidified with dilute *hydrochloric acid*, and a few drops of barium chloride solution are then added. If the solution contains sulfate ions, a white precipitate of barium sulfate is formed.

Key words

actinides   tensile strength
catalyst   transition metals
orbital
oxidation state
shell

Characteristics of transition metals

- The *transition metals* are any of the metallic elements with an incomplete inner electronic structure. While the outermost *shell* contains at most two electrons, their next-to-outermost shells have incompletely filled *orbitals*, which fill up going across a period. The filling is not always regular.
- The 40 transitional metals are organized into four series: The first series, shown in the table, runs from element 21 (scandium) to element 30 (zinc) and is in period 4. The second series, elements 39 (yttrium) to 48 (cadmium), is in period 5. The third, elements 71 (lanthanum) to 80 (mercury), is in period 6. The fourth series, from 103 (lawrencium) to 112 (ununbium), is the *actinides* and transactinides.
- Moving away from the nucleus, successive electron shells become progressively closer in energy. The energy levels of the third and fourth orbitals are close in the first series of transition metals.
- The electronic structure of all of the elements in period 4 can be written as that of the element argon together with additional electrons filling the 3d and 4s orbitals (see table).
- Transition metals often have colored compounds because their ions contain electrons in the 3d orbitals that can move between energy levels, giving out light.
- Transition metals tend to have high *tensile strength* (the maximum stress a material can withstand without breaking), density, and melting and boiling points. They have a variety of different *oxidation states* and are often good *catalysts*.

The transition metals: electron structure

Table to show the electron structures of atoms and ions of elements from scandium to zinc

Element	Symbol	Electronic structure of atom	Common ion	Electronic structure of ion
Scandium	Sc	$(Ar)3d^14s^2$	Sc^{3+}	(Ar)
Titanium	Ti	$(Ar)3d^24s^2$	Ti^{4+}	(Ar)
Vanadium	V	$(Ar)3d^34s^2$	V^{3+}	$(Ar)3d^2$
Chromium	Cr	$(Ar)3d^54s^1$	Cr^{3+}	$(Ar)3d^3$
Manganese	Mn	$(Ar)3d^54s^2$	Mn^{2+}	$(Ar)3d^5$
Iron	Fe	$(Ar)3d^64s^2$	Fe^{2+}	$(Ar)3d^6$
			Fe^{3+}	$(Ar)3d^5$
Cobalt	Co	$(Ar)3d^74s^2$	Co^{2+}	$(Ar)3d^7$
Nickel	Ni	$(Ar)3d^84s^2$	Ni^{2+}	$(Ar)3d^8$
Copper	Cu	$(Ar)3d^{10}4s^1$	Cu^+	$(Ar)3d^{10}$
			Cu^{2+}	$(Ar)3d^9$
Zinc	Zn	$(Ar)3d^{10}4s^2$	Zn^{2+}	$(Ar)3d^{10}$

(Ar) = electron structure of argon

Note: As the shells of electrons get further and further from the nucleus successive shells become closer in energy

The transition metals: ionization energies and physical properties

Key words

boiling point
conductor
ionization energy
melting point
transition metals

1 Graphs showing the second and third ionization energies of the elements from scandium to zinc

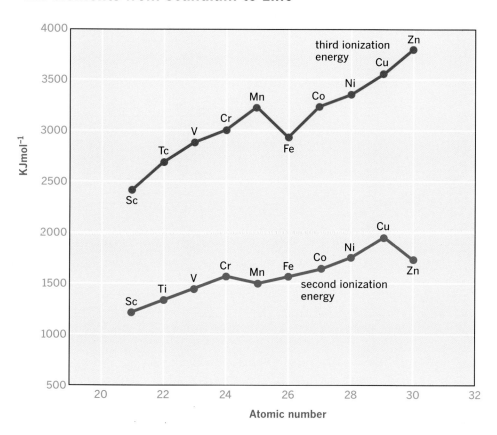

1 Ionization energies

- *Ionization energy* is the energy needed to remove an electron from a neutral gaseous atom or ion against the attraction of the nucleus.
- The second ionization energy is the energy needed to go from M^+ to M^{2+}, (where M = metal), and the third ionization energy is the energy needed to go from M^{2+} to M^{3+}.
- The second ionization energy increases across period 4 because there is an increasing positive charge on the nucleus of the ion, making it increasingly more difficult to remove the second electron.
- The third ionization energy for all elements is significantly higher than the second. Removal of the second electron results in a greater net difference between the positive charge on the nucleus of the ion and the negative charge surrounding it, so it requires more energy to remove a third electron.

2 Physical properties of the elements from scandium to zinc

Element		Atomic radius/nm	m.p./°C	b.p./°C	Density/ gcm–3	Ionic radius/nm M2+	M3+
Scandium	Sc	0.16	1540	2730	3.0		0.081
Titanium	Ti	0.15	1680	3260	4.5	0.090	0.076
Vanadium	V	0.14	1900	3400	6.1	0.088	0.074
Chromium	Cr	0.13	1890	2480	7.2	0.084	0.069
Manganese	Mn	0.14	1240	2100	7.4	0.080	0.066
Iron	Fe	0.13	1540	3000	7.9	0.076	0.064
Cobalt	Co	0.13	1500	2900	8.9	0.074	0.063
Nickel	Ni	0.13	1450	2730	8.9	0.072	0.062
Copper	Cu	0.13	1080	2600	8.9	0.070	
Zinc	Zn	0.13	420	910	7.1	0.074	

2 Physical properties

- Like other metals, *transition metals* are good *conductors* of both heat and electricity.
- The transition metals in general have higher *melting points* and *boiling points* than groups 1 and 2 metals.
- The atomic radii and ionic radii for the M^{2+} ion decrease across period 4 because the increasing positive charge on the nucleus of the atom and of the ion provides a greater attraction for the surrounding electrons.

Key words

acid	electrolysis
alkali	electrolyte
aluminum	filtrate
amphoteric	ore
cryolite	precipitate

1 Extraction

- Bauxite, the *ore* from which *aluminum* is obtained, contains impurities, principally iron(III) oxide (Fe_2O_3), that must be removed before the ore can be processed to obtain aluminum.
- Aluminum oxide is an *amphoteric* oxide (it reacts with both *acids* and *alkalis*). After grinding, the ore is mixed with an excess of sodium hydroxide solution, forming sodium tetrahydroxoaluminate(III) solution.
- Iron(III) oxide and the other impurities remain undissolved in the sodium hydroxide solution and are filtered off.
- The *filtrate*, containing sodium tetrahydroxoaluminate(III), is transferred into a precipitation tank, where the solution decomposes, giving a *precipitate* of pure solid aluminum oxide.

2 Manufacture

- Aluminum oxide is reduced by *electrolysis* in a Hall-Hérault cell.
- For electrolysis to occur, the *electrolyte* must be molten so that the ions are mobile and able carry electric charge. The electrolyte consists of a solution of aluminum oxide and molten *cryolite* (a compound of aluminum fluoride and sodium fluoride).
- Aluminum oxide dissociates in the cryolite solution, giving aluminum ions, Al^{3+}, and oxide ions, O^{2-}.
- Aluminum ions are reduced to aluminum metal, which is tapped off molten from the bottom of the cell. Oxide ions are oxidized to oxygen.
- The graphite anode readily reacts with the oxygen produced to give carbon dioxide. The graphite anode is gradually eaten away and must be replaced at regular intervals.

Aluminum

1 Extraction of pure aluminum oxide (Al_2O_3)

Addition of NaOH solution

Bauxite (impure Al_2O_3)

Grinder

Filter to remove Fe_2O_3 and other insoluble matter

Reactor

$Al(OH)_3$ precipitate

Filter to obtain $Al(OH)_3$

Seed crystals or carbon dioxide added

Solid $Al(OH)_3$

Heater to decompose $Al(OH)_3$

Pure Al_2O_3

2 The electrolytic manufacture of aluminum

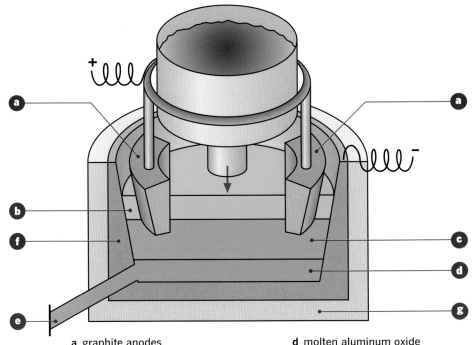

a graphite anodes
b solid crust of electrolyte
c molten electrolyte (aluminum oxide dissolved in cryolite)
d molten aluminum oxide
e tapping hole
f graphite lining to cell (cathode)
g insulation

Iron: smelting

1 The blast furnace

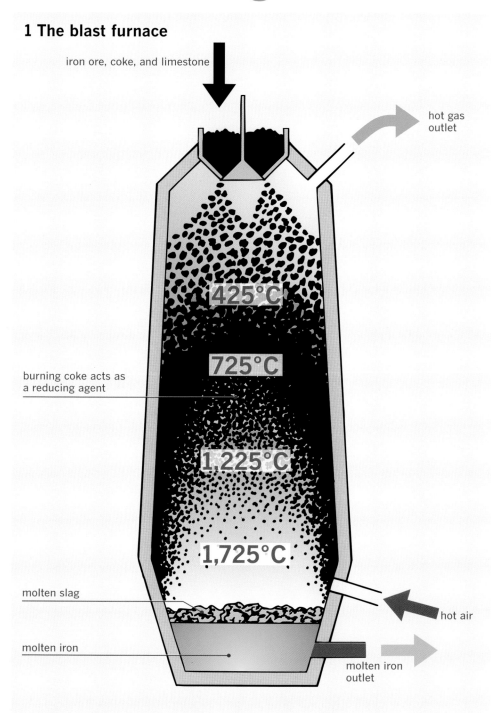

iron ore, coke, and limestone

hot gas outlet

425°C

725°C

burning coke acts as a reducing agent

1,225°C

1,725°C

molten slag

molten iron

hot air

molten iron outlet

2 Table of impurities of pig iron

Impurity	% impurity in pig iron
Carbon	3 to 5
Silicon	1 to 2
Sulfur	0.05 to 0.10
Phosphorus	0.05 to 1.5
Manganese	0.5 to 1.0

Key words

flux	*smelting*
ore	
reducing agent	
reduction	
slag	

1 The blast furnace

- Iron *ores* such as hematite and magnetite contain oxygen. To create pure iron, the ores are smelted in a blast furnace to remove the oxygen.
- A charge of iron ore, limestone, and coke is fed into the top of the furnace, and hot air is blown in toward the bottom through pipes called tuyeres.
- The coke is used as a fuel, as a *reducing agent*, and also to supply carbon, which dissolves in the molten iron formed.
- The limestone acts as a *flux* (cleaning agent), combining with acidic impurities in the iron ore to form a liquid *slag* (the waste produce of *smelting*).
- Molten iron falls to the bottom of the furnace, where it is tapped.
- Molten slag floats on the molten iron and is drawn off.
- Hot gases (carbon monoxide, carbon dioxide, sulfur dioxide, nitrogen, and unreacted oxygen) are removed at the top of the furnace.
- The conversion of iron oxide to iron is a *reduction*. The main reducing agent is carbon monoxide.
- Iron oxide is reduced to iron by carbon monoxide, which itself is oxidized to carbon dioxide.
- The temperature inside the blast furnace is sufficient to decompose limestone into calcium oxide and carbon dioxide. Calcium oxide then combines with impurities such as silicon dioxide to form slag.

2 Impurities

- The iron that leaves the blast furnace (called pig iron) contains a variable amount of impurities, including carbon, silicon, sulfur, phosphorus, and manganese.

Key words

alloy
slag

1 Basic oxygen process

- Steel is an *alloy* of iron, carbon, and other metals and non-metals.
- In the basic oxygen process, the furnace is charged with controlled amounts of steel scrap and molten iron from a blast furnace. An oxygen lance, cooled by circulating water, is lowered into the furnace, and high purity oxygen is injected into the vessel at twice the speed of sound. Impurities are readily oxidized. Molten iron is also oxidized.
- With the exception of carbon monoxide, the remaining oxides all react with calcium oxide, which is added during the oxygen blow, to form a *slag*.
- The resulting steel is highly oxidized and not suitable for casting. It is deoxidized by adding controlled amounts of aluminum and silicon in a separate reaction vessel. Additional metals and non-metals are added at this point to make different types of steel.

2 Electric arc furnace

- The electric arc furnace process uses only cold scrap metal. The furnace is a circular bath with a moveable roof through which carbon electrodes can be raised or lowered as required.
- Scrap steel is placed in the furnace, the roof closed, and the electrodes lowered into position. When a current is passed, an arc forms between the scrap steel and the electrodes, and the heat generated melts the scrap steel.
- Lime, fluorspar, and iron ore are added, and these combine with impurities forming a slag. When the steel has reached the correct composition, the slag is poured off, and the steel is tapped from the furnace.

The manufacture of steel

1 Basic oxygen process

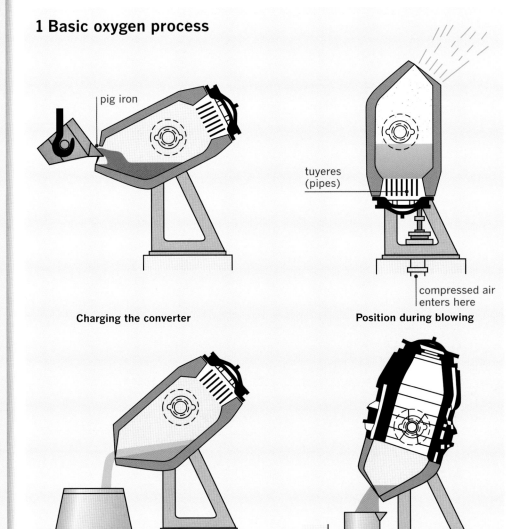

Charging the converter

Position during blowing

Discharging the slag

Discharging the steel

2 Electric arc furnace

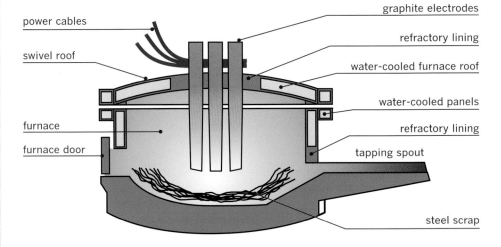

Rusting

1 Rust experiment

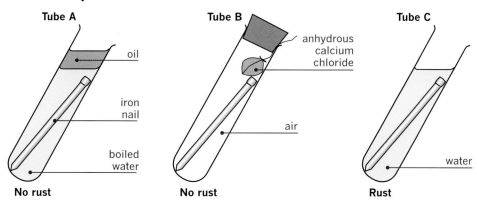

Tube A

oil

iron nail

boiled water

No rust

Tube B

anhydrous calcium chloride

air

No rust

Tube C

water

Rust

2 Chemical process

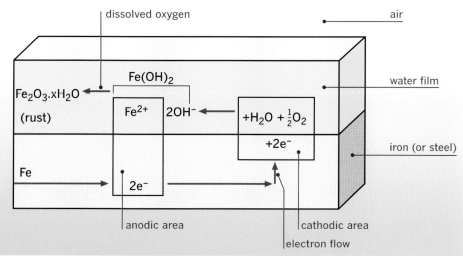

dissolved oxygen

air

$Fe_2O_3.xH_2O$ (rust)

$Fe(OH)_2$

Fe^{2+} $2OH^-$ $+H_2O + \frac{1}{2}O_2$

$+2e^-$

water film

iron (or steel)

Fe

$2e^-$

anodic area

cathodic area

electron flow

3 Rust prevention

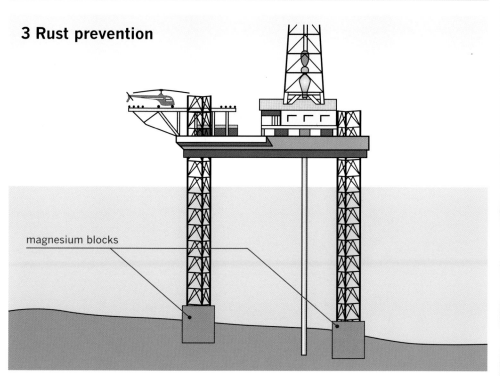

magnesium blocks

Key words

galvanizing
hydroxide ion
iron
magnesium
rust

Rusting

- Rusting is the result of a chemical cell being formed on the surface of *iron* when it is in contact with water and oxygen from the air.

1 Rust experiment

- The experiment at left proves that both water and oxygen are needed for rusting.
- Tube A: When water is boiled, the air it contains is expelled, and oil prevents any air redissolving in the water. The nail is exposed to water but not oxygen and does not *rust*.
- Tube B: Anhydrous calcium chloride removes moisture from the air. The nail is exposed to oxygen but not water and does not rust.
- Tube C: The nail is exposed to both water and oxygen, and rust forms on it.

2 Chemical process

- Iron atoms are oxidized to form first iron(II) ions, Fe^{2+}, and then iron(III) ions, Fe^{3+}, present in rust, $Fe_2O_3.xH_2O$.
- Oxygen is reduced and combined with water to form *hydroxide ions*, OH^-.

3 Rust prevention

- Most methods of rust prevention involve stopping iron or, more commonly, steel from coming into contact with water and/or oxygen in air. These methods include painting, greasing, coating in plastic, coating in zinc (*galvanizing*), and coating in tin.
- Sacrificial protection involves bolting blocks of a more reactive metal, such as *magnesium*, to a steel structure. The magnesium will oxidize more readily than the iron and will thus "sacrifice itself" in order to prevent iron from rusting.

© Diagram Visual Information Ltd.

Key words

anode
cathode
electrolyte
slag

1 Matte smelting

- Matte smelting is used to produce a liquid sulfide phase (matte) containing as much copper as possible, and an immiscible liquid *slag*, which contains virtually no copper.
- Copper sulfide ores, such as chalcopyrite (**CuFeS$_2$**) are mixed with sand and blown into the flash furnace:

  $$4CuFeS_2(s) + 5O_2(g) + 2SiO_2(s) \rightarrow$$
  $$\underbrace{2Cu_2S.FeS(l)}_{matte} + \underbrace{2FeSiO_3(l)}_{slag} + 4SO_2(g)$$

- As the iron content of the matte falls to about 1 percent, copper starts to form. This product is called "blister copper" and is 98–99.5 percent pure. It is porous and brittle and requires further refining to be commercially useful.
- Blister copper is melted to drive off sulfur dioxide, and air is blown through it to remove any sulfur. The impure copper is cast into *anodes* for electro-refining.

2 Electro-refining

- In electro-refining, a large impure copper anode and a small pure copper *cathode* are suspended in an *electrolyte* consisting of copper(II) sulfate solution and sulfuric acid.
- At the anode, copper atoms are oxidized to copper ions and pass into solution. The anode gradually becomes smaller:

  $$Cu(s) \rightarrow Cu^{2+}(aq) + 2e^-$$

- At the cathode, copper ions are removed from solution as they are reduced to copper atoms. The cathode gradually becomes larger:

  $$Cu^{2+}(aq) + 2e^- \rightarrow Cu(s)$$

- Impurities that are insoluble in the electrolyte fall to the bottom of the cell. These may include gold, silver, platinum, and tin, and in some circumstances may be more valuable than the copper produced.

Copper smelting and converting

1 Matte smelting

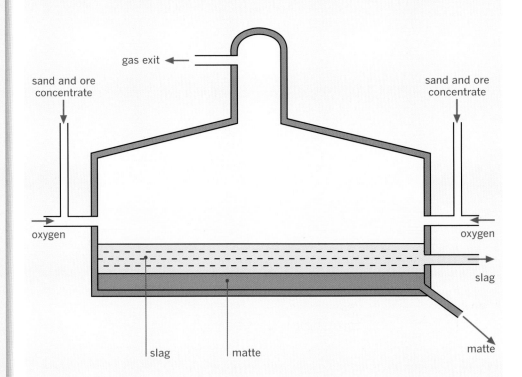

gas exit

sand and ore concentrate

sand and ore concentrate

oxygen

oxygen

slag

matte

slag   matte

2 Electro-refining

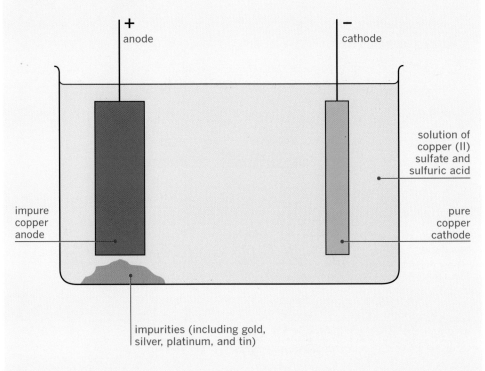

+
anode

−
cathode

solution of copper (II) sulfate and sulfuric acid

impure copper anode

pure copper cathode

impurities (including gold, silver, platinum, and tin)

Reactions of copper

Key words

hydrochloric acid	sulfuric acid
nitric acid	transition metals
oxidation state	
oxidizing agent	

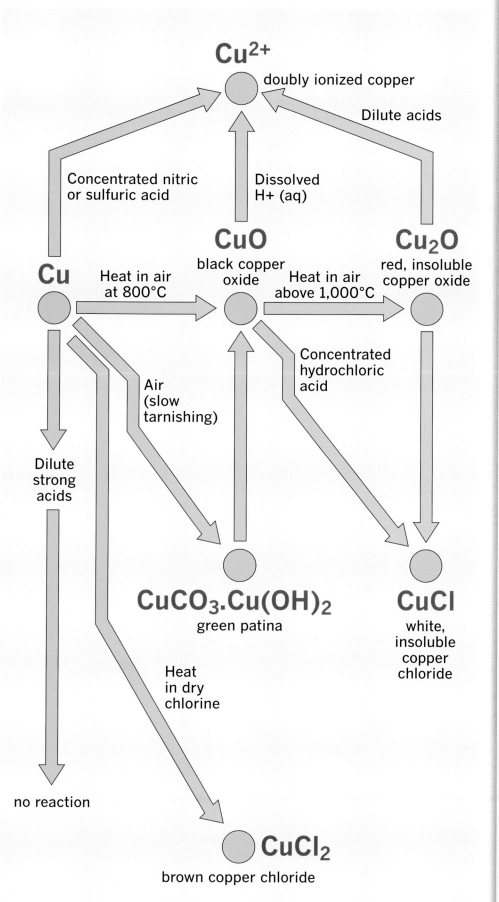

Reactions of copper

- Copper is a *transition metal*. Its normal *oxidation state* is copper(II), Cu^{2+}, but it also forms some copper(I), Cu^+, compounds. Copper is a relatively unreactive metal. It does not react with dilute strong acids, water, or steam.

- When heated in air at 800°C, copper is oxidized to black copper(II) oxide:
  $$2Cu(s) + O_2(g) \rightarrow 2CuO(s)$$
  At temperatures over 1,000°C, red copper(I) oxide is formed:
  $$4Cu(s) + O_2(g) \rightarrow 2Cu_2O(s)$$
  Both oxides react with dilute acids to form copper(II) salts.

- When heated in chlorine, copper forms brown copper(II) chloride.
  $$Cu(s) + Cl_2(g) \rightarrow CuCl_2(s)$$

- White copper(I) chloride also exists and can be made by strongly heating copper(II) chloride:
  $$2CuCl_2(s) \rightarrow 2CuCl(s) + Cl_2(g)$$
  It is also formed by the reaction of copper(II) oxide with concentrated *hydrochloric acid* via an complex ion, $[CuCl_2]^-$. When a solution containing this ion is poured into water, copper(I) chloride is precipitated.

- Copper tarnishes slowly in air, forming basic copper(II) carbonate, a compound of copper(II) carbonate, and copper(II) hydroxide, $CuCO_3.Cu(OH)_2$. It is this compound that produces the green coloration, referred to as patina, on weathered copper.

- Copper reacts with both concentrated nitric and concentrated *sulfuric acid*. Both of these concentrated acids are powerful *oxidizing agents* and react with copper in a different way than a dilute acid reacts with a metal. Copper does not react with dilute acids.
  With concentrated sulfuric acid:
  $$Cu(s) + 2H_2SO_4(l) \rightarrow$$
  $$CuSO_4(aq) + 2H_2O(l) + SO_2(g)$$
  With concentrated *nitric acid*:
  $$Cu(s) + 4HNO_3 \rightarrow$$
  $$Cu(NO_3)_2(aq) + 2H_2O(l) + 2NO_2(g)$$

Key words

aluminum	iron
amphoteric	oxidation state
carbonate	oxide
copper	transition metals
hydroxide	valency

Reactivity

- *Aluminum* is the most reactive and *copper* is least reactive of the three metals.
- All three metals react directly with non-metals.

Oxides

- Aluminum has one *oxide*, Al_2O_3, which is *amphoteric* and thus reacts with both acids and alkalis. *Iron* has three oxides: FeO, Fe_2O_3, and Fe_3O_4. Copper has two: Cu_2O and CuO. All metal oxides react with dilute acids to form salts and water.

Hydroxides

- Aluminum *hydroxide*, like aluminum oxide, is amphoteric. Iron forms two hydroxides by the addition of sodium hydroxide solution to solutions of its salts. Iron(II) salts produce a dirty green precipitate of iron(II) hydroxide, while iron(III) salts produce a red-brown precipitate of iron(III) hydroxide. Copper(II) hydroxide forms as a blue precipitate when sodium hydroxide is added to a solution of a copper salt.
- All metal hydroxides react with alkalis to give metal salts and water.

Carbonates

- Aluminum and iron(III) do not form *carbonates*. Iron(II) carbonate and copper(II) carbonate decompose on heating to the corresponding metal oxide with the loss of carbon dioxide gas. The carbonates also react with dilute acids to forms metal salts, carbon dioxide, and water.

Valency

- Aluminum is in group 3 of the periodic table and exhibits only one *oxidation state*, +3, in its compounds. Iron and copper are both *transition metals* and exhibit two oxidation states in their compounds.

Reaction summary: aluminum, iron, and copper

Aluminum	
Preparation	Electrolysis of aluminum oxide $Al^{3+} + 3e^- \rightarrow Al$ at cathode
Reaction of elements	$4Al + 3O_2 \rightarrow 2Al_2O_3$ oxide layer formed $2Al + 3Cl_2 \rightarrow Al_2Cl_6$ $2Al + 3H_2SO_4 \rightarrow Al_2(SO_4)_3 + 3H_2$
Oxide	$Al_2O_3 + 3H_2SO_4 \rightarrow Al_2(SO_4)_3 + 3H_2O$ $Al_2O_3(s) + 2NaOH(aq) \rightarrow Na[Al(OH)_4](aq)$
Hydroxide	$AlCl_3 + 3NaOH \rightarrow Al(OH)_3 + 3NaCl$ $Al(OH)_3 + 3HCl \rightarrow AlCl_3 + 3H_2O$ $Al(OH)_3(s) + NaOH(aq) \rightarrow 2Na[Al(OH)_4](aq)$ (amphoteric)
Carbonate	Not formed
Change of valency	Only on oxidation

Iron	
Preparation	Chemical reduction in blast furnace $Fe_2O_3 + 3CO \rightarrow 2Fe + 3CO_2$
Reaction of elements	$2Fe + 2H_2O + O_2 \rightarrow 2Fe(OH)_2$ rust $Fe + 2HCl \rightarrow FeCl_2 + H_2$ $2Fe + 3Cl_2 \rightarrow 2FeCl_3$ $Fe + S \rightarrow FeS$ $Fe + H_2SO_4 \rightarrow FeSO_4 + H_2$
Oxide	$FeO + H_2SO_4 \rightarrow FeSO_4 + H_2O$ $Fe_2O_3 + 3H_2SO_4 \rightarrow Fe_2(SO_4)_3 + 3H_2O$
Hydroxide	$FeCl_2 + 2NaOH \rightarrow Fe(OH)_2 + 2NaCl$ $FeCl_3 + 3NaOH \rightarrow Fe(OH)_3 + 3NaCl$ $Fe(OH)_2 + 2HCl \rightarrow FeCl_2 + 2H_2O$ $Fe(OH)_3 + 3HCl \rightarrow FeCl_3 + 3H_2O$
Carbonate	Unstable to heat. $FeCO_3 \rightarrow FeO + CO_2$ $FeCO_3 + H_2SO_4 \rightarrow FeSO_4 + CO_2 + H_2O$
Change of valency	$2Fe^{2+}_{(aq)} + Cl_{2(g)} \rightarrow 2Fe^{3+}_{(aq)} + 2Cl^-_{(aq)}$

Copper	
Preparation	Thermal decomposition in furnace $Cu_2S \xrightarrow{air} 2Cu + SO_2$
Reaction of elements	$2Cu + O_2 \rightarrow 2CuO$ $Cu + Cl_2 \rightarrow CuCl_2$ $2Cu + S \rightarrow Cu_2S$ $CuCl_2 + H_2SO_4 \rightarrow$ no reaction with dilute acid $Cu + 2H_2SO_4 \rightarrow CuSO_4 + SO_2 + 2H_2O$ with conc. acid
Oxide	$CuO + H_2SO_4 \rightarrow CuSO_4 + H_2O$
Hydroxide	$CuCl_2 + 2NaOH \rightarrow Cu(OH)_2 + 2NaCl$ $Cu(OH)_2 + 2HCl \rightarrow CuCl_2 + 2H_2O$
Carbonate	Unstable to heat. $CuCO_3 \rightarrow CuO + CO_2$ $CuCO_3 + H_2SO_4 \rightarrow CuSO_4 + CO_2 + H_2O$
Change of valency	$2Cu^{2+}_{(aq)} + 2I^-_{(aq)} \rightarrow 2Cu^+_{(aq)} + I_{2(s)}$ then $Cu^+_{(aq)} + I^-_{(aq)} \rightarrow CuI_{(s)}$

The extraction of metals from their ores

Metal (Date of discovery) Ranked from highest to lowest in reactivity series	Main ore from which it is obtained	Main method of extraction
Sodium (1807) Group 1	Rock salt NaCl	Electrolysis of molten NaCl
Magnesium (1808) Group 2	Magnesite $MgCO_3$ and Mg^{2+} ions in seawater	Electrolysis of molten $MgCl_2$
Aluminum (1827) Group 3	Bauxite $Al_2O_3.2H_2O$	Electrolysis of Al_2O_3 in molten cryolite (Na_3AlF_6)
Zinc (1746) Transition metal	Zinc blende ZnS	Heat sulfide in air → oxide. Dissolve oxide in H_2SO_4, electrolyze
Iron (ancient) Transition metal	Hematite Fe_2O_3	Reduce Fe_2O_3 with carbon monoxide
Tin (ancient) Group 4	Tinstone SnO_2	Reduce SnO_2 with carbon
Lead (ancient) Group 4	Galena PbS	Heat sulfide in air → oxide. Reduce oxide with carbon
Copper (ancient) Transition metal	Copper pyrites $CuFeS_2$ (CuS + FeS)	Controlled heating with correct amount of air → Cu + SO_2
Mercury (ancient) Transition metal	Cinnabar HgS	Heat in air → Hg + SO_2

Key words

electrolysis
ore
reactivity series
reduction

Extraction of metals

- The ease with which a metal is obtained from its *ore* is directly related to its position in the *reactivity series* of metals.

Electrolytic reduction

- All of the group 1 and group 2 metals and aluminum from group 3 are reactive metals and in the upper half of the reactivity series. They cannot be obtained from their ores by chemical *reduction*, i.e., by heating the ore with a reducing agent such as carbon monoxide or carbon. These metals can only be obtained by electrolytic reduction or *electrolysis*.
- Consequently, it was impossible to obtain these metals before the discovery and development of electricity at the end of the eighteenth century. All of these metals were first made in the early years of the nineteenth century, several by English chemist Sir Humphrey Davy.

Heating

- Zinc oxide and iron oxide are reduced by heating with carbon monoxide. Although zinc can be obtained by chemical reduction, approximately 80 percent of the world's annual production is, in fact, obtained by electrolysis.
- All of the metals from iron and below in the reactivity series are relatively easy to obtain from their ores by heating.
- Iron is obtained by reduction with carbon monoxide
- Tin is obtained by reduction with carbon
- Lead is obtained by heating lead sulfide in air to produce an oxide, which is then reduced with carbon.
- Copper is obtained by controlled heating with the correct amount of air
- Mercury is obtained by heating in air.

Key words

oxide
reactivity
reactivity series

Reactivity summary: metals

Reactivity summary

- Metals can be arranged in order of their *reactivity*, starting with the most reactive. This is called the *reactivity series*. The relative reactivity of metals is reflected through all of their chemistry.

Reaction with oxygen

- Metals at the top of the reactivity series readily burn in oxygen. Less reactive metals do not burn but form a surface layer of *oxide*. Metals at the bottom of the reactivity series are not oxidized by atmospheric oxygen.

Reaction with cold water

- Metals at the top of the reactivity series react readily with cold water but with decreasing vigor down to magnesium. The metals below magnesium do not react with cold water.

Reaction with steam

- Metals react more vigorously with steam than with cold water. All of the metals down to iron react with steam with decreasing vigor. The metals below iron do not react with steam.

Reaction with dilute acid

- All of the metals down to lead react with dilute acids, with decreasing vigor. The metals below lead do not react with dilute acids.

	K Na	**Ca Mg Al Zn Fe**	**Pb Cu Hg**	**Ag Pt Au**
Reaction with $O_{2(g)}$ on heating	form oxides (e.g.,Na_2O) in limited supplies of O_2, but peroxides (e.g., Na_2O_2) with excess O_2	burn with decreasing vigor to form oxides	do *not* burn, but only form a surface layer of oxide	do *not* burn or oxidize on surface
Heat evolved when metal reacts with 1 mole of O_2 to form oxide shown /kJ	**K** K_2O 723 **Na** Na_2O 832	**Ca** CaO 1272 **Mg** MgO 1204 **Al** Al_2O_3 1114 **Zn** ZnO 697 **Fe** Fe_2O_3 548	**Pb** PbO 436 **Cu** CuO 311 **Hg** HgO 182	**Ag** Ag_2O 61 **Pt** — — **Au** Au_2O_3 54
Reaction with cold water	displace $H_{2(g)}$ from cold water with decreasing reactivity **K**, violently	displace $H_{2(g)}$ from cold water with decreasing reactivity **Mg**, very slowly	do *not* displace $H_{2(g)}$ from cold water	do *not* displace $H_{2(g)}$ from cold water
Reaction with steam	displace $H_{2(g)}$ from steam with decreasing vigor **K**, very violently	displace $H_{2(g)}$ from steam with decreasing vigor **Fe**, very slowly)	do *not* displace $H_{2(g)}$ from steam	do *not* displace $H_{2(g)}$ from steam
Reaction with dilute acid	displace $H_{2(g)}$ from dilute acid with decreasing vigor **K**, explosively	**Mg**,very vigorous **Fe**,steadily	do *not* displace $H_{2(g)}$ from dilute acid **Pb**, very slowly	do *not* displace $H_{2(g)}$ from dilute acid

Tests on metals: flame test

Key words

ion
salt
solution

1 Flame test

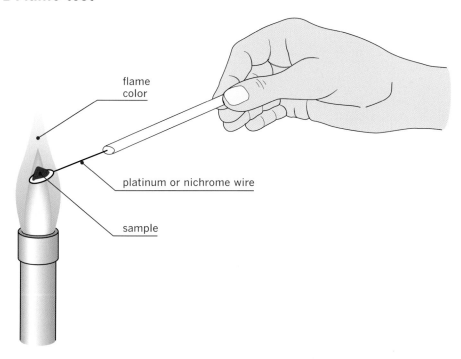

flame
color

platinum or nichrome wire

sample

1 Flame test
- Several metal *ions* produce characteristic colors when introduced to a bunsen flame either as a solid or as a *solution* of a *salt*.
- A clean platinum or nichrome wire is dipped in concentrated hydrochloric acid and then into the solid or solution.
- The sample is introduced to the middle of a non-luminous bunsen flame.

2 Flame coloration
- The following metals produce the following colors in the flame test:
  barium: apple green
  calcium: brick red
  copper: blue-green
  lithium: red
  potassium: lilac
  sodium: orange-yellow
  strontium: crimson
- The lilac color of potassium is sometimes difficult to see and is better observed through blue glass that makes the flame appear purple.
- The orange-yellow color of sodium is very intense and may mask the color of other metal ions present.

2 Table of flame coloration

Color of flame	Likely ion present	Metal
Apple green	Ba^{2+}	barium
Blue-green	Cu^{2+}	copper
Brick red	Ca^{2+}	calcium
Crimson	Sr^{2+}	strontium
Lilac	K^+	potassium
Orange-yellow	Na^+	sodium
Red	Li^+	lithium

Key words

amphoteric   transition metals
hydroxide
precipitate
salt
sodium hydroxide

1 Producing the hydroxide

- Group 1 metal *hydroxides* are very
  soluble and form strong alkaline
  solutions. Group 2 metal hydroxides
  are less soluble but still dissolve
  sufficiently to form weak alkaline
  solutions. All other metals form
  insoluble hydroxides. If several drops
  of sodium hydroxide (**NaOH**) solution
  are added to a solution of a metal *salt*,
  a *precipitate*, often gelatinous, is
  formed. Care must be taken when
  carrying out this reaction because
  some metals form precipitates that
  redissolve in excess *sodium hydroxide*
  solution. If sodium hydroxide solution
  is added too quickly, the initial
  precipitate may not be seen.

2 The reactions

- The reactions of metal salt solutions
  with sodium hydroxide solution can be
  used to identify the metal.
- Aluminum, zinc, and lead hydroxides
  are all *amphoteric*. When sodium
  hydroxide solution is added to
  solutions of salts of these metals, an
  initial white precipitate is formed.
  However, if excess sodium hydroxide
  solution is added, the precipitate
  dissolves, forming a solution of a
  soluble complex compound.
  $Al(OH)_3(s) + NaOH(aq) \rightarrow$
    $Na[Al(OH)_4](aq)$
  sodium tetrahydroxoaluminate(III)

  $Zn(OH)_2(s) + 2NaOH(aq) \rightarrow$
    $Na_2[Zn(OH)_4](aq)$
  sodium tetrahydroxozincate(II)

  $Pb(OH)_2(s) + 2NaOH(aq) \rightarrow$
    $Na_2[Pb(OH)_4](aq)$
  sodium tetrahydroxoplumbate(II).
- Iron and copper are *transition metals*
  and form characteristic colored
  precipitates with sodium hydroxide
  solution.

© Diagram Visual Information Ltd.

Tests on metals: metal hydroxides

1 Producing the hydroxide from the metallic salt

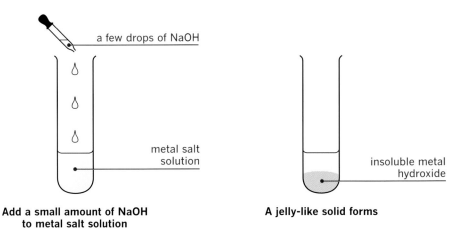

a few drops of NaOH

metal salt
solution

insoluble metal
hydroxide

**Add a small amount of NaOH
to metal salt solution**

A jelly-like solid forms

2 The reactions

Aluminum nitrate $\rightarrow$ white precipitate of aluminum hydroxide
$Al(NO_3)_3 + 3NaOH \rightarrow 3NaNO_3 + Al(OH)_3 \downarrow$

Zinc nitrate $\rightarrow$ white precipitate of zinc hydroxide
$Zn(NO_3)_2 + 2NaOH \rightarrow 2NaNO_3 + Zn(OH)_2 \downarrow$

Lead nitrate $\rightarrow$ white precipitate of lead hydroxide
$Pb(NO_3)_2 + 2NaOH \rightarrow 2NaNO_3 + Pb(OH)_2 \downarrow$

Iron(II) nitrate $\rightarrow$ green precipitate of iron(II) hydroxide
$Fe(NO_3)_2 + 2NaOH \rightarrow 2NaNO_3 + Fe(OH)_2 \downarrow$

Iron(III) nitrate $\rightarrow$ rust-brown precipitate of iron(III) hydroxide
$Fe(NO_3)_3 + 3NaOH \rightarrow 3NaNO_3 + Fe(OH)_3 \downarrow$

Copper nitrate $\rightarrow$ royal blue precipitate of copper hydroxide
$Cu(NO_3)_2 + 2NaOH \rightarrow 2NaNO_3 + Cu(OH)_2 \downarrow$

Tests on metals: metal ions

Key words

hydroxide
reagent

Reacations with reagents

● In addition to flame tests and the properties of their hydroxides, the presence of some metal ions in solution can be demonstrated by their reactions with particular reagents.

Metal ion in solution	To the test solution	Positive result
Alumnum Al^{3+}	Add 1 or 2 drops of litmus solution followed by dilute hydrochloric acid until the mixture is just acidic. Then add ammonia solution until just alkaline.	Blue lake – a gelatinous precipitate of aluminum hydroxide – is formed, and this absorbs the litmus, leaving the solution almost colorless.
Barium Ba^{2+}	Add several drops of potassium chromate solution.	A yellow precipitate of barium chromate. Lead ions also give a yellow precipitate, but lead chromate is deeper yellow and turns orange on heating.
Copper Cu^{2+}	Add ammonia solution drop by drop until it is in excess.	An initial blue precipitate of copper(II) hydroxide that dissolves in excess ammonia solution to give a deep blue solution containing the complex ion $[Cu(NH_3)_4]^{2+}$.
Iron(II) Fe^{2+}	Add several drops of potassium hexacyanoferrate(III) solution.	A deep blue solution is formed.
Iron(III) Fe^{3+}	Add several drops of ammonium thiocyanate solution.	Deep blood-red coloration.
Lead Pb^{2+}	Add several drops of potassium iodide solution.	A yellow precipitate of lead(II) iodide.
Silver Ag^+	Add several drops of potassium chromate solution.	A brick-red precipitate of silver chromate.
Zinc Zn^{2+}	Add ammonium chloride and ammonia solution, then pass hydrogen sulfide through the mixture.	A white, or more often dirty white, precipitate of zinc sulfide.

Key words

alloy	*iron*
aluminum	*lead*
copper	*reactivity series*
ductile	*zinc*
galvanizing	

Uses of metals

- The uses of metals are related to both their physical and chemical properties. The physical properties of a metal are sometimes altered by mixing it with other metals or non-metals to form *alloys*.

Aluminum

- *Aluminum* has a low density but is too soft for many applications. It is frequently used as duralumin (an alloy of aluminum and *copper*) as a structural material in the manufacture of airplanes.

Zinc

- *Zinc* is above *iron* in the *reactivity series*. During *galvanizing*, iron is dipped in molten zinc, and the layer of zinc formed on the iron protects it from rusting. If the galvanized iron is scratched, exposing the iron, an electrolytic cell forms between the iron and zinc, and the zinc corrodes in preference to the iron.

Iron

- Iron is used for all sorts of structures, most often as steel (an alloy of iron and carbon). The one serious problem with iron and steel is that they rust on exposure to water and oxygen in the air.

Lead

- *Lead* has a high density and is impervious to water, so it used as flashing on roofs. It is also used as in the manufacture of car batteries. In the past, before its toxic nature was understood, lead was also used for water pipes and in paints. Solder (an alloy of lead and tin) is widely used to join copper wires and copper pipes.

Uses of metals

Metal	Use	Reason
Aluminum 	Structural material for ships, planes, cars, cookware Electric cables	Strong but light; oxide layer prevents corrosion. Light, but good conductor.
Zinc 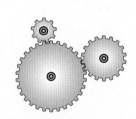	Coating (galvanizing) steel Alloys: brass (Zn/Cu) bronze (Zn/Sn/Cu)	Reactive — gives sacrificial protection to iron; does not corrode easily. Modifies the properties of the other elements.
Iron 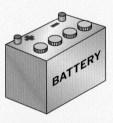	Structural material for all industries (in the form of steel)	Strong and cheap; properties can be made suitable by alloying.
Lead 	Roofing Car batteries Solder (Pb/Sn alloy)	Very malleable and does not corrode. Design of battery makes recharging possible. Low melting point.
Copper	Electric cables Pipes Alloys (see above) Coins (alloyed with nickel)	Very good conductor. Very ductile, does not corrode easily.

Copper

- Copper is very *ductile* and can be easily drawn into wires. It is a good conductor of electricity and is used for the conducting parts of electric cables. Copper does not react with water and is a good conductor of heat. It is used for water pipes and radiators.

Reactivity of metals 1

Key words

alkali	hydroxide
calcium	magnesium
chloride	oxide
copper	sodium
iron	

1 Forming oxides and chlorides

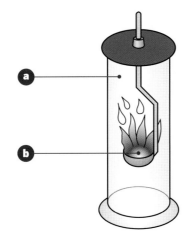

a oxygen or chlorine
b burning piece of reactive metal

2 Forming hydroxides

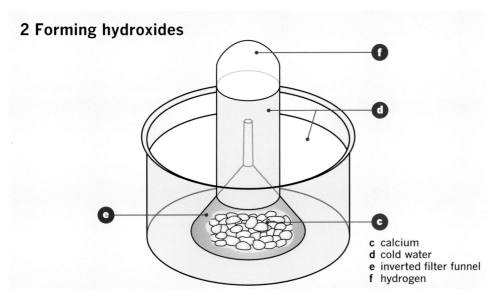

c calcium
d cold water
e inverted filter funnel
f hydrogen

3 Less reactive metals

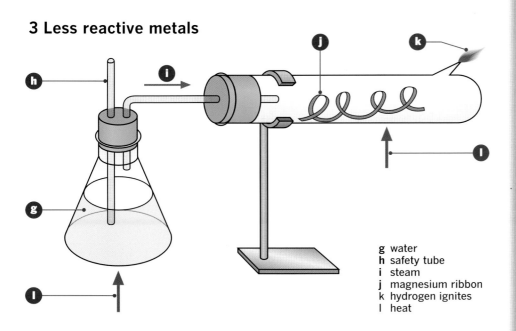

g water
h safety tube
i steam
j magnesium ribbon
k hydrogen ignites
l heat

1 Forming oxides and chlorides

- Most metals react with air to form metal *oxides*. Reactive metals like *magnesium* burn, producing light and heat. Less reactive metals like *copper* simply change color on heating:

$2Mg(s) + O_2(g) \rightarrow 2MgO(s)$
$2Cu(s) + O_2 \rightarrow 2CuO(s)$

- Metals will also form *chlorides* when heated in chlorine:

$Mg(s) + Cl_2(g) \rightarrow MgCl_2(s)$
$Cu(s) + Cl_2 \rightarrow CuCl_2(s)$

2 Forming hydroxides

- Very reactive metals like *calcium* and *sodium* react with water to form solutions of metal *hydroxides* and hydrogen gas:

$Ca(s) + 2H_2O(l) \rightarrow$
$\quad Ca(OH)_2(aq) + H_2(g)$
$2Na(s) + 2H_2O(l) \rightarrow$
$\quad 2NaOH(aq) + H_2(g)$

- Calcium hydroxide is less soluble in water and forms a weak *alkali*.
- Sodium hydroxide is very soluble in water and forms a strong alkali.

3 Less reactive metals

- Less reactive metals, which react with water very slowly or not at all, react with steam to form metal oxides and hydrogen gas.
- Magnesium reacts very slowly with water but readily with steam:

$Mg(s) + H_2O(g) \rightarrow MgO(s) + H_2(g)$

- Iron does not react with water but reacts with steam to form iron(II) diiron(III) oxide:

$3Fe(s) + 4H_2O(g) \rightarrow Fe_3O_4(s) + 4H_2(g)$

- The least reactive metals, such as copper, do not react with water or steam.

Reactivity of metals 2

1 Metal compounds

- The *oxides* of metals that are low in the *reactivity series*, like copper, can be reduced by heating them in a stream of hydrogen gas.
- All group 1 metal *carbonates*, with the exception of lithium carbonate, are not decomposed on heating. All other metal carbonates decompose on heating, forming the metal oxide and carbon dioxide gas:

$$Li_2CO_3(s) \rightarrow Li_2O(s) + CO_2(g)$$
$$MgCO_3(s) \rightarrow MgO(s) + CO_2(g)$$
$$CuCO_3(s) \rightarrow CuO(s) + CO_2(g)$$

- Carbon dioxide gas is more dense than air and can be poured from one test tube into another. Carbon dioxide turns *limewater* milky.

2 Generating electric current

- When rods of zinc and copper are placed in dilute *sulfuric acid*, a simple electrical cell is formed, and there is a potential voltage difference between the two metals. If the two metals are connected externally, electric current flows.
- The zinc rod becomes the positive electrode (*anode*) of the cell. Zinc atoms are oxidized to form zinc ions:

$$Zn(s) \rightarrow Zn^{2+}(aq) + 2e^-$$

- The copper rod becomes the negative electrode (*cathode*) of the cell. Hydrogen ions are reduced to hydrogen gas:

$$2H^+(aq) + 2e^- \rightarrow H_2(g)$$

- If the copper rod is surrounded by a porous vessel containing copper(II) sulfate solution, a different reaction occurs at the cathode:

$$Cu^{2+}(aq) + 2e^- \rightarrow Cu(s)$$

- Zinc atoms are oxidized to zinc ions, while copper ions are reduced to copper atoms.

1 Reactions of metal compounds

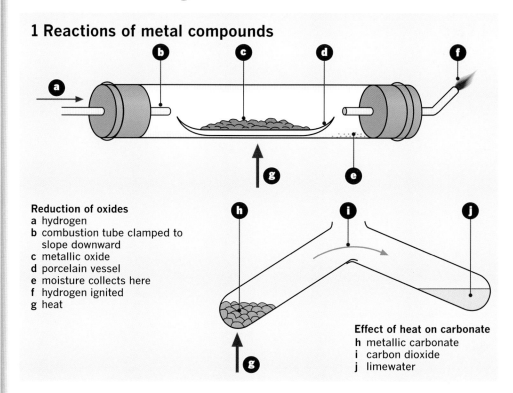

Reduction of oxides
a hydrogen
b combustion tube clamped to slope downward
c metallic oxide
d porcelain vessel
e moisture collects here
f hydrogen ignited
g heat

Effect of heat on carbonate
h metallic carbonate
i carbon dioxide
j limewater

2 Generation of electric current by mechanical reaction

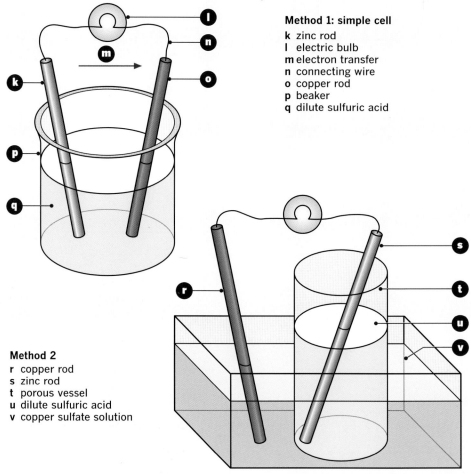

Method 1: simple cell
k zinc rod
l electric bulb
m electron transfer
n connecting wire
o copper rod
p beaker
q dilute sulfuric acid

Method 2
r copper rod
s zinc rod
t porous vessel
u dilute sulfuric acid
v copper sulfate solution

Electrolysis

1 Electrolysis: schematic

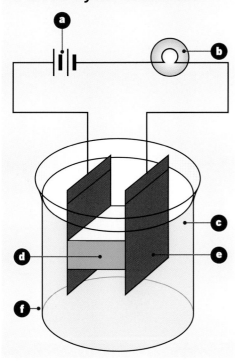

2 Electrolysis of salt solutions

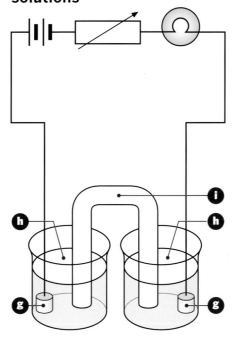

3 Electrolysis of water

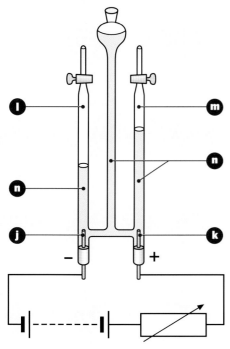

4 U tube

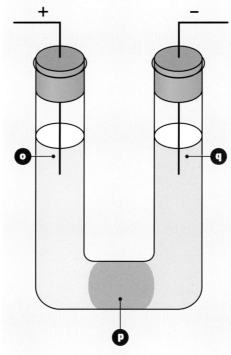

1 Electrolysis
- *Electrolysis* is the process by which an *electrolyte* (a substance that conducts electricity) is decomposed when a direct current is passed through it between *electrodes*. Positive *cations* move to the *cathode* to gain electrons; negative *anions* move to the *anode* to lose electrons.
- Substances are either deposited or liberated at the electrodes depending on the nature of the electrodes and electrolyte.

2 Salt solutions
- Two electrolytes undergo electrolysis at the same time when they are connected in a circuit by a salt bridge.
- The platinum electrode in the left-hand beaker is the anode and attracts negative ions, which are oxidized.
- The platinum electrode in the right-hand beaker is the cathode and attracts positive ions, which are reduced.

3 Water
- The electrolysis of water yields hydrogen at the cathode and oxygen at the anode. Hydrogen and oxygen are formed in the ratio of 2:1.

4 U tube
- The ions present in dilute sulfuric acid are H^+, OH^-, and SO_4^{2-}. Hydroxide ions are discharged at the anode, leaving a surplus of hydrogen ions, so the electrolyte in the left side of the U tube becomes increasingly acidic.
- The ions present in sodium sulfate solution are H^+, Na^+, OH^-, and SO_4^{2-}. Hydrogen ions are discharged at the cathode, leaving a surplus of hydroxide ions, so the electrolyte in the right side of the U tube becomes increasingly alkaline.

a battery
b electric bulb
c liquid under test
d poly(ethene) support
e copper plates
f glass vessel
g platinum electrodes
h electrolyte solution in beakers
i salt bridge

j platinum cathode
k platinum anode
l hydrogen
m oxygen
n water acidified with dilute sulfuric acid
o dilute sulfuric acid
p agar jelly colored pink by phenolphthalein and alkali
q sodium sulfate solution

Key words

anode
cathode
electrode
electrolysis
inert

Electrode activity and concentration

- The results of *electrolysis* differ depending on the concentration of the solution and type of *electrodes* used.
- *Inert* electrodes take no part in the reaction; active electrodes take part in the reaction.

1 Dilute solution

- Reaction at the *anode*: oxygen produced
- Reaction at the *cathode*: hydrogen produced

2 Concentrated solution

- Reaction at the anode: chlorine produced
- Reaction at the cathode: hydrogen produced

3 Inert electrodes

- The following reactions occur at the electrodes when copper(II) sulfate undergoes electrolysis using carbon (inert) electrodes.
- Reaction at the anode: oxygen is produced
- Reaction at the cathode: copper metal is deposited on the cathode.

4 Active electrodes

- The following reactions occur at the electrodes when copper(II) sulfate undergoes electrolysis using copper (active) electrodes.
- Reaction at the anode: copper goes into solution as copper ions, and the anode grows smaller.
- Reaction at the cathode: copper metal is deposited, and the cathode grows bigger.

Electrolysis: electrode activity and concentration

1 Dilute solution sodium chloride

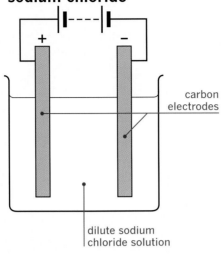

carbon electrodes

dilute sodium chloride solution

2 Concentrated solution sodium chloride

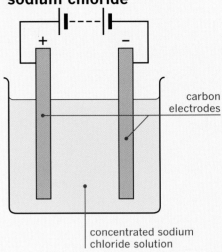

carbon electrodes

concentrated sodium chloride solution

3 Inert electrodes

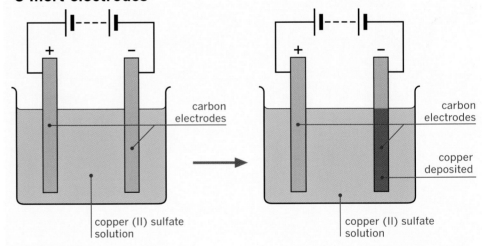

carbon electrodes

copper (II) sulfate solution

carbon electrodes

copper deposited

copper (II) sulfate solution

4 Active electrodes

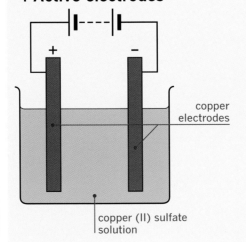

copper electrodes

copper (II) sulfate solution

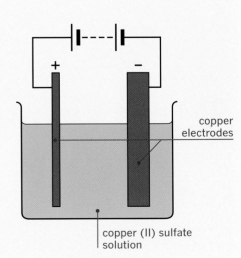

copper electrodes

copper (II) sulfate solution

Acids: reactions

Key words

acid	oxidation
base	oxide
carbonate	salt
catalyst	
hydroxide	

1 Main reactions of an acid

acid → carbonate → salt + CO_2 + H_2O

acid → metal → salt + H_2

acid → base → salt + H_2O

2 Examples of reaction type

Acid with carbonate	$Na_2CO_3(s) + 2HNO_3(aq) \rightarrow$ $2NaNO_3(aq) + CO_2(g) + H_2O(l)$
Acid with base	$HCl(aq) + NaOH(s) \rightarrow NaCl(s) + H_2O(l)$
Acid with metal	$Zn(s) + 2HCl(aq) \rightarrow ZnCl_2(aq) + H_2(g)$
Acid neutralized by oxide	$CuO(s) + H_2SO_4(aq) \rightarrow CuSO_4(aq) + H_2O(l)$

3 Laboratory preparation of sulfur trioxide

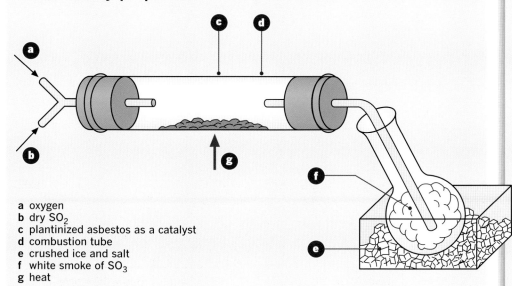

a oxygen
b dry SO_2
c plantinized asbestos as a catalyst
d combustion tube
e crushed ice and salt
f white smoke of SO_3
g heat

1 Main reactions of an acid

- Dilute *acids* react with all metal *carbonates* to give a metal *salt*, carbon dioxide, and water.
- Dilute acids react with *bases* to give salts plus water.
- Dilute acids react with most metals to give a metal salt and hydrogen.
- Dilute acids are neutralized by metal *oxides* and metal *hydroxides* to form a metal salt and water.

2 Example of reaction type

- Sodium carbonate reacts with dilute nitric acid to give sodium nitrate, carbon dioxide, and water.
- Hydrochloric acid reacts with sodium hydroxide to form a salt and water.
- Zinc reacts with dilute hydrochloric acid to give zinc chloride and hydrogen.
- Copper(II) oxide reacts with dilute sulfuric acid to give copper(II) sulfate and water.

3 Sulfur trioxide

- Sulfur trioxide is a white crystalline solid obtained by *oxidation* of sulfur dioxide. It dissolves in water with a hissing noise and the production of heat, forming sulfuric acid. Sulfur trioxide is employed as a dehydrating agent.
- Sulfur trioxide is made in the laboratory by passing a mixture of dry sulfur dioxide and dry oxygen over a heated platinum *catalyst*. Sulfur trioxide melts at 17°C and condenses as a solid in a suitably cooled beaker.
- Industrially it is made using the contact process (see pages 75 & 76).

Preparation of acids

Key words

hydrochloric acid   sulfuric acid
hydrogen
  chloride
nitric acid
soluble

1 Preparing HCl gas

- *Hydrogen chloride* gas is made by the reaction of sodium chloride and concentrated sulfuric acid:
$$2NaCl(s) + H_2SO_4(aq) \rightarrow$$
$$Na_2SO_4(aq) + 2HCl(g)$$
The gas is more dense than air and is collected by downward delivery.

2 Preparing HCl acid

- Hydrogen chloride is extremely *soluble* in water, forming *hydrochloric acid*. It cannot be dissolved simply by placing a delivery tube carrying the gas directly into water because the water would be sucked back into the reaction vessel.
- The gas is dissolved in water by passing it into an inverted funnel positioned so the lip is just under the surface of the water. The funnel prevents suck back.

3 Preparing nitric acid

- *Nitric acid* can be made by the reaction of solid sodium or potassium nitrate with concentrated *sulfuric acid*:
$$KNO_3(s) + H_2SO_4(aq) \rightarrow$$
$$KHSO_4(aq) + HNO_3$$
- The product of this reaction is normally yellow due to the presence of nitrogen dioxide, formed by the thermal decomposition of the acid:
$$4HNO_3(l) \rightarrow$$
$$4NO_2(g) + 2H_2O(g) + O_2(g)$$

4 Industrial preparation of HNO₃

- Nitric acid is made industrially by the oxidation of ammonia in a process involving three stages (see page 76): production of nitrogen oxide gas, oxidation of nitrogen oxide to nitrogen dioxide gas, reaction of nitrogen dioxide and water.
- This process can be modeled in the laboratory by passing ammonia vapor over a heated platinum catalyst.

1 Preparation of hydrogen chloride (gas)

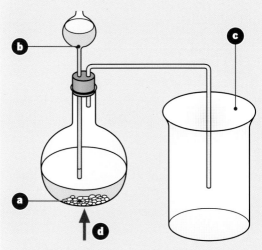

a rock salt
b concentrated sulfuric acid
c HCl gas collected
d heat

2 Preparation of hydrochloric acid

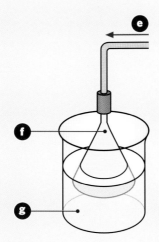

e HCl filter
f filter funnel
g water (to become dilute HCl acid)

3 Laboratory preparation of nitric acid

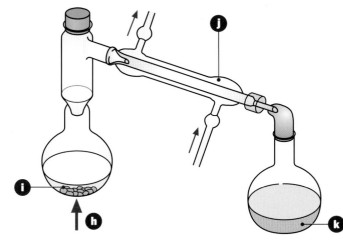

h heat
i solid sodium nitrate plus concentrated sulfuric acid
j water jacket
k pure nitric acid

4 Industrial preparation of nitric acid

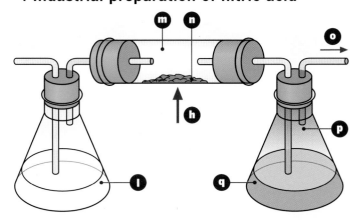

l concentrated ammonia diluted with water (50%)
m combustion tube
n platinized asbestos
o pump sucks gases through apparatus
p brown gas
q litmus goes red

Bases: reactions

1 General reactions of a base with an acid

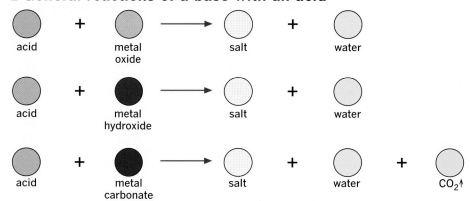

acid + metal oxide ⟶ salt + water

acid + metal hydroxide ⟶ salt + water

acid + metal carbonate ⟶ salt + water + CO₂↑

2 Metal oxide and acid

heat is applied

Magnesium oxide is added to hydrochloric acid and indicator

Neutral solution, indicator is green

3 Carbonate and acid

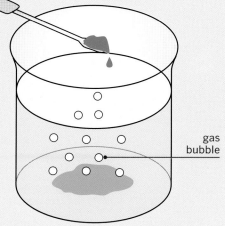

gas bubble

Cabonate is added to hydrochloric acid and indicator

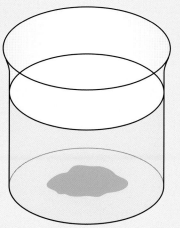

Neutral solution, indicator is green

Key words

acid	*salt*
base	*universal*
carbonate	*indicator*
hydroxide	
oxide	

Bases

● A *base* is a compound that reacts with an *acid* to form a *salt*. Common bases are metal *oxides*, metal *hydroxides*, and metal *carbonates*.

1 General reactions with acids

● Metal oxides react with acids to form salts and water.
● Metal hydroxides also react with acids to form salts and water.
● Metal carbonates react with acids to form salts, water, and carbon dioxide.

2 Metal oxide and acid

● The reaction of magnesium oxide (MgO) with hydrochloric acid (HCl) can be followed by adding a few drops of *universal indicator* to the acid.
● Initially the indicator is red. When magnesium oxide is added to the reaction, the following reaction occurs:
$MgO(s) + 2HCl(aq) \rightarrow MgCl_2(aq) + H_2O(l)$
● When there are equivalent amounts of magnesium oxide and hydrochloric acid, the indicator turns green, signifying all of the acid has reacted and the mixture is neutral.

3 Carbonate and acid

● The reaction of magnesium carbonate ($MgCO_3$) with hydrochloric acid (HCl) can be followed by observing the carbon dioxide gas evolved.
● Initially bubbles of gas are evolved as the following reaction occurs:
$MgCO_3(s) + 2HCl(aq) \rightarrow MgCl_2(aq) + H_2O(l) + CO_2(g)$
● When all of the hydrochloric acid has reacted, no gas is produced, and excess insoluble magnesium carbonate remains in the beaker.

Bases: forming pure salts

Key words

acid
base
indicator
insoluble
neutral
salt
soluble
titration

1 From a soluble base

- *Titration* is used to make *salts* from *acids* and *soluble bases*, e.g., sodium chloride from hydrochloric acid and sodium hydroxide.
- The burette is filled with hydrochloric acid, and a known volume of sodium hydroxide solution is placed in a conical flask. A few drops of a suitable *indicator* are added to the sodium hydroxide solution. Hydrochloric acid is run into the flask until the color of the indicator changes, showing that the reaction mixture is *neutral*. The volume of hydrochloric acid in the burette is noted before and after addition so the volume of acid needed can be calculated.
- The flask contains a solution of sodium chloride, which is impure due to the presence of the indicator. The procedure must be repeated using exactly the same volumes of hydrochloric acid and sodium hydroxide solution but no indicator.
- Sodium chloride crystals are obtained by boiling off some of the water from the sodium chloride solution and allowing the remaining solution to cool.

2 From an insoluble base

- Salts are made from *insoluble* bases by adding an excess of the base to an acid. For example, copper(II) sulfate is formed by the reaction of copper(II) oxide and sulfuric acid.
- An excess of copper(II) oxide is used to ensure that all of the sulfuric acid has reacted and no acid residue remains. The excess is filtered off, leaving a blue solution of copper(II) sulfate.
- Copper(II) sulfate crystals are obtained by boiling off some of the water from the copper(II) sulfate solution and allowing the remaining solution to cool.

1 From a soluble base (alkali)
Example: sodium chloride from sodium hydroxide and hydrochloric acid

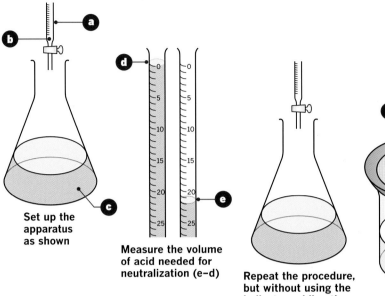

Set up the apparatus as shown

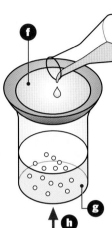

Measure the volume of acid needed for neutralization (e–d)

Repeat the procedure, but without using the indicator, adding the amount of acid measured above (i.e., e–d)

Evaporate off excess water

2 From an insoluble base
Example: copper oxide and sulfuric acid

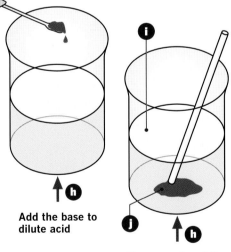

Add the base to dilute acid

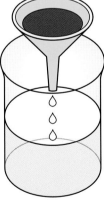

Warm gently, adding the base until no more will dissolve

Filter off excess solid and collect the filtrate

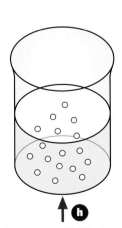

Evaporate off filtrate

a burette
b acid
c alkali and phenolphthalein indicator
   Add the acid until the solution just turns colorless.
d volume of acid in the burette before carrying out the procedure

e volume of acid remaining when the indicator has turned colorless
f salt solution
g boiling water
h heat
i neutralized acid
j excess solid

Proton transfer: neutralization of alkalis

Key words

ammonium	proton
hydroxide	species
ammonium ion	
hydronium ion	
hydroxide ion	

1 Water particles

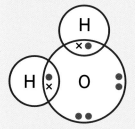 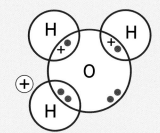 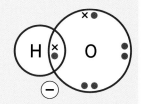

Neutral water molecule

Hydronium ion: protonated water molecule

Hydroxide ion: deprotonated water molecule

2 Ammonia solution turns universal indicator blue

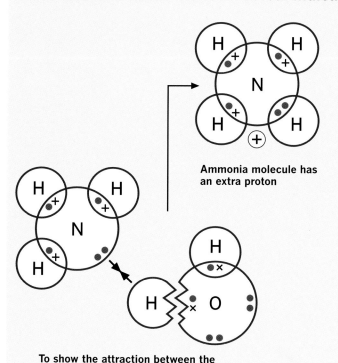

Ammonia molecule has an extra proton

To show the extra-electron in the hydroxide ion

To show the attraction between the molecules and the breaking of the bond in the molecule

3 Schematic of proton transfer in diagram 2

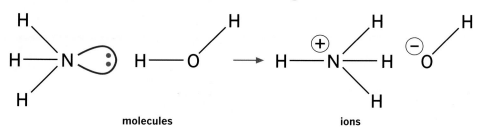

molecules   ions

1 Water particles

- In a water molecule, the oxygen atom forms bonds with two hydrogen atoms. The oxygen atom and the hydrogen atom each donate one electron to the bond. The oxygen atom also has two pairs of non-bonding electrons, which can be donated to form bonds with other *species*.
- In acidic solutions, each proton reacts with a water molecule to form a *hydronium ion*. A pair of non-bonding electrons forms the new **H-O** bond: $H^+ + H_2O \rightarrow H_3O^+$
- An *hydroxide ion* is formed by the loss of a *proton* from a water molecule: $H_2O \rightleftharpoons H^+ + OH^-$

2 Ammonium ions

- The ammonia molecule, NH_3, has a similar structure to the water molecule, H_2O, in the sense that the nitrogen atom has a pair of non-bonding electrons that it can donate to form a bond with another species.
- Ammonia reacts with the protons in an acid to form the *ammonium ions*: $NH_3 + H^+ \rightarrow NH_4^+$
- The four **N-H** bonds in the ammonium ion are directed toward the corners of a tetrahedron, giving a similar structure to methane. This keeps the bonding pairs of electrons as far away from each other as possible.

3 Schematic of proton transfer

- Ammonia is very soluble in water and dissolves to form a weak alkaline solution that is sometimes referred to as *ammonium hydroxide*: $NH_3 + H_2O \rightleftharpoons NH_4OH \rightleftharpoons NH_4^+ + OH^-$
- Ammonia solution contains ammonium ions, NH_4^+, and hydroxide ions, OH^-, and has similar reactions to solutions of soluble metal hydroxides, such as sodium hydroxide.

© Diagram Visual Information Ltd.

Key words	
acid	magnesium oxide
base	oxide
hydronium ion	proton
lattice	salt

Neutralizing bases
- Metallic *bases* neutralize *acids* to form a *salt* plus water.

1 MgO in acid
- *Magnesium oxide* consists of a regular *lattice* of magnesium ions, Mg^{2+}, and *oxide* ions, O^{2-}.
- An acid contains *hydronium ions*, H_3O^+.

2 Attractions
- Hydronium ions carry a positive charge, while oxide ions carry a negative charge. When solid magnesium oxide is added to an acid, these oppositely charged ions are attracted to each other.

3 Transfer
- In an oxide ion, there are eight electrons in the outer orbital of the oxygen atom. Two pairs of electrons are donated to form bonds with oppositely charged hydronium ions:
$$2H_3O^+ + O^{2-} \rightarrow 3H_2O$$

4 Neutral solution
- Each hydronium ion transfers a *proton* to the oxide ion, forming a molecule of water.
- The magnesium oxide lattice breaks down, releasing magnesium ions into solution.
- The acid is neutralized, and a solution of a magnesium salt is formed. The nature of the salt depends on the acid used.
$$MgO(s) + 2HCl(aq) \rightarrow$$
$$MgCl_2(aq) + H_2O(l)$$
Hydrochloric acid → magnesium chloride

$$MgO(s) + 2HNO_3(aq) \rightarrow$$
$$Mg(NO_3)_2(aq) + H_2O(l)$$
Nitric acid → magnesium nitrate

$$MgO(s) + H_2SO_4(aq) \rightarrow$$
$$MgSO_4(aq) + H_2O(l)$$
Sulfuric acid → magnesium sulfate

Proton transfer: neutralization of bases

1 Magnesium oxide (MgO) solid and dilute acid

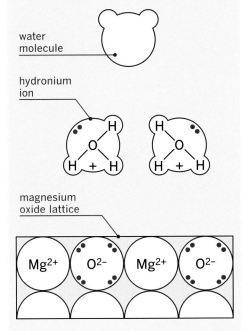

water molecule

hydronium ion

magnesium oxide lattice

2 The oxide ions attract the hydronium ions

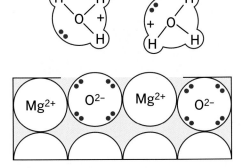

3 Proton transfer takes place

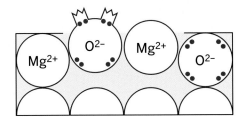

4 A neutral solution is produced and part of the oxide lattice has dissolved

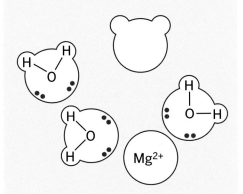

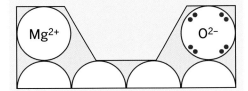

Proton transfer: metallic carbonates

Key words

carbonate	orbital
carbonic acid	salt
hydronium ion	

1 Carbonate ions attract hydronium ions

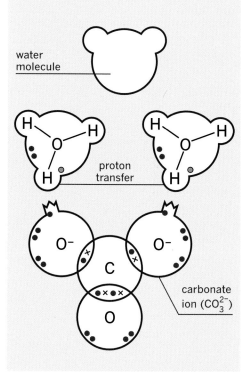

water
molecule

proton
transfer

carbonate
ion (CO_3^{2-})

2 Hydrogen carbonate molecules and water molecules are produced

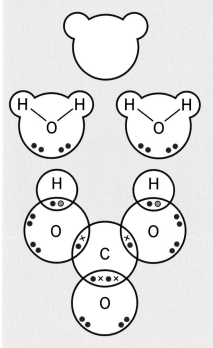

3 A hydrogen carbonate molecule splits

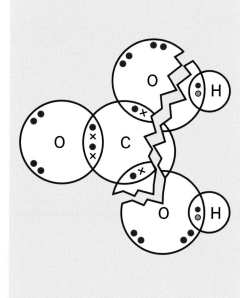

4 A carbon dioxide molecule and water molecule are produced

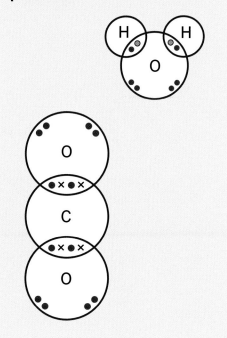

Metallic carbonates

- Metallic *carbonates* neutralize acids to form a metal *salt*, carbon dioxide, and water.

1 Attraction

- Group 1 metal carbonates are soluble in water and can be used as solids or in solution. Other metal carbonates are insoluble in water and are used as solids.
- All metal carbonates contain the carbonate ion, CO_3^{2-}. All acids contain the *hydronium ion*, H_3O^+.
- Hydronium ions carry a positive charge, while carbonate ions carry a negative charge. When a carbonate is added to an acid, these oppositely charged ions are attracted to each other.
- In a carbonate ion, each of the three oxygen atoms has eight electrons in its outer *orbital*. A pair of electrons is donated from two of the oxygen atoms to form bonds with oppositely charged hydronium ions.

2 H_2CO_3 and water

- The result is the formation of *carbonic acid*, H_2CO_3, and water:
  $$2H_3O^+ + CO_3^{2-} \rightarrow H_2CO_3 + 2H_2O$$

3 H_2CO_3 splits

- Carbonic acid is a weak acid that only exists in solution. It readily breaks down to carbon dioxide and water:
  $$H_2CO_3 \rightleftharpoons H_2O + CO_2$$

4 CO_2 and water

- In an acid–carbonate reaction, some of the carbon dioxide will remain in solution, but most will be given off as bubbles of gas.
- The gas can be identified by bubbling it into limewater. Carbon dioxide turns limewater milky due to the formation of insoluble calcium carbonate.
- The acid is neutralized by the carbonate, and a salt is formed. The nature of the salt depends on the metal carbonate and the acid used.

© Diagram Visual Information Ltd.

Key words

ammonia	hydrogen
covalent bond	chloride

Neutralizing acids

- Bases react with acids to produce a salt and water.

1 Molecules

- A chlorine atom has seven electrons in its outer orbit. In *hydrogen chloride*, the chlorine atom forms a *covalent bond* with one hydrogen atom, forming the molecule HCl.
- An oxygen atom has six electrons in its outer orbit. In hydrogen oxide (water), the oxygen atom forms covalent bonds with two hydrogen atoms, forming the molecule H_2O.
- A nitrogen atom has five electrons in its outer orbit. In *ammonia*, the nitrogen atom forms covalent bonds with three hydrogen atoms, forming the molecule NH_3.

2 Schematic

- In a hydrogen chloride molecule, each chlorine atom is surrounded by eight electrons: one pair of bonding electrons and three pairs of non-bonding electrons (lone pairs).
- In a water molecule, each oxygen atom is surrounded by eight electrons: two pairs of bonding electrons and two lone pairs of electrons.
- In an ammonia molecule, each nitrogen atom is surrounded by eight electrons: three pairs of bonding electrons and one pair lone pair of electrons.

3 & 4 Proton transfer and schematic

- Hydrogen chloride gas is a covalent compound and exists as diatomic molecules.
- When hydrogen chloride dissolves in water, an acidic solution is formed: $H_2O + HCl \rightarrow H_3O^+ + Cl^-$
- A lone pair of electrons from an oxygen atom is donated to create a covalent bond between the oxygen atom and a hydrogen atom, forming a hydronium ion and a chloride ion.
- When hydrogen chloride is dissolved in water, it forms an ionic compound.

Proton transfer: neutralization of acids

1 Examples of molecules

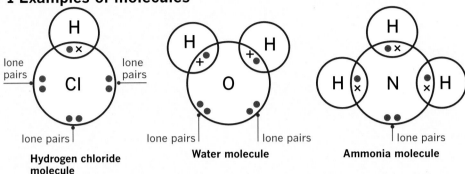

Hydrogen chloride molecule

Water molecule

Ammonia molecule

2 Schematic of the molecules shown in diagram 1

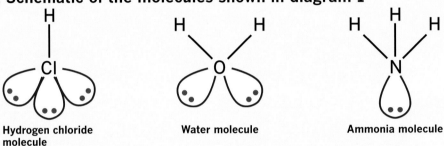

Hydrogen chloride molecule

Water molecule

Ammonia molecule

3 Proton transfer

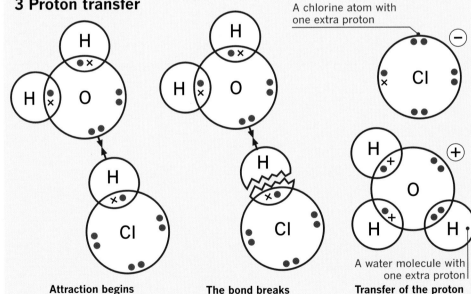

A chlorine atom with one extra proton

A water molecule with one extra proton

Attraction begins

The bond breaks

Transfer of the proton is complete

4 Schematic of proton transfer

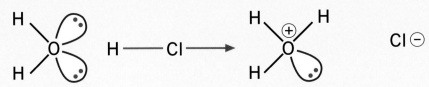

Collision theory

1 Collision theory

No collision between the particles of the reactants: no reaction

Weak collision: no reaction

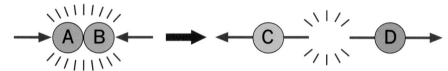

Effective collision: reaction

2 Maxwell-Boltzman distribution

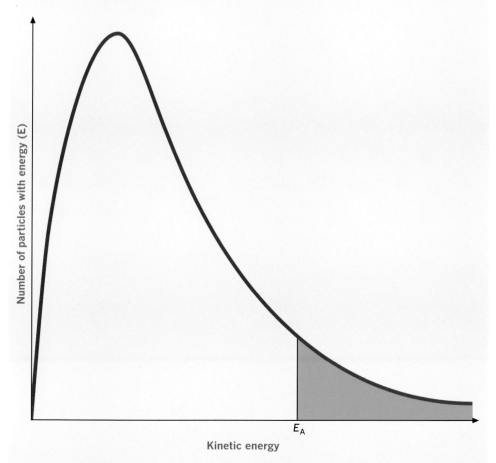

Key words

activation energy
effective collision
product
reactant

1 Collision theory

- Reactions occur when particles collide with sufficient force to provide the energy needed to start a reaction.
- If particles collide with insufficient force to start a reaction, they simply bounce off each other.
- A collision that brings about a reaction is called an *effective collision*. Particles of *reactant* collide, and particles of *product* are formed:

$$\underbrace{A + B}_{\text{reactants}} \quad \rightarrow \quad \underbrace{C + D}_{\text{products}}$$

- Not every collision between particles gives rise to a reaction, but every set of particles that do react have to collide.

2 Maxwell-Boltzman distribution

- Because all the particles of a particular chemical, element, or compound have the same mass, the energy of the particles is directly related to their speed.
- In any mixture of moving particles, the energy at which an individual particle is moving will vary.
- The Maxwell-Boltzman distribution shows how the number of particles in a sample is distributed at different energies at a particular temperature.
- There are no particles at zero energy. There are relatively few particles at very high energy, but there is no maximum energy value.
- In order to react, particles need to have a minimum amount of energy, called *activation energy*. The activation energy is marked on the graph by a line, parallel to the Y axis, at a point on the X axis that symbolizes the activation energy (E_A).

© Diagram Visual Information Ltd.

Rates of reaction: surface area and mixing

Key words

diffusion
immiscible
reactant
surface area

Surface area

- In order for a reaction to take place, the *reactants* must come into contact with each other. Thus, for a given mass of reactant, the smaller the objects, the greater the *surface area* on which the chemical reaction can occur. If all of the reactants are gases or liquids, it is easy for them to mix, giving the maximum opportunity for the particles to collide.

1 Total surface area

- The reaction can only take place on the surface of the solid.
- A cube with sides 2 cm has a total surface area of $2 \times 2 \times 6 = 24$ cm^2. If the same cube is divided into 8 cubes with sides 1 cm, the total surface area now becomes $1 \times 1 \times 6 \times 8 = 48$ cm^2.

2 Reduced surface area

- Zinc reacts with dilute hydrochloric acid to form zinc chloride and hydrogen gas:
  $$Zn + 2HCl \rightarrow ZnCl_2 + H_2$$
- This reaction proceeds much more quickly if zinc dust (fine powder) is used rather than granulated zinc (large lumps).

3 Mixing

- When reactant particles are added together, they will eventually mix by *diffusion*, and a reaction will take place.
- Stirring reactants speeds the process of mixing so the reaction takes place more quickly.

4 Interface surface area

- If one of the reactants is a liquid and one a gas, or if the two reactants are *immiscible* liquids, then the reaction can only take place at the interface. The larger the surface area of the interface, the faster the reaction will take place.

1 Total suface area

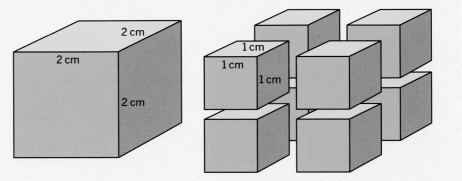

2 Reduced surface area reaction

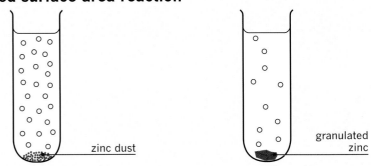

zinc dust

granulated zinc

3 Mixing

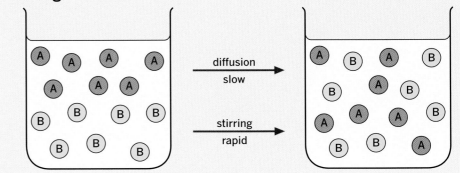

diffusion slow

stirring rapid

4 Interface surface area

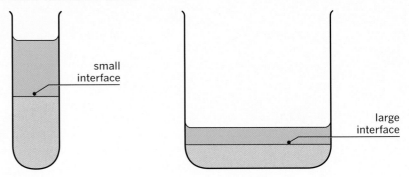

small interface

large interface

Rates of reaction: temperature and concentration

Key words

activation energy
product
reactant

1 Temperature (distribution of molecular energies at T_1 and T_2)

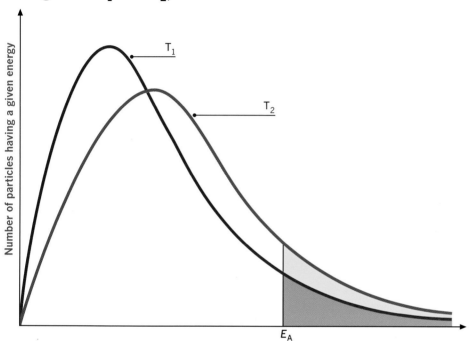

Number of particles having a given energy (y-axis)

T_1

T_2

E_A

Kinetic energy

2 Concentration

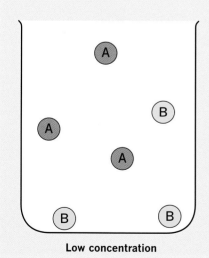

Low concentration

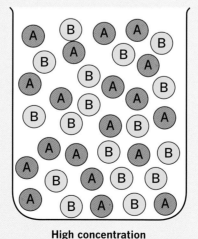

High concentration

3 Rate of reaction

$$\text{Rate of reaction} = \frac{\text{Change in concentration}}{\text{Time}}$$

1 Temperature
- Temperature is an important factor in determining rate of reaction.
- When temperature increases, the average speed of the particles in a substance increases. The graph shows the Maxwell-Boltzman distribution at two temperatures, T_2 is greater than T_1.
- The number of particles is constant, so the area under the two curves is the same. However, the average energy of the particles at T_2 is greater. The area of the curve to the right of the *activation energy* line (E_A) is greater for T_2. Therefore, at this temperature a higher proportion of particles have sufficient energy to react.

2 Concentration
- An increase in the concentration of a chemical, or the pressure of a gas, means that there will be more particles within a given space, so particles will collide more often.

3 Rate of reaction
- The rate of any reaction is the speed at which the *reactants* are converted to *products*. This can be qualified as the change of concentration of reactants or products.
- Changes in concentration can be measured by:
  1. appearance or disappearance of color in reactants or products
  2. volume of gas evolved
  3. changes in pH
  4. heat produced
  5. changes in pressure.

© Diagram Visual Information Ltd.

Key words
concentration   *rate of reaction*

Concentration over time

- Bromine reacts with an excess of methanoic acid in aqueous solution according to the following equation. The reaction is catalyzed by acid:

$$H^+$$
$$Br_2(aq) + HCOOH(aq) \rightarrow$$
$$2Br^-(aq) + 2H^+(aq) + CO_2(g)$$

- The reaction can be followed by measuring the intensity of the red-brown at different time intervals and relating this to the *concentration* of bromine.
- The concentration of bromine, $[Br_2]$, falls during the reaction, so the rate of the reaction can be expressed in terms of the rate at which the bromine concentration changes.
- The *rate of reaction* =
  - rate of change of bromine concentration =

$$- \frac{d[Br_2]}{dt}$$

- The rate of change of bromine concentration is negative because the bromine is being used up. The negative sign in the expression is necessary to give the rate of reaction a positive value.
- In order to obtain the rate of reaction at any given time, a tangent to the curve must be drawn at that particular time and the gradient measured. The concentration of bromine after 300 seconds (s) is 0.0035 mol dm^{-3}. The rate of reaction at this time is 1.2 x 10^{-5} mol dm^{-3} s^{-1}.

Rates of reaction: concentration over time

Graph to show the variation of bromine concentration with time in the reaction between methanoic scid and bromine

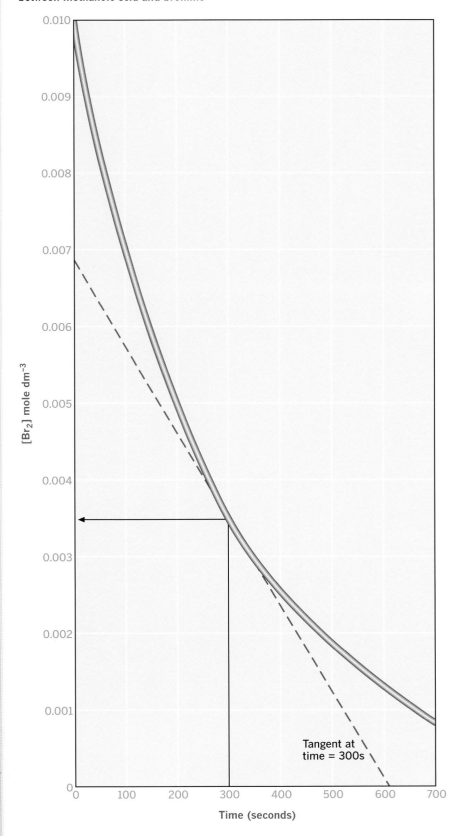

Rate of reaction vs. concentration

Graph to show the variation of reaction rate with bromine concentration

Key words

concentration
rate of reaction

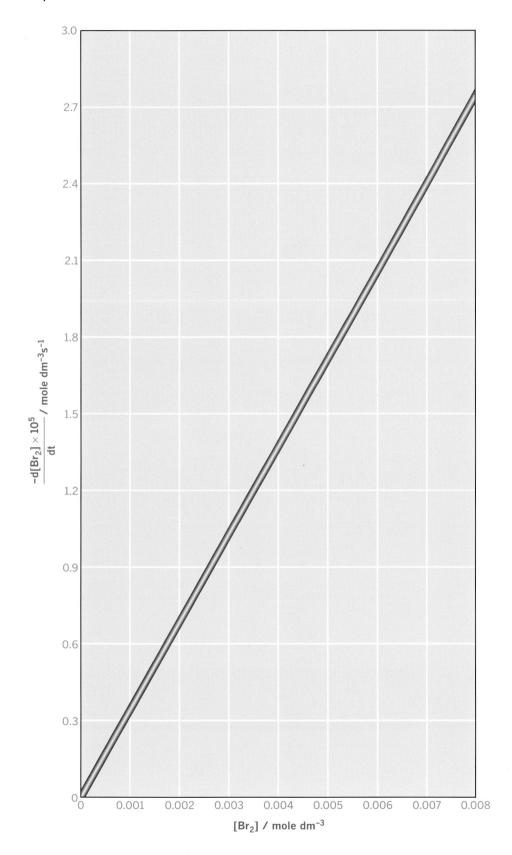

[Br$_2$] / mole dm^{-3}

$\dfrac{-d[Br_2] \times 10^5}{dt}$ / mole dm^{-3}s^{-1}

Rate vs. concentration

- In order to draw a graph showing how the *rate of reaction* varies with bromine *concentration*, it is necessary to find the rate of reaction at different times and, therefore, different bromine concentrations.
- The graph shows that the rate of reaction is directly proportional to the bromine concentration.
  Reaction rate $\propto$[Br$_2$], therefore,
  Rate of reaction = k[Br$_2$] where k is a constant, known as the rate constant or the velocity constant for the reaction.
- This reaction is said to be first rate with respect to bromine since doubling the concentration of bromine doubles the rate of the reaction.
- Since rate of reaction = k[Br$_2$], then to find the units of k:
  k = $\dfrac{\text{rate of reaction}}{[Br_2]}$ =
  $\dfrac{\text{mol dm}^{-3} \text{ s}^{-1}}{\text{mol dm}^{-3}} = s^{-1}$
  The unit of the rate constant, k, for first order reactions is s^{-1}.

© Diagram Visual Information Ltd.

Key words
concentration
product
rate of reaction
reactant

1 Clock technique

- *Rate of reaction =*

$$\frac{\text{change in concentration of a substance}}{\text{time}}$$

- In order to monitor the progress of a reaction, we could measure the *concentration* of a *reactant* or a *product* at regular time intervals, say every 10 seconds.

- Strictly speaking, this would give us the average reaction rate during the 10 second period. By measuring the change in concentration over shorter and shorter time periods, we would obtain an increasingly more accurate estimate of the rate of reaction at any particular moment.

- Using a clock technique, the rate is obtained as the inverse of the time for a certain proportion of the reaction to occur. Provided the reaction has only gone a small way toward completion, the error is very small, but the error increases as the reaction moves further to completion.

2 Increasing concentration

- If doubling the concentration of a reactant has no effect on the rate of a reaction, then the reaction is said to be zero order with respect to the reactant. The rate equation is:
rate = k[reactant]^0 = k

- If doubling the concentration of a reactant doubles the rate of a reaction, then the reaction is said to be first order with respect to the reactant. The rate equation is:
rate = k[reactant]

- If doubling the concentration of a reactant quadruples the rate of a reaction, then the reaction is said to be second order with respect to the reactant. The rate equation is:
rate = k[reactant]^2

Variation of reaction rate

1 Clock technique for measuring reaction rates

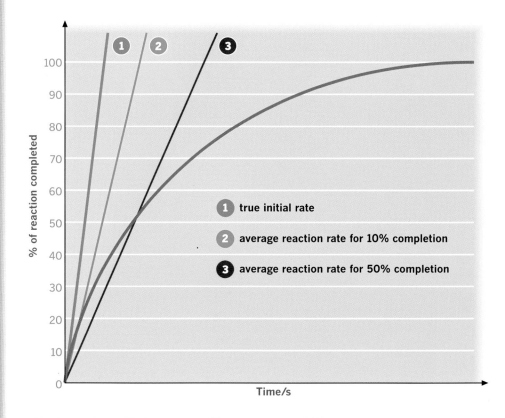

1 true initial rate

2 average reaction rate for 10% completion

3 average reaction rate for 50% completion

2 Increasing concentration

The variation of reaction rate with concentration for reactions which are zero, first, and second order

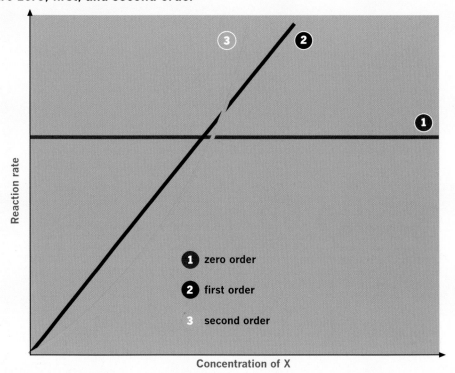

1 zero order

2 first order

3 second order

Rates of reaction: effect of temperature 1

The effect of temperature on different reactions

Key words

effective collision
enzyme
kinetic energy
polymer
rate of reaction

1 Most reactions

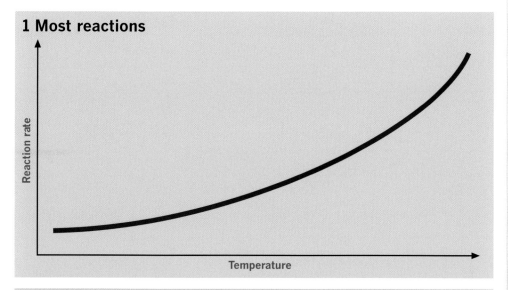

2 Enzyme-catalyzed reactions

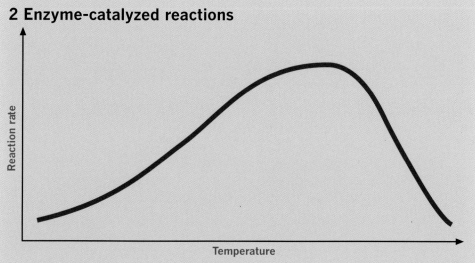

3 Explosive reactions

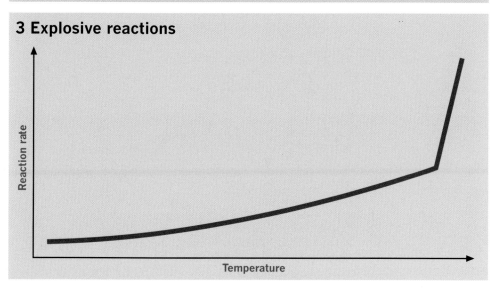

Effect of temperature

● When a substance is heated, its particles gain *kinetic energy* and move around more quickly. The frequency of collisions increases, and because the particles have a greater momentum, the frequency of *effective collisions* also increases. The result is an increase in the *rate of reaction*.

1 Most reactions

● In most chemical reactions, the rate of reaction increases steadily with rising temperature. It is for this reason that chemical reactions are often heated.

2 Enzyme-catalyzed reactions

● *Enzymes* catalyze chemical reactions with a high degree of specificity and efficiency. An enzyme molecule is a *polymer* composed of a long chain of amino acids that folds over on itself, giving it a particular shape. Reacting molecules, called the substrate, fit into this shape rather like a key in a lock.

● Up to a point, the rate of an enzyme-catalyzed reaction increases with rising temperature in the same way as most other reactions. However, after reaching an optimum temperature at which the activity of the enzyme is greatest, the reaction rate rapidly falls.

● Heating an enzyme causes its shape to change, and thus the enzyme ceases to be able to catalyze the reaction. It is said to be denatured.

3 Explosive reactions

● In an explosive reaction, the reaction rate increases with rising temperature up to some point where the reaction rate suddenly rises sharply.

Key words
activation energy

Rates of reaction: effect of temperature 2

1 Rate constant for reaction

- As a general rule of thumb, the rate of a reaction doubles for every 10 K rise in temperature. This would seem to suggest that there is an exponential relationship between rate and temperature.
- The exact relationship was proposed by the Swedish chemist Svante Arrhenius in 1889. The Arrhenius equation relates the rate constant (not the rate of reaction) to temperature.
- The equation can be expressed in a logarithmic form and in terms of log to the base 10. The latter form of the equation is the most useful for calculation purposes.

$$k = Ae^{-Ea/RT}$$

$$\ln k = \ln A - E_a/RT$$

$$\log k = \log A - E_a/2.303RT$$

k = rate constant for the reaction

A = constant for the reaction (Arrhenius constant)

E_a = activation energy

R = gas constant

T = absolute temperature

2 Plotting the Arrhenius constant

- The constants A and E_a for a given reaction can be obtained by plotting $\log k$ against $1/T$: the temperature, T, must be expressed in kelvin. The slope of the graph is equal to $E_a / 2.303R$.
- The Arrhenius constant, A, can be obtained by substituting values for the slope ($E_a / 2.303R$), $\log k$ and T in the Arrhenius equation.
- The *activation energy*, E_a, can also be found from the slope of the graph. Slope = $- E_a / 2.303 R$ The slope of the graph is negative, and its unit is K therefore $E_a = 2.303 \times R \times$ slope The gas constant, R, = 0.008314 kJ K^{-1} mol^{-1} therefore $E_a = 2.303 \times 0.008314 \times$ slope kJ mol^{-1}

2 Plotting the Arrhenius constant

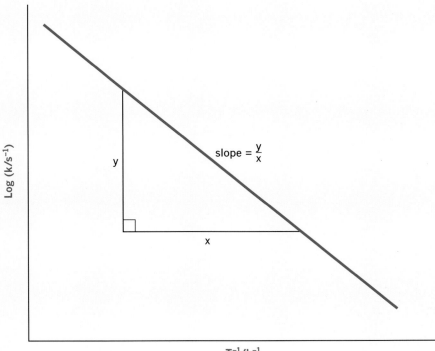

Exothermic and endothermic reactions

1 Exothermic

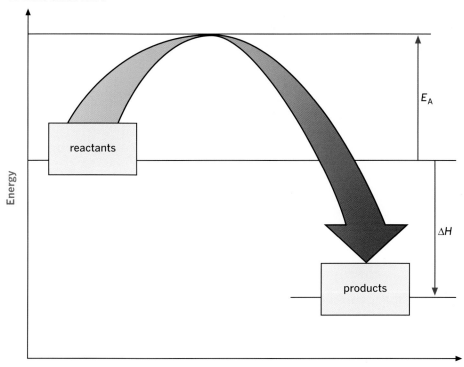

E_A = activation energy ΔH = heat of reaction

2 Endothermic

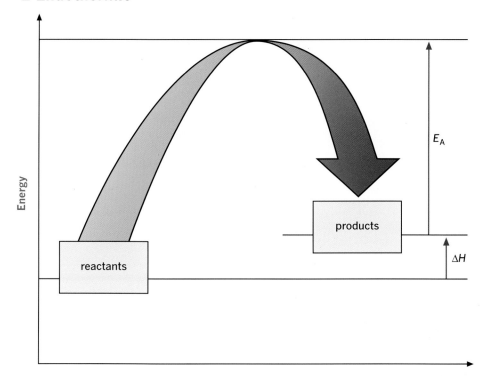

1 Exothermic

- In an *exothermic* reaction, energy is given out, and the temperature of the reaction mixture increases as the reaction proceeds. The *products* are at a lower energy than the *reactants*.
- The energy released is due to a decrease in the *enthalpy*, ΔH, of the system. Enthalpy is a measure of the stored heat energy of a substance. Therefore, ΔH is negative for an exothermic reaction.
- The following equation represents the combustion of methane in a good supply of air:
  $$CH_4(g) + 2O_2(g) \rightarrow CO_2(g) + 2H_2O(g)$$
  $$\Delta H = -890 \text{ kJ mol}^{-1}$$
  This is an exothermic reaction. 890 kJ of energy are released per mole of methane combusted.

2 Endothermic

- In an *endothermic* reaction, energy is taken in, and the temperature of the reaction mixture decreases as the reaction proceeds. The products are at a higher energy than the reactants.
- The energy taken in is due to an increase in the enthalpy, ΔH, of the system. Therefore, ΔH is positive for an endothermic reaction.
- The following equation represents the steam reforming of methane:
  $$CH_4(g) + H_2O(g) \rightarrow 3H_2(g) + CO(g)$$
  $$\Delta H = +206 \text{ kJ mol}^{-1}$$
  This reaction is an endothermic reaction. 206 kJ of energy are taken in per mole of methane reformed.

Key words

dissociation
enthalpy

1 Average bond enthalpy

- Bond *dissociation* energy is the energy change when one mole of bonds is broken. It refers to a specific bond in a molecule. However, the exact value depends on the local environment of the bond. For example, if the C-H bonds in methane are broken one after another, each will have a different bond dissociation *enthalpy*:

$CH_4(g) \rightarrow CH_3(g) + H(g)$
$\Delta H = +425$ kJ mol^{-1}
$CH_3(g) \rightarrow CH_2(g) + H(g)$
$\Delta H = +470$ kJ mol^{-1}
$CH_2(g) \rightarrow CH(g) + H(g)$
$\Delta H = +416$ kJ mol^{-1}
$CH(g) \rightarrow C(g) + H(g)$
$\Delta H = +335$ kJ mol^{-1}

- For this reason, in a molecule composed of more than one atom, it is more useful to know the average amount of energy needed to break a particular bond.

2 Estimating enthalpy change

- The table at right utilizes the complete combustion of propane to illustrate how bond enthalpies can be used to estimate the enthalpy change in a reaction.
- 6,488 kJ mol^{-1} of total energy is taken in to break the bonds.
- 8,542 kJ mol^{-1} of total energy is given out when the bonds are formed.
- The enthalpy change when 1 mole of propane is completely combusted is 6,488 − 8,542 = 2,054 kJ mol^{-1}.

Average bond dissociation energies

1 Average bond enthalpy

Bond	Average bond enthalpy / kJ mol^{-1}	Bond	Average bond enthalpy / kJ mol^{-1}
C-C	347	C=O	805
C=C	612	H-Cl	432
C-Cl	346	H-H	436
C-H	413	N-H	391
C-N	286	O-H	464
C-O	336	O=O	498

2 Estimating the enthalpy change in a reaction.

Complete combustion of propane.

$C_3H_8(g) + 5O_2(g) \rightarrow 3CO_2(g) + 4H_2O(g)$

Energy is taken in to break bonds:

Bond	Average bond dissociation energy / kJ mol^{-1}	Number of bonds	Energy taken in / kJ mol^{-1}
C-H	413	8	3,304
C-C	347	2	694
O=O	498	5	2,490
Total energy taken in			6,488

Energy is given out when bonds are formed:

Bond	Average bond dissociation energy / kJ mol^{-1}	Number of bonds	Energy taken in / kJ mol^{-1}
C=O	805	6	4,830
O-H	464	8	3,712
Total energy taken in			8,542

The enthalpy change when 1 mole of propane is completely combusted is 6,488 − 8,542 = 2,054 kJ mol^{-1}.

Catalysts: characteristics

1 Characteristics of catalysts

Stoichiometry	The overall stoichiometry of a reaction is unaltered.
Specificity	Catalysts may alter the rate of one reaction but have no effect on others.
Reaction mechanism	A catalyst provides an alternative reaction pathway for a reaction to take place.
Chemical involvement	A catalyst is chemically involved in a reaction. It is consumed during one step and regenerated in another. A catalyst does not undergo a net chemical change, but it may change its physical form.
Equilibrium	A catalyst speeds up the rates of both forward and backward reactions, and this speeds up the rate at which equilibrium is attained.
Yield	A catalyst does not alter the yield of a reaction.

2 Increasing reaction rate

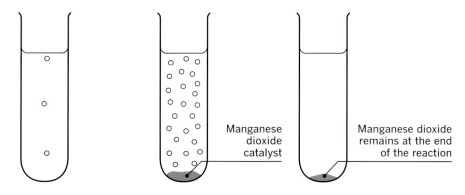

Manganese dioxide catalyst

Manganese dioxide remains at the end of the reaction

3 Distribution of the kinectic energies of reacting particles and the activation energies for catalyzed and uncatalyzed reactions

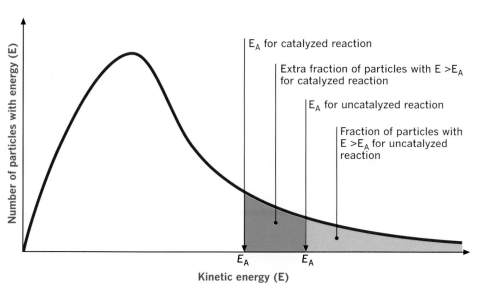

E_A for catalyzed reaction

Extra fraction of particles with $E > E_A$ for catalyzed reaction

E_A for uncatalyzed reaction

Fraction of particles with $E > E_A$ for uncatalyzed reaction

Number of particles with energy (E)

E_A E_A

Kinetic energy (E)

Catalysts
- A *catalyst* is a substance that alters the rate of a chemical reaction but remains chemically unchanged by it.

1 Characteristics of catalysts
- Catalysts may be classified as homogenous or heterogeneous. Homogenous catalysts are in the same phase (solid, liquid, or gas) as the reactants; heterogeneous catalysts are in a different phase.
- A large number of reactions are catalyzed on the surface of solid catalysts. The surface provides *active sites* where reactions can occur. Thus, an increase in the surface area will increase the effect of the catalyst.

2 Increasing reaction rate
- Hydrogen peroxide decomposes very slowly on its own to form water and oxygen gas:
$$2H_2O_2(aq) \rightarrow 2H_2O(l) + O_2(g)$$
The rate of this reaction is greatly increased by adding manganese dioxide, MnO_2.
- Manganese dioxide acts as a catalyst and remains unchanged after all of the hydrogen peroxide has decomposed.

3 Activation energies
- A catalyst lowers the minimum energy, or *activation energy* (E_A), required for a reaction to occur. The frequency of *effective collisions* is, therefore, increased, resulting in an increase in the rate of a reaction.

© Diagram Visual Information Ltd.

Key words

catalyst	oxidation
equilibrium	oxidation state
exothermic	reduction
Le Chatelier's	transition metals
principle	vanadium

1 Reaction catalyzed
- *Catalysts* are often *transition metals* or transition metal compounds. Transitional metals are useful as catalysts because or their ability to exist in different *oxidation states*.

2 V$_2$O$_5$ as catalyst
- The contact process is an important step in the manufacture of sulfuric acid (see pages 85 and 86). Sulfur dioxide is oxidized to sulfur trioxide in the presence of a *vanadium pentoxide*, V$_2$O$_5$, catalyst.
- This reaction involves the *reduction* and subsequent *oxidation* of the catalyst. In the reduction reaction, the oxidation state of vanadium changes from +5 to +4. In the oxidation reaction, it changes back from +4 to +5.

3 Iron as catalyst
- The Haber process for the manufacture of ammonia uses finely divided iron as the catalyst (see pages 74 and 75):

$$\text{N}_2 + 3\text{H}_2 \xrightarrow{\text{Fe(s)}} 2\text{NH}_3$$
$$\Delta H = -92 \text{ kJ mol}^{-1}$$

- This reaction is *exothermic*. According to *Le Chatelier's principle*, a low temperature would produce more ammonia in the *equilibrium* mixture, but it would take longer to reach equilibrium.
- The catalyst does not alter the yield of ammonia in the equilibrium mixture, but it does increase the speed with which equilibrium is attained. Using a catalyst, a reasonable rate of reaction is achieved at a lower temperature than would otherwise be the case.

Catalysts: transition metals

1 Transition metals and reaction catalyzed

Transition metal/compound	Reaction catalyzed
TiCl$_3$	polymerization of ethene to poly(ethene)
V$_2$O$_5$	contact process in production of sulfuric acid
Fe	Haber process on production of ammonia
Ni	hydrogenation of alkenes in hardening of vegetable oils
Cu	oxidation of ethanol to ethanal
Pt	oxidation of ammonia in manufacture of nitric acid

2 Vanadium oxide as catalyst in contact process

$$2\text{SO}_2(g) + \text{O}_2(g) \xrightarrow{\text{V}_2\text{O}_5(s)} \rightleftharpoons 2\text{SO}_3(g)$$

$$\text{SO}_2 + \text{V}_2\text{O}_5 \longrightarrow \text{SO}_3 + \text{V}_2\text{O}_4$$

$$2\text{V}_2\text{O}_4 + \text{O}_2 \longrightarrow 2\text{V}_2\text{O}_5$$

3 Iron as catalyst in Haber process
(Energy profiles for the reaction $\text{N}_2 + 3\text{H}_2 \xrightarrow{\text{Fe(s)}} 2\text{NH}_3$)

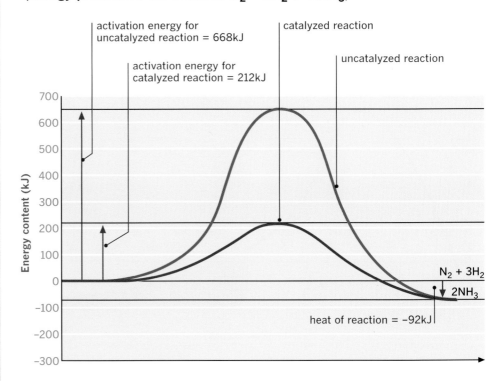

Oxidation and reduction

Key words

oxidation
oxidation state
redox reaction
reduction

1 Oxygen

Oxidation is the addition of oxygen to a substance

Reduction is the removal of oxygen from a substance

2 Hydrogen

Oxidation is the removal of hydrogen from a substance

Reduction is the addition of hydrogen to a substance

3 Modern definition

Oxidation is the loss of electrons from a substance

Reduction is the gain of electrons by a substance

4 Redox reaction

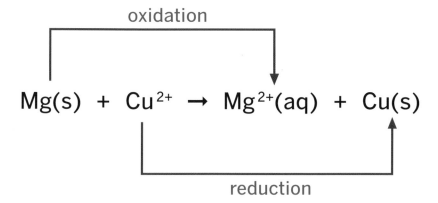

$$Mg(s) \ + \ Cu^{2+} \ \rightarrow \ Mg^{2+}(aq) \ + \ Cu(s)$$

Evolving definition
- Over time, scientists have extended the definitions of *oxidation* and *reduction*.

1 Oxygen
- Historically the terms oxidation and reduction were applied to reactions involving either the addition or the removal of oxygen. For example:
$2Cu(s) + O_2 \rightarrow 2CuO(s)$
copper is oxidized
$Fe_2O_3(s) + 3CO(g) \rightarrow 2Fe(s) + 3CO_2(g)$
iron is reduced

2 Hydrogen
- The terms were extended to include the removal or addition of hydrogen:
$CH_3\text{-}CH_3(g) \rightarrow CH_2{=}CH_2(g) + H_2(g)$
ethane is oxidized
$CH_3COH(l) + H_2(g) \rightarrow CH_3CH_2OH(l)$
ethanal is reduced

3 Modern definition
- The terms oxidation and reduction are now used more widely to describe changes in *oxidation state*:
$Cu(s) \rightarrow Cu^{2+}(aq) + 2e^-$
copper is oxidized to copper(II)
$Fe^{3+}(aq) + e^- \rightarrow Fe^{2+}(aq)$
iron(III) is reduced to iron(II)
- This definition covers all of those reactions involving the gain or loss of oxygen and other reactions that do not involve oxygen.

4 Redox reaction
- Reactions that involve a reduction must also involve an oxidation. If one reactant is reduced, then another must be oxidized. Such reactions are described as *redox reactions*.

© Diagram Visual Information Ltd.

Key words

displacement reaction
oxidation
redox reaction
reduction

Redox reactions

- *Reduction* and *oxidation* reactions always occur together and are collectively referred to as *redox reactions*.

1 Oxidation and reduction

- When magnesium is heated in air, it forms magnesium oxide:
$2Mg(s) + O_2(g) \rightarrow 2MgO(s)$
- Magnesium atoms are oxidized to magnesium ions by losing two electrons.
- Oxygen atoms are reduced to oxide ions by gaining two electrons.
- This is true of all metals when they are converted to metal oxides.

2 Electron transfer

- A more reactive metal displaces the ions of a less reactive metal from a solution of its salts. This type of reaction is called a *displacement reaction*:
$Zn(s) + Cu^{2+}(aq) \rightarrow Zn^{2+}(aq) + Cu(s)$
Zinc atoms are oxidized to zinc ions by losing two electrons.
- Copper ions are reduced to copper atoms by gaining two electrons.

3 Balancing redox reactions

- In balancing redox reactions, the electrons lost must equal the electrons gained.
- In the example at right, bromine (a) is gaining two electrons and iron (b) is losing 1 electron.
- In order to balance the equation, the entire reaction has to be multiplied by 2 (c).
- The result is a balanced equation (d).

Redox reactions 1

1 Redox reactions: oxidation and reduction

$$2Mg + O_2 \rightarrow 2Mg^{2+} + 2O^{2-}$$

$$4Na + O_2 \rightarrow 2(Na^2)_2O^{2-}$$

When metals react with oxygen they form oxides

$$2Mg \rightarrow 2Mg^{2+} + \boxed{4e^-}$$

$$O_2 + \boxed{4e^-} \rightarrow 2O^{2-}$$

The metal is oxidized and the metal is reduced. The oxygen takes the electrons given up by the metal

2 Electron transfer in redox reactions

$$Zn(s) + Cu^{2+}_{(aq)} \rightarrow Zn^{2+}_{(aq)} + Cu(s)$$

When powered zinc is added to copper sulfate (II) solution, an exothermic reaction occurs

$$Zn(s) \rightarrow Zn^{2+}_{(aq)} + \boxed{2e^-}$$

$$Cu^{2+}_{(aq)} + \boxed{2e^-} \rightarrow Cu(s)$$

Redox equations for the reaction

3 Balancing redox reactions

$$Br_2 + 2e^- \rightarrow 2Br^-$$

(a) The oxidizing agent is Br^2

$$Fe^{2+} \rightarrow Fe^{3+} + e^-$$

(b) The reducing agent is Fe^{2+}

$$2Fe^{2+} \rightarrow 2Fe^{3+} + \boxed{2e^-}$$

$$Br_2 + \boxed{2e^-} \rightarrow 2Br^-$$

(c) Redox reaction

$$2Fe^{2+} + Br_2 \rightarrow 2Fe^{3+} + 2Br^-$$

(d) Balance equation

Redox reactions 2

Key words

redox reaction

1 The reaction of metals with non-metals

$$Fe + S \rightarrow Fe^{2+}S^{2-}$$

Iron and sulfur

$$Fe \rightarrow Fe^{2+} + \boxed{2e^-}$$
$$S + \boxed{2e^-} \rightarrow S^{2-}$$

Redox equation

$$2Fe + 3Cl_2 \rightarrow 2FeCl_3$$

Iron and chlorine

$$2Fe \rightarrow 2Fe^{3+} + \boxed{6e^-}$$
$$3Cl_2 + \boxed{6e^-} \rightarrow 6Cl^-$$

Redox equation

2 The reaction of metals with water

$$Ca + 2H_2O \rightarrow Ca^{2+}(OH^-)_2 + H_2$$

Calcium and water

$$Ca \rightarrow Ca^{2+} + \boxed{2e^-}$$
$$2H_2O + \boxed{2e^-} \rightarrow 2OH^- + H_2$$

Redox equation

3 The reaction of metals with acids

$$Zn(s) + 2H^+_{(aq)} \rightarrow Zn^{2+}_{(aq)} + H_2\uparrow$$

The reaction of zinc

$$Zn \rightarrow Zn^{2+} + \boxed{2e^-}$$
$$2H^+ + \boxed{2e^-} \rightarrow H^2$$

Redox equation

1 Metals with non-metals
- Iron undergoes *redox reactions* with non-metals.
  Iron and sulfur:
  $Fe(s) + S(s) \rightarrow Fe^{2+}S^{2-}(s)$
  Iron atoms are oxidized to iron(II) ions by losing two electrons.
  Sulfur is reduced to sulfide ions by gaining two electrons.
  Iron and chlorine:
  $2Fe(s) + 3Cl_2(s) \rightarrow 2Fe^{3+}Cl^-_3(s)$
  Iron atoms are oxidized to iron(III) ions by losing three electrons.
  Chlorine is reduced to chloride ions by gaining one electron.

2 Metals with water
- Metals are oxidized when they react with water.
  Metal + water →
      metal hydroxide + hydrogen
  $Ca(s) + 2H_2O(l) \rightarrow$
      $Ca(OH)_2(aq) + H_2(g)$
  $H_2O(l) \rightleftharpoons H^+(aq) + OH^-(aq)$
  $Ca(s) + 2H^+(aq) \rightarrow Ca^{2+}(aq) + H_2(g)$
  In the example at left, calcium atoms are oxidized to calcium ions by the loss of two electrons. Hydrogen ions are reduced to hydrogen atoms by gaining one electron.

3 Metals with acids
- Metals are oxidized when they react with acids.
  Metal + acid → metal salt + hydrogen
  $Zn(s) + 2HCl(aq) \rightarrow ZnCl_2(aq) + H_2(g)$
  $Zn(s) + 2H^+(aq) \rightarrow Zn^{2+}(aq) + H_2(g)$
  In the example at left, zinc atoms are oxidized to zinc ions by the loss of two electrons. Hydrogen ions are reduced to hydrogen atoms by gaining one electron.

Key words

reactivity series
redox reaction

1 Electron transfer in redox reactions

- The movement of electrons during *redox reactions* can be demonstrated using a simple cell consisting of two metals rods, suspended in solutions of their salts, connected by a wire and a salt bridge.
- At the zinc rod, zinc atoms lose two electrons to become zinc ions. The electrons pass along the wire and through the bulb to the copper rod. The zinc ions pass into solution.
- At the copper rod, copper ions gain two electrons to become copper atoms. The copper ions come out of solution and are deposited as copper metal on the copper rod.
- Electric current passes through the wire in the external circuit as a flow of negatively charged electrons.
- Ions flow through the salt bridge: positive ions from the zinc sulfate solution to the copper sulfate, and negative ions in the opposite direction from the copper sulfate solution to the zinc sulfate solution.
- Electric current passes through ionic solutions as a flow of positively charged and negatively charged ions.

2 Reaction equations

- Zinc is higher than copper in the *reactivity series*. Zinc atoms are oxidized to zinc ions, while copper ions are reduced to copper atoms.
- When any two metals are placed in a cell, the direction of electrons in the external circuit depends on their reactivities. The metal that is higher in the reactivity series will be oxidized, while the ions of the metal that is lower in the reactivity series will be reduced.

Demonstrating redox reactions

1 Electron transfer in redox reactions

Experimental set-up

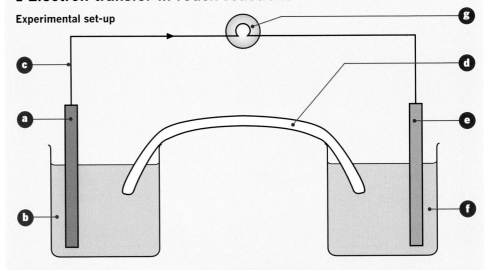

Movement of charge around the circuit

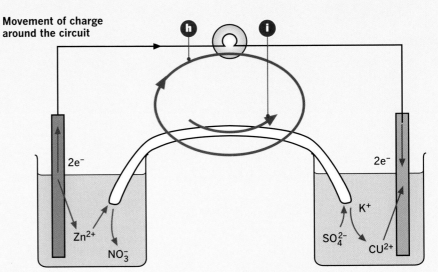

a zinc rod
b zinc sulfate solution
c electron flow
d filter paper soaked in potassium nitrate as a salt bridge
e copper rod

f copper sulfate solution
g small light bulb
h movement of negative charge (electrons and anions)
i movement of positive charge (cations)

2 Reaction equations

$$Zn(s) + Cu^{2+} \rightarrow Zn^{2+}_{(aq)} + Cu(s)$$

$$Zn(s) \rightarrow Zn^{2+}_{(aq)} + 2e^-$$

$$Cu^{2+}_{(aq)} + 2e^- \rightarrow Cu(s)$$

Copper ions are reduced to a deposit of red-brown

Assigning oxidation state

Key words

oxidation state
transition metals

1 Oxidation state

Component	Oxidation state
uncombined elements	0
Group 2 metals in compounds	+2
Group 1 metals in compounds	+1
combined hydrogen except in metal hydrides	+1
combined hydrogen in metal hydrides	−1
combined halogens	−1
combined oxygen	−2

1 Oxidation state

- The ability of *transition metals* to exhibit different *oxidation states* in different compounds is central to the behavior of these elements.
- The oxidation state of simple ions is given by the charge they carry, e.g.: Na^+ has an oxidation state of $+1$ O^{2-} has an oxidation state of -2
- The situation is more complicated in a complex ion. The oxidation state of the central atom in a complex ion is the charge that the ion would have if it were a simple ion. This is found by adding the oxidation states of the various components in the complex ion.

2 Tetrachlorocuprate ion

$$CuCl_4^{2-}$$

the tetrachlorocuprate ion contains the transition metal copper

2 Tetrachlorocuprate ion

- Total oxidation number due to chlorine $= 4 \times -1 = -4$.
- Overall charge on the ion $= -2$.
- Oxidation state of the central copper atom $= -2 - (-4) = +2$.
- This complex ion is more correctly called the tetrachlorocuprate(II) ion.

3 Manganate ion

$$MnO_4^-$$

the manganate ion contains the transition metal manganese

3 Manganate ion

- Total oxidation number due to oxygen $= 4 \times -2 = -8$.
- Overall charge on the ion $= -1$.
- Oxidation state of the central manganese atom $= -1 - (-8) = +7$.
- This complex ion is more correctly called the manganate(VII) ion.

4 Dichromate ion

$$Cr_2O_7^{2-}$$

the dichromate ion contains the transition metal chromium

4 Dichromate ion

- Total oxidation number due to oxygen $= 7 \times -2 = -14$.
- Overall charge on the ion $= -2$.
- Total oxidation state of the two central chromium atoms $= -2 - (-14) = +12$.
- Oxidation state of each chromium atom $= +12 / 2 = +6$.
- This complex ion is more correctly called the dichromate(VI) ion.

Key words

allotrope
carbon
diamond
fullerenes
graphite

Carbon allotropes

● *Carbon* exists in three *allotropes: diamond*, *graphite*, and *fullerenes*.

1 Diamond

● In diamond, each carbon atom is covalently bonded to four other carbon atoms.

● The four bonds are directed toward the corners of a pyramid or tetrahedron, and all bonds are the same length, 0.154 nm. The angle between any two bonds is 109.5°.

● All four of the outer electrons on the carbon atom form bonds with other carbon atoms so there are no mobile electrons. Diamond does not, therefore, conduct electricity.

● Diamond has a rigid structure and is very hard.

2 Graphite

● The carbon atoms in graphite are arranged in layers consisting of interlocking hexagons in which each carbon atom is covalently bonded to three other carbon atoms. The length of the bond is 0.141 nm, and the angle between bonds is 120°.

● The fourth outer electron on each carbon atom forms bonds with adjacent layers. The bond length is much greater than between carbon atoms within a layer.

● The electrons between the layers are mobile; therefore, graphite conducts electricity. Also, the layers are able to slide over each other relatively easily.

● Graphite is soft.

The allotropes of carbon: diamond and graphite

Diamond

Bond angle 109.5°
Bond length 0.154 nm

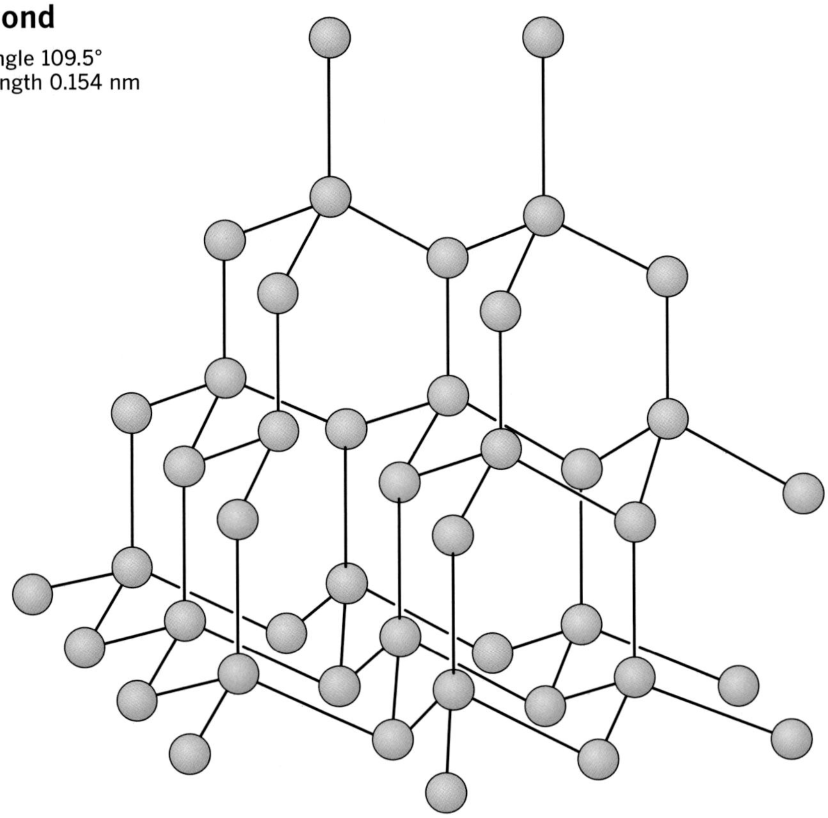

Graphite

Bond angle 120°
Bond lengths
– in layers 0.141 nm
– between layers
  0.335 nm

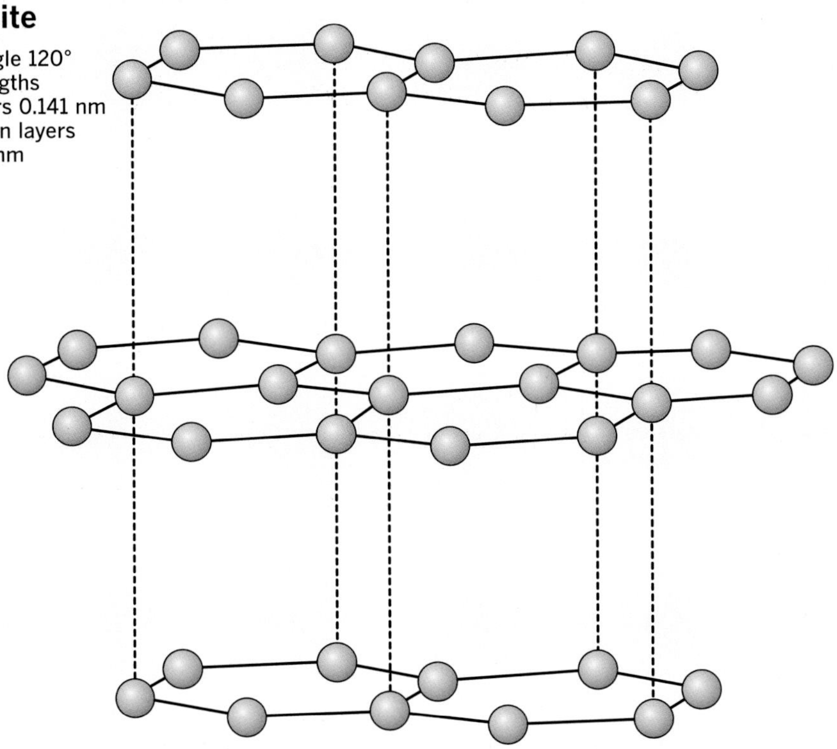

The allotropes of carbon: fullerenes

Buckyball

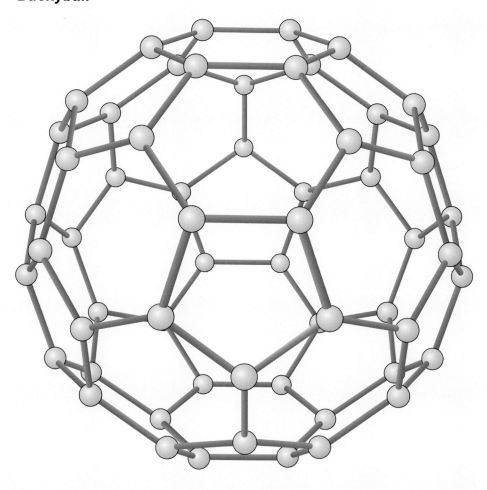

Nanotube

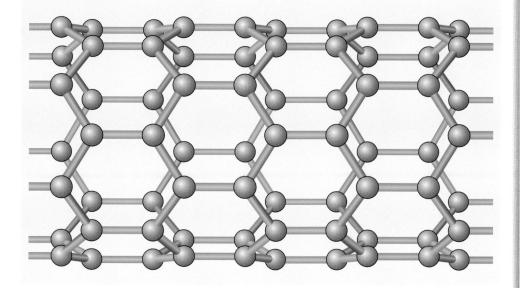

Key words

allotrope	fullerenes
buckyball	graphite
carbon	nanotube

Fullerenes

- *Fullerenes* are *allotropes* of *carbon* in the form of a hollow sphere or tube. Spherical fullerenes are sometimes called *buckyballs*, and cylindrical fullerenes are called *nanotubes*.
- Because the allotrope was only discovered in the late twentieth century, its physical and chemical properties are still being studied.
- Fullerenes are not very reactive and are only slightly soluble in many solvents. They are the only known allotrope of carbon that can be dissolved.

Buckminsterfullerene

- This form of carbon is composed of 60 carbon atoms bonded together in a polyhedral structure composed of pentagons and hexagons. The molecules are made when an electric arc is struck between *graphite* electrodes in an inert atmosphere. This method also produces small amounts of other fullerenes that have less symmetrical molecular structures, such as C_{70}.
- Buckminsterfullerene was first identified in 1985 and named after the architect Richard Buckminster Fuller because of the resemblance of its structure to the geodesic dome.
- The substance is a yellow crystalline solid that is soluble in benzene, an organic solvent.
- It is possible to trap metal ions within the C_{60} sphere. Some of these structures are semiconductors.

Nanotubes

- Nanotubes, first identified in 1991, are long thin cylinders of carbon closed at either end with caps containing pentagonal rings.
- Nanotubes have a very broad range of electronic, thermal, and structural properties that change depending on the kind of nanotube (defined by its diameter, length, and twist).

Key words

atmosphere	photosynthesis
carbon	respiration
carbon cycle	
chlorophyll	
glucose	

The carbon cycle

- *Carbon* is the fourth most abundant element in the Universe.
- The total amount of carbon on planet Earth is fixed. The same carbon atoms have been used in countless other molecules since Earth began. The *carbon cycle* is the complex set of processes through which all carbon atoms rotate.
- Carbon exists in Earth's *atmosphere* primarily as carbon dioxide.
- All green plants contain *chlorophyll*, a pigment that gives them their characteristic color. During *photosynthesis*, chlorophyll traps energy from sunlight and uses it to convert carbon dioxide and water into *glucose* and oxygen.
- Carbon is transferred from green plants to animals when animals eat plants or other animals.
- All animals and plants need energy to drive their various metabolic processes. This energy is provided by *respiration*. During this process, glucose reacts with oxygen to form carbon dioxide and water. These waste products are subsequently released into the atmosphere. In essence, respiration is the opposite process to photosynthesis.
- When plants and animals die, their bodies decompose. In the presence of air, the carbon they contain becomes carbon dioxide, which is released into the atmosphere.
- When plants and animals decay in the absence of air, carbon cannot be converted into carbon dioxide. Instead, it remains and forms fossil fuels such as coal, crude oil, and natural gas.
- When fossil fuels are burned, the carbon they contain becomes carbon dioxide and is released into the atmosphere.

The carbon cycle

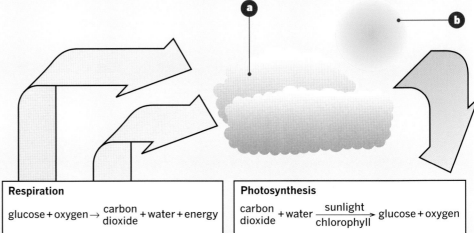

Respiration

$$glucose + oxygen \rightarrow \underset{dioxide}{carbon} + water + energy$$

$$C_6H_{12}O_{8(aq)} + 6O_{2(g)} \rightarrow 6CO_{2(g)} + 6H_2O_{(l)}$$

Photosynthesis

$$\underset{dioxide}{carbon} + water \xrightarrow[chlorophyll]{sunlight} glucose + oxygen$$

$$6CO_{2(g)} + 6H_2O_{(l)} \rightarrow C_6H_{12}O_{6(aq)} + 6O_{2(g)}$$

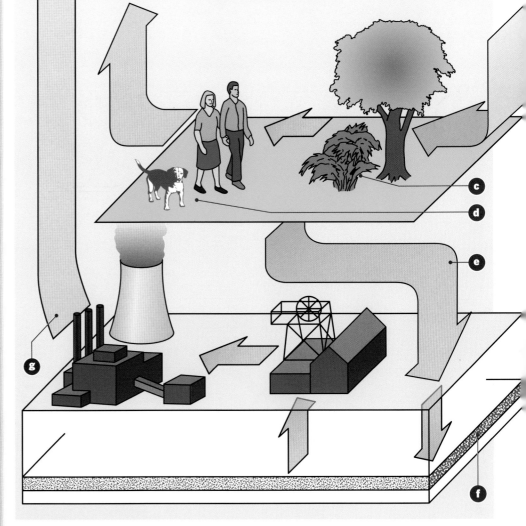

a carbon dioxide in the air
b sunlight
c plants take in carbon dioxide and give out oxygen
d animals take in oxygen, eat plants and vegetables, and breath out CO_2
e death and decay
f carbon compounds (e.g., in oil and coal)
g burning fuel produces CO_2

Laboratory preparation of carbon oxides

Key words

carbonate
carbon dioxide
carbon monoxide

1 Preparation of carbon dioxide

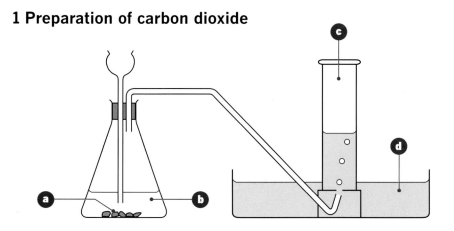

2 Preparation of dry carbon dioxide

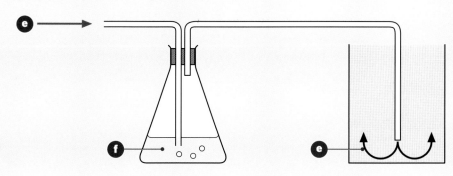

3 Preparation of carbon monoxide

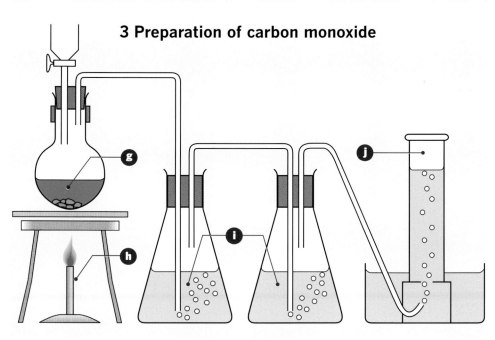

a marble chips
b dilute hydrochloric acid
c carbon dioxide
d water
e carbon dioxide
f concentrated sulfuric acid
g ethanedioic (oxalic) acid crystals and concentrated sulfuric acid
h heat
i concentrated potassium hydroxide solution
j carbon monoxide

Carbon oxides

- The most common forms of carbon oxides are *carbon dioxide*, which is instrumental in the carbon cycle, and *carbon monoxide*, a colorless, odorless gas that is the result of the incomplete combustion of fuels. They can be prepared in the laboratory using the following techniques.

1 Carbon dioxide

- Carbon dioxide is formed when a metal *carbonate* reacts with a dilute acid:

  metal carbonate + dilute acid →
  metal salt + carbon dioxide + water

- When calcium carbonate (marble chips) reacts with dilute hydrochloric acid:

  $CaCO_3(s) + 2HCl(aq) →$
  $CaCl_2(aq) + CO_2(g) + H_2O(l)$

- Carbon dioxide is not very soluble in water, so it can be conveniently collected over water.

2 Dry carbon dioxide

- Carbon dioxide can be dried by passing it through concentrated sulfuric acid and collected by downward delivery (upward displacement) because it is denser than air.

3 Carbon monoxide

- Carbon monoxide is formed by the dehydration of ethanedioic (oxalic) acid using concentrated sulfuric acid:

$$HOOC\text{-}COOH(l) \xrightarrow{\text{conc. sulfuric acid}}$$
$$CO_2(g) + CO(g) + H_2O(l)$$

- Acid residues and carbon dioxide are removed by passing the gas through a potassium hydroxide solution. Carbon monoxide can be collected over water because it is only slightly soluble.

© Diagram Visual Information Ltd.

Key words

fractional
 distillation
hydrocarbon

Fractional distillation

● *Fractional distillation* is one of
 several processes used to refine crude
 oil. Refining converts crude oil into a
 range of useful products.

● Crude oil is a complex mixture of
 hydrocarbons. During fractional
 distillation, this mixture is separated
 into a series of fractions (components)
 on the basis of boiling point.

● The crude oil is passed through a
 furnace, where it is heated to 400°C
 and turns mostly into vapor. The gases
 pass into a distillation column within
 which there is a gradation of
 temperature. The column is hottest at
 the bottom and coolest at the top.

● Hydrocarbons with the highest boiling
 points are the first to condense at the
 bottom of the column, along with any
 remaining liquid residue from the
 crude oil. This fraction provides
 bitumen for use in road building.

● Rising up the column, other fractions
 condense out: first diesel oil, then
 kerosene, and finally gasoline. All of
 these fractions are used as fuels.

● The hydrocarbons with the lowest
 boiling points remain as gases and rise
 to the top of the column. This fraction
 is used as a fuel in the refinery.

● The hydrocarbon vapor moves up the
 column through a series of bubble
 caps. At each level, the hydrocarbon
 vapor passes through condensed
 hydrocarbon liquid. This helps to
 ensure a good separation into the
 various fractions.

Crude oil composition

● Crude oil varies in composition,
 depending on where it was obtained.
 Fractional distillation of different crude
 oils provides different proportions of
 the various fractions.

The fractional distillation of crude oil

1 Fractional distillation of crude oil

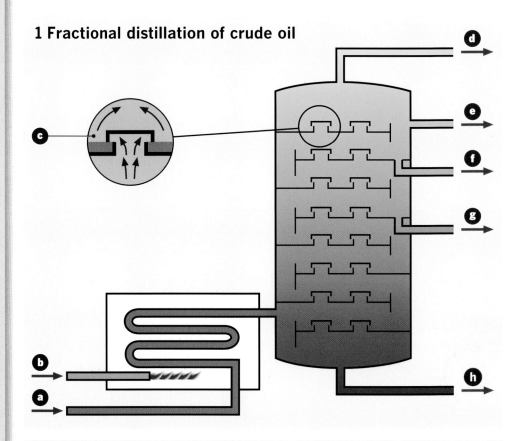

2 Crude oil composition (percent yields and uses of oil)

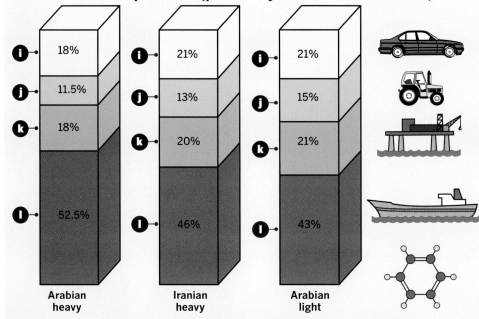

	Arabian heavy	Iranian heavy	Arabian light
i	18%	21%	21%
j	11.5%	13%	15%
k	18%	20%	21%
l	52.5%	46%	43%

a crude oil
b heater
c bubble cap
d refinery gas
e gasoline (110°C)
f kerosine (180°C)

g diesel oil (260°C)
h residue — bitumen tar (400°C)
i gasoline and chemical feedstock
j kerosine
k gas oil
l fuel oil

Other refining processes

1 Other refining processes

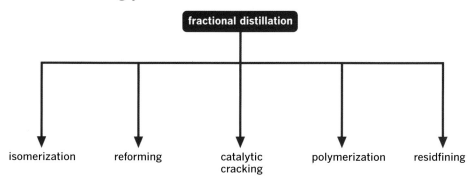

fractional distillation

→ isomerization

→ reforming

→ catalytic cracking

→ polymerization

→ residfining

2 Isomerization

$$CH_3-CH_2-CH_2-CH_2-CH_2-CH_3 \rightarrow CH_3-CH_2-CH_2-\underset{\underset{CH_3}{|}}{CH}-CH_3$$

pentane → 2-methylbutane

3 Reforming
Dehydration

methylcyclohexane → methylbenzene $+$ $3H_2$

Cyclization

$$CH_3-CH_2-CH_2-CH_2-CH_2-CH_2-CH_3 \rightarrow$$

heptane → methylcyclohexane

4 Catalytic cracking

Octane → propane and pent-1-ene

$$CH_3CH_2CH_2CH_2CH_2CH_2CH_2CH_3 \rightarrow CH_3CH_2CH_3 + CH_3CH_2CH_2CH=CH_2$$

octane → propane + pent-1-ene

5 Polymerization

Two propene molecules combine to form hexene

$$CH_3CH=CH_2 + CH_3CH=CH_2 \rightarrow CH_3CH_2CH_2CH_2CH=CH_2$$

propene + propene → hex-1-ene

Key words

alkane	isomerization
alkene	polymerization
catalytic cracking	reforming
fractional distillation	residfining

1 Other processes
- Other refining processes are used to modify the products of *fractional distillation*. These include *isomerization*, *reforming*, *catalytic cracking*, *polymerization*, and *residfining*.

2 Isomerization
- Isomerization changes the shape of hydrocarbon molecules. For example, pentane is converted into 2-methylbutane.

3 Reforming
- Reforming converts straight chain molecules into branched molecules in order to improve the efficiency of gasoline. One type of reaction involves the dehydration of saturated compounds to unsaturated compounds. Another involves the cyclization of hydrocarbons.

4 Catalytic cracking
- In general, smaller hydrocarbon molecules, such as those in gasoline, are in greater demand than larger ones. Catalytic cracking redresses this balance by breaking (cracking) large alkane molecules into smaller *alkane* and *alkene* molecules.

5 Polymerization
- Polymerization combines small molecules to form larger molecules that can be used to make various products.

Residfining
- Resifining is the process used on the residue fraction to convert it into usable products. It also removes impurities that would damage the catalyst used in catalytic cracking.

CHEMISTRY OF CARBON

Key words

alkane	catenation
alkene	van der Waals
alkyne	forces
bond	
carbon	

1 Catenation

● *Carbon* has the ability to form long chains of carbon atoms in its compounds. This is called *catenation*.

2 Melting and boiling points

● Forces of attraction, called *van der Waals forces*, exist between molecules. As molecular size increases, there is more overlap between the molecules, and the intermolecular forces of attraction increase.
● In order to melt and to boil, the forces of attraction between molecules must be overcome. The greater these forces, the more energy is needed. This is reflected in a steady increase in melting point and boiling point as molecules increase in size.

3 Types of bonds

● A carbon atom may form one, two, or three *bonds* with another carbon atom in its compounds. These bonds are described as single bonds (**C–C**), double bonds (**C=C**), and triple bonds (**C≡C**).
● *Alkanes* contain only carbon–carbon single bonds.
● *Alkenes* contain a carbon–carbon double bond.
● *Alkynes* contain a carbon–carbon triple bond.
● Alkanes, alkenes, and alkynes are all hydrocarbons since they consist only of hydrogen and carbon atoms.

Carbon chains

1 Catenation

Chain length

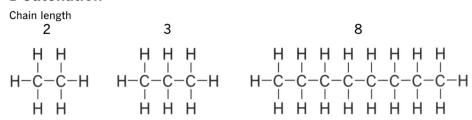

2 Melting and boiling points of some chains

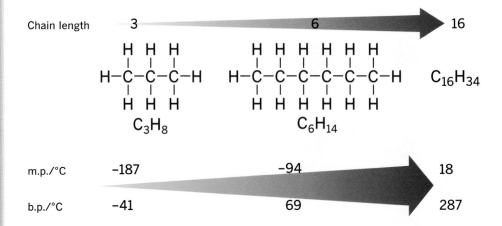

Chain length	3	6	16
m.p./°C	−187	−94	18
b.p./°C	−41	69	287

3 Types of bonds

Alkanes

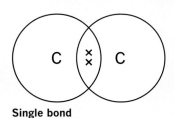

Single bond

Alkenes

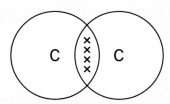

Double bond

H–C≡C–H

Alkynes

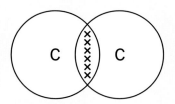

Triple bond

Naming hydrocarbons

1 Chain length gives first part of name

Chain length	C_1	C_2	C_3	C_4	C_5	C_6
First part of name	meth-	eth-	prop-	but-	pent-	hex-

2 Functional group gives second part of name

	Alkane	Alkene	Alkyne
Functional group	H | −C−H | H	C=C	C≡C
Second part of name	-ane	-ene	-yne

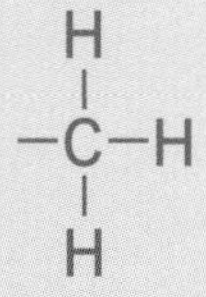

3 Examples of organic compound names

Molecule	Chain length	Functional group	Name
H | H−C−H | H	1 → meth-	H | −C−H → -ane | H	methane
H H H H | | | | H−C−C−C−C−H | | | | H H H H	4 → but-	H | −C−H → -ane | H	butane
H C−H H ∥ H−C−C | | H H	3 → prop-	C=C → -ene	propene
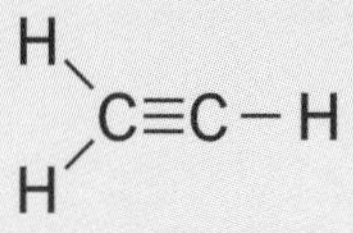 H \\ C≡C−H / H	2 → eth-	C≡C → -yne	ethyne

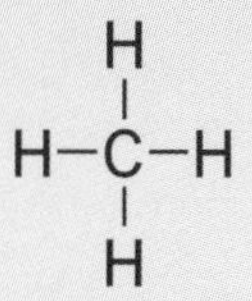

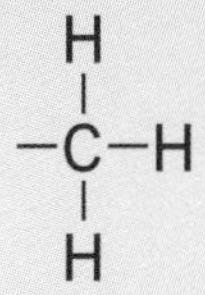

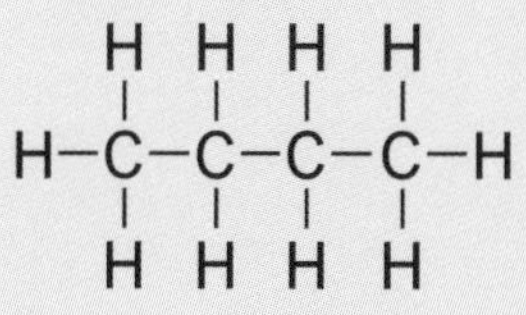

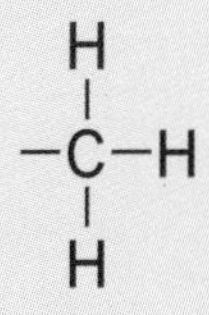

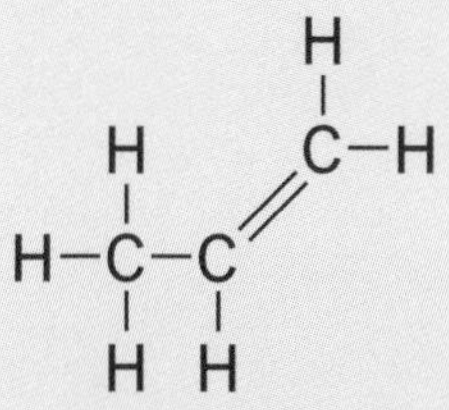

Naming hydrocarbons

- The name of a *hydrocarbon* indicates the number of carbon atoms in the molecule and what sort of carbon–carbon bonds is present.

1 Chain length

- The first part of name is determined by the number of carbon atoms in the molecule. The same prefixes are used for all groups of organic compounds.

2 Functional group

- The second part of the name is determined by the type of carbon–carbon bonds present. Each *functional group* has a unique suffix.
- The position of the functional group in a carbon chain is identified by numbering the carbon atoms in the carbon chain.

3 Examples of compound names

- The first two examples in the diagram are *alkanes*. If there is one carbon atom in the molecule it is:
  "meth" (1 carbon atom in the chain) + "ane" (for alkane): methane.
  If there are four carbon atoms in the molecule it is:
  "but" (4 carbon atoms in the chain) + "ane" (for alkane): butane.
- The third example is propane, an *alkene* with three carbon atoms:
  "pro" (3 carbon atoms in the chain) + "ene" (for alkene).
- The fourth example is ethyne, an *alkyne* with a two carbon chain:
  "eth" (2 carbon atoms in the chain) + "yne" (for alkyne).

Key words

alkane	van der Waals
homologous	forces
series	
hydrocarbon	

The first six alkanes

- The *alkanes* form an *homologous series* of compounds that have the general formula C_nH_{2n+2}, where n is a positive integer. Each alkane molecule differs from the previous one in the series by -CH_2-.
- They have similar chemical properties and show a gradation of physical properties, such as melting point and boiling point, as the molecular size increases.
- Alkane molecules are attracted to each other by *van der Waals forces*. As molecular size increases, there is more overlap between the molecules, and the intermolecular forces of attraction increase.
- Alkane molecules are frequently shown as having a flat two-dimensional structure because this is easy to draw, but in reality, the four bonds around each carbon atom are directed toward the corners of a tetrahedron. The angle between any two bonds is 109.5°.
- Alkanes are relatively unreactive substances when compared with other groups of *hydrocarbons*. Their most important reaction is combustion, and they are the main constituent of a range of fuels. Natural gas is largely composed of methane:

$$CH_4 + 2O_2 \rightarrow CO_2 + 2H_2O$$

- In a good supply of air, hydrocarbons burn to give carbon dioxide and water. In a restricted supply of air, carbon monoxide and/or carbon may be formed:

$$C_2H_6 + 2O_2 \rightarrow CO + C + 3H_2O$$

Table of the first six alkanes

Alkane	Methane	Ethane	Propane
Formula	CH_4	C_2H_6	C_3H_8
Structural formula	H–C–H with H above and below	H–C–C–H with H above and below each C	H–C–C–C–H with H above and below each C
Boiling point (°C)	−164	−87	−42
Physical state at room temperature	Gas	Gas	Gas
Molecular model			

Alkane	Butane	Pentane	Hexane
Formula	C_4H_{10}	C_5H_{12}	C_6H_{14}
Structural formula	H–C–C–C–C–H with H above and below each C	H–C–C–C–C–C–H with H above and below each C	H–C–C–C–C–C–C–H with H above and below each C
Boiling point (°C)	0	36	69
Physical state at room temperature	Gas	Liquid	Liquid
Molecular model			

Table of the first five alkenes

Key words

addition reaction   van der Waals
alkene   forces
functional group
homologous
  series

	Ethene	Propene	Butene	Pentene	Hexene
Molecular model					
Physical state at room temperature	Gas	Gas	Gas	Liquid	Liquid
Boiling point (°C)	–104	–47	–6	30	64
Structural formula					
Number of carbon atoms per molecule	2	3	4	5	6
Formula	C_2H_4	C_3H_6	C_4H_8	C_5H_{10}	C_6H_{12}

The first five alkenes

- The *alkenes* form an *homologous series* of compounds with the general formula C_nH_{2n}, where **n** is a positive integer. Each alkene molecule differs from the previous one in the series by $-CH_2-$.
- Alkene molecules are attracted to each other by *van der Waals forces*. As molecular size increases, there is more overlap between the molecules, and the intermolecular forces of attraction increase. The series thus shows a gradation of physical properties, such as melting point and boiling point.
- Alkenes all contain the same *functional group*, a carbon–carbon double bond, represented by $C=C$.
- The bonds around each of the carbon atoms in a carbon–carbon double bond are in the same plane and directed toward the corners of an equilateral triangle. The angle between any two bonds is 120°.
- Alkenes undergo combustion in the same way as alkanes. However, they have other chemistry resulting from the reactive carbon–carbon double bond.
- Alkenes undergo addition reactions in which a molecule is added across the carbon–carbon double bond. For example, ethene undergoes the following *addition reactions*:

$$CH_2=CH_2 + H\text{-}H \rightarrow CH_3\text{-}CH_3$$
ethene + hydrogen → ethane

$$CH_2=CH_2 + H\text{-}OH \rightarrow CH_3\text{-}CH_2\text{-}OH$$
ethene + steam → ethanol

$$CH_2=CH_2 + H\text{-}Br \rightarrow CH_3\text{-}CH_2Br$$
ethene + hydrogen bromide → bromoethane

$$CH_2=CH_2 + Br\text{-}Br \rightarrow CH_2Br\text{-}CH_2Br$$
ethene + bromine → 1,2-dibromoethane

Key words

alkene	geometric
ethane	isomerism
ethene	halogens
ethanol	isomer

Ethene

- *Ethene* is the first member of the *alkene* series. It is a colorless, flammable gas.

1 Preparation

- In the laboratory, ethene can be made by the dehydration of *ethanol* using concentrated sulfuric acid.

2 Structure

- Ethene, like all alkenes, contains a carbon–carbon double bond about which rotation is impossible.

3 Isomerism

- *Isomers* are compounds having the same molecular formula and relative molecular mass but different three-dimensional structures.
- The existence of two compounds with the same molecular formula but where groups are distributed differently around a carbon–carbon double bond is described as *geometric isomerism* or cis / trans isomerism.
- The prefix "cis" is used when the substituent groups (an atom or group of atoms substituted in place of a hydrogen atom or chain) of a hydrocarbon are or the same side of a plane through the carbon–carbon double bond. The prefix "trans" is used when the substituent groups are on the opposite side.
- In trans-1,2-dibromoethene the bromine atoms are on opposite sides of a plane through the carbon–carbon double bond.
- In cis-1,2-dibromoethene the bromine atoms are on the same side.

4 Reactivity

- The carbon–carbon double bond in ethene is very reactive and will undergo various addition reactions. Ethene reacts with: *halogens* (such as chlorine) to form 1,2-dihaloethane, hydrogen to form *ethane*, and hydrogen halides to form haloethane.

Ethene

1 Dehydration of ethanol to produce ethene

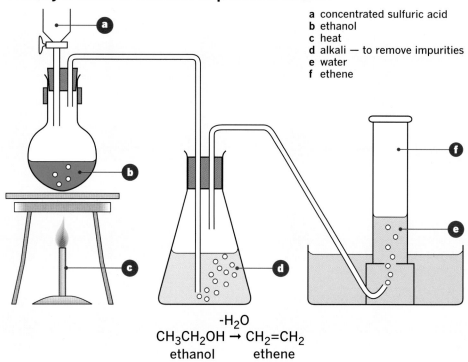

a concentrated sulfuric acid
b ethanol
c heat
d alkali — to remove impurities
e water
f ethene

$$-H_2O$$
$$CH_3CH_2OH \rightarrow CH_2=CH_2$$
ethanol   ethene

2 Structure

Ethene

3 Isomerism

Trans-1, 2-dibromoethene

Cis-1, 2-dibromoethene

4 Reactivity

$$CH_2 = CH_2 + Cl_2 \longrightarrow CH_2Cl-CH_2Cl$$

Reaction with chlorine to form 1, 2-dichloroethane

$$CH_2 = CH_2 + H_2 \xrightarrow{Ni} CH_3CH_3$$

Reaction with hydrogen to form ethane

$$CH_2 = CH_2 + HX \longrightarrow CH_3CH_2X$$

Reaction with hydrogen halides to form haloethane

Polymers

1 Types of branching

A

Polymer with few branched chains, e.g., high-density polyethene

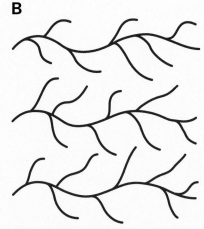

B

Polymer with many branched chains, e.g., low-density polyethene

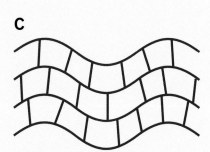

C

Polymer with much cross-linking, e.g., bakelite

2 Additional polymerization (illustrating how ethene can be restructured to form poly(ethylene) i.e., polyethene)

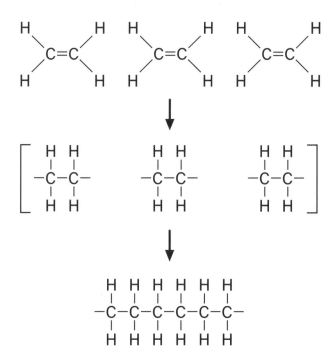

Key words

addition polymerization	polyethene
bakelite	polymer
ethene	polymerization

Polymers

- A *polymer* is a large organic molecule composed of repeating carbon chains. The physical properties of a polymer depend on the nature of these carbon chains and how they are arranged.

1 Types of branching

- A certain amount of side branching occurs during *polymerization*, depending on the reaction conditions.
- Low pressure and low temperature results in a high-density polymer.
- Very high pressure and moderate temperatures produce a low-density polymer.
- In high-density polymers, the carbon chains are unbranched, and they can be packed closely together forming a dense substance, e.g., high-density *polyethene* (1A).
- In low-density polymers, the carbon chains are branched, and it is not possible to pack them as closely together, e.g., low-density polyethene (1B).
- In polymers like *bakelite*, there are cross links between the carbon chains, producing a hard, rigid structure (1C).

2 Addition polymerization

- *Ethene* forms a polymer by a process called *addition polymerization*.
- In this process, one of the bonds from the carbon–carbon double bond is used to form a bond with an adjacent molecule. This process is repeated many times, resulting in long chains containing thousands of carbon atoms.

Key words

alkene   polymer
monomer

Monomers
- *Monomers* are the basic units from which a polymer is made.
- The systematic name for a *polymer* is derived from the name of the monomer. For example, polypropene is "poly" (for polymer) + the *alkene* propene.
- The diagrams at right illustrate the formation of some alkene polymers.

1 Forming polypropene
- Propene molecules combine to form polypropene.
- Most polypropene is produced as a monopolymer (a polymer formed from propene only).

2 Forming polychloroethene
- Chloroethene molecules combine to form polychloroethene.
- 1,2-dichloroethane is made by chlorinating ethene. This product is then cracked to form chloroethene.

3 Forming polyphenylethene
- Phenylethene molecules combine to form polyphenylethene.
- Phenylethane is made from ethene and benzene by a Friedel-Crafts reaction using aluminum(III) chloride/hydrochloric acid catalyst. This is dehydrogenated to give the phenylethene monomer.

4 Forming polytetrafluoroethene
- Tetrafluoroethene molecules combine to form polytetrafluoroethene.
- Trichloromethane is produced by the reaction of methane with controlled amounts of chlorine/hydrochloric acid. This is reacted with anhydrous hydrogen fluoride in the presence of antimony(III) chloride to give chlorodifluoromethane, which is subsequently cracked to produce tetrafluoroethene.

Polymers: formation

1 Restructuring of propene to make poly(propene)

2 Restructuring of chloroethene to make poly(chloroethene) i.e., polyvinylchloride

3 Poly(phenylethene)

4 Poly(tetrafluoroethene)

Polymers: table of properties and structure

Key words

monomer
polymer
polymerization

Polymer systematic name	Polymer common name	Properties	Uses	Structure of monomer
Poly(ethene)	Polyethene	low density; high density	film and bags; molding rigid articles	$CH_2=CH_2$ (H, H / H, H)
Poly(propane)	Polypropylene	high density	molding rigid articles, film and fibers	substituents CH_3 and H
Poly(chloroethene)	PVC (polyvinylchloride)	flexible	coating fabrics and insulation on wires and cables	substituents Cl and H
Poly(phenylethene)	Polystyrene	brittle but cheap	plastic toys, expanded with air and used for insulation	substituents C_6H_5 and H
Poly(ethene)	PTFE (polytetrafluoroethene)	low friction and stable to heat	non-stick coating on pans	$CF_2=CF_2$ (F, F / F, F)
Poly(methyl-2-methyl-propenoate)	Perspex	transparent	substitute for glass	substituents CH_3, $C(=O)OCH_3$
Poly(propenenitrile)	Acrilan	strong fibers	wool substitute in textiles	substituents CN and H

Polymers

- Most *polymers* have common names that are used in everyday language.
- The uses of polymers depend on their properties.

Classification

- There are several ways in which polymers can be classified.
- Heat. Thermoplastics soften when heated and harden on cooling, so they can be reshaped many times without changing their chemical structure. Thermosets are chemically altered on heating and produce a permanently hard material that cannot be softened by heating.
- Method of polymerization. Addition polymers are usually formed from *monomers* containing a –CH=CH– unit to which different atoms or groups are attached. On *polymerization*, one of the carbon–carbon bonds becomes a bond to another unit. Condensation polymers are formed from condensation reactions in which a small molecule, sometimes but not always water, is lost.
- Formula. Homopolymers are formed from one monomer unit. Co-polymers are formed from two or more monomers.
- Chemical structure. Linear chains may have straight, zigzag, coiled, or random spatial arrangements. Branched chains have side branch chains attached to the main chains. Cross-linked chains have two or three dimensional cross-linkage between chains.
- Steric structure. Isotactic: in which all side groups are on the same side of the main chain. Syndiotactic: in which each alternative side group has the same orientation. Atactic: in which there is no specific pattern to the distribution of side groups.

Key words	
alcohol	homologous
alkene	series
carboxylic acid	oxidation
ester	
functional group	

Functional groups

- A *functional group* is the atom or group of atoms present in a molecule that determines the characteristic properties of the molecule.
- A *homologous series* is a group of compounds that contain the same functional group. The physical properties of a homologous series show a gradation as molecular size increases. The chemical properties of a homologous series are similar because they are determined by the functional group.

1 Alkenes

- *Alkenes* contain the functional group C=C.
- Their general formula is C_nH_{2n}.
- Alkenes are reactive and undergo additional reactions.

2 Alcohols

- *Alcohols* contain the functional group C-OH.
- Their general formula is $C_nH_{2n+1}OH$.
- Alcohols can also undergo *oxidation* to give carboxylic acids, or they can be dehydrated to alkenes. They can also react to form ester compounds

3 Carboxylic acids

- *Carboxylic acids* contain the functional group -COOH.
- Carboxylic acids are typically weak acids that partially dissociate into H+ cations and RCOO- anions in aqueous solution.
- Carboxylic acids are widespread in nature.

4 Esters

- *Esters* contain the functional group –COOC-.
- Esters are formed by a reaction between a carboxylic acid and an alcohol.
- Esters are used in flavorings and perfumes.

Functional groups and homologous series

Functional group	**Example**

1 Alkenes

Propene

2 Alcohols

Ethanol

3 Carboxylic acids

Ethanoic acid

4 Esters

Methylethanoate

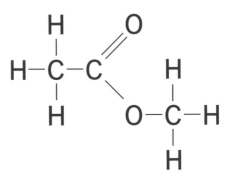

Alcohols

Key words

alcohol
alkane
functional group
hydrogen bond

1 The first six alcohols

Structure	Name
$CH_3\text{-}OH$	methanol
$CH_3CH_2\text{-}OH$	ethanol
$CH_3CH_2CH_2\text{-}OH$	propan-1-ol
$CH_3CH_2CH_2CH_2\text{-}OH$	butan-1-ol
$CH_3CH_2CH_2CH_2CH_2\text{-}OH$	pentan-1-ol
$CH_3CH_2CH_2CH_2CH_2CH_2\text{-}OH$	hexan-1-ol

2 Classification

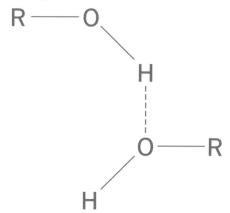

Primary alcohol   Secondary alcohol   Tertiary alcohol

3 Sharing of electrons

$$R \longrightarrow O^{\delta-}$$
$$H^{\delta+}$$

4 Hydrogen bonding

$$R \longrightarrow O$$
$$H$$
$$O \longrightarrow R$$
$$H$$

1 Naming

- *Alcohols* are named by dropping the terminal "e" from the *alkane* chain and adding "ol." For example, methane is the alkane; methanol is the alkanol, or alcohol. When necessary, the position of the hydroxyl (**-OH**) group is indicated by a number between the alkane name and the "ol," e.g., propan-1-ol, or in front of the name, e.g., 2-propanol.

2 Classification

- Alcohols may be classified as primary, secondary, or tertiary on the basis of the number of carbon atoms bonded to the carbon carrying the *functional group* (**-OH**).

3 Sharing of electrons

- An oxygen atom is more electronegative than a hydrogen atom, and this leads to an unequal sharing of the electrons in the **O-H** bond. The bonding electrons are drawn more toward the oxygen atom and, because the electrons carry a negative charge, the oxygen atom becomes slightly negative. This is described as delta minus and is denoted by δ-. Conversely, the hydrogen atom becomes slightly positive—delta plus, denoted by δ+. (**R** represents the carbon group attached to the oxygen.)

4 Hydrogen bonding

- The **-OH** functional group generally makes the alcohol molecule polar. It has a positive charge at one end and a negative at the other. Molecules can form *hydrogen bonds* with one another and other compounds when the oppositely charged parts are attracted to each other, forming hydrogen bonds.

Key words

alkali	pH
carbonate	salt
carboxylic acid	
dissociation	
homologous series	

1 Naming

- *Carboxylic acids* are named by adding the suffix "anoic acid" to the prefixes used for all *homologous series* of organic compounds. For example, the carboxylic acid containing three carbon atoms is "prop" + "anoic acid" = "propanoic acid."

2 Hydrogen bonding

- Hydrogen bonding is present between carboxylic acid molecules, resulting in higher boiling points than might otherwise be expected and miscibility with water.

3 Ionization

- Carboxylic acids ionize to give hydrogen ions, H^+; however, they are weak acids because they are only partially ionized.
- The *dissociation* constant for ethanoic acid, for example, is 1.75×10^{-5} $mol^3 dm^{-6}$. This means that only about 4 molecules in every 1,000 are ionized at any one time.

Characteristics

- Carboxylic acids have a *pH* value of approximately 3–5.
- Carboxylic acids react with *carbonates* and hydrogencarbonates to produce carbon dioxide:
  $2H^+(aq) + CO_3^{2-}(aq) \rightarrow$
  $H_2O(l) + CO_2(g)$
  $H^+(aq) + HCO_3^-(aq) \rightarrow$
  $H_2O(l) + CO_2(g)$
- Carboxylic acids form *salts* with *alkalis*:
  $CH_3COOH(aq) + NaOH(aq) \rightarrow$
  ethanoic acid   sodium hydroxide
  $CH_3COO^-Na^+(aq) + H_2O(l)$
  sodium ethanoate water

Carboxylic acids

1 The first six carboxylic acids

Structure	Name
CHOOH	methanoic acid
CH_3COOH	ethanoic acid
CH_3CH_2COOH	propanoic acid
$CH_3CH_2CH_2COOH$	butanoic acid
$CH_3CH_2CH_2CH_2COOH$	pentanoic acid
$CH_3CH_2CH_2CH_2CH_2COOH$	hexanoic acid

2 Hydrogen bonding

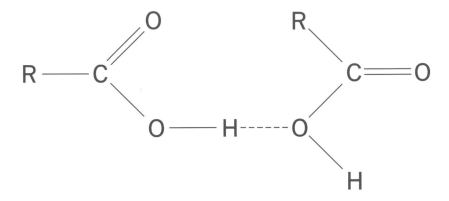

3 Ionization

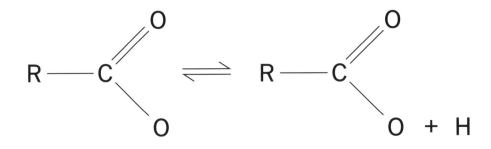

Esters

1 Forming esters

concentrated sulfuric acid

2 Naming

Structure of ester	Name of ester
	methyl ethanoate
	ethyl ethanoate
	propyl ethanoate
	methyl propanoate

3 Saponification

$$R-C \begin{smallmatrix} O \\ \\ O-R' \end{smallmatrix} + NaOH \longrightarrow R-C \begin{smallmatrix} O \\ \\ O^- Na^+ \end{smallmatrix} + R'-OH$$

Key words

alcohol	ester
alkyl	functional group
aryl	saponification
carbon	
carboxylic acid	

Esters

- *Esters* contain the *functional group* –COOR, where R is an *alkyl* or an *aryl* group.

1 Forming esters

- Esters are formed by the reaction of *carboxylic acids* with *alcohols* in the presence of a strong acid catalyst, such as concentrated sulfuric acid. The reaction involves the loss of water.
- Esters generally have a fruity smell that can be used to identify their presence. They are used for food flavorings and in cosmetics.
- Esters have no –OH group, so they cannot form hydrogen bond like carboxylic acids and alcohols. Consequently, they are more volatile and are insoluble in water.

2 Naming

- The name of an ester is derived from the carboxylic acid and the alcohol from which it is formed.
- The alcohol part of an ester is written at the beginning of the ester name; from methanol we get methyl, from ethanol we get ethyl, etc.
- The acid part of an ester is written at the end of the ester name. It is written as if it was an ionic carboxylate group in a salt; from ethanoic acid we get ethanoate, from propanoic acid we get propanoate, etc.

3 Saponification

- When esters are heated with an alkali, such as sodium hydroxide, they are readily hydrolyzed to form an alcohol and a carboxylic acid salt.
- This may be described as a *saponification* reaction. It is important in the production of soaps from fats and oils.

Key words

carboxylic acid	hydrophobic
detergent	soap
ester	
fatty acid	
hydrophilic	

Soaps and Detergents

- *Soaps* are cleansing agents made from *fatty acids* derived from natural oils and fats. *Detergents* are made from synthetic chemical compounds.

1 Fatty acids

- *Carboxylic acids* occur in animal and plant fats and oils. They may contain from 7 to 21 carbon atoms and are often referred to as fatty acids.

2 Making soap

- Most naturally occurring fats and oils are *esters* of propane-1,2,3-triol (glycerine). When the fats are boiled with sodium hydroxide, propane1,2,3,-triol and a mixture of sodium salts of the three carboxylic acids are formed. These salts are what we call soaps.

3 Soap molecule

- One end of a soap molecule is ionic, while the other end is covalent. The ionic end is described as *hydrophilic* because it dissolves in water. Conversely, the covalent end is described as *hydrophobic* because it does not dissolve in water, but it will dissolve in organic substances like oils.

4 Cleaning action

- The cleaning action of soap is the result of the different affinities of the two ends of the soap molecule.
- The hydrophobic end of the molecule dissolves in oils and fats on the fabric, while the hydrophilic end of the molecule remains in the water.
- The oil and fat particles are lifted off the fabric and held in the water by soap molecules.

5 Detergent molecule

- Alkylbenzene sulfonates are common examples of detergents.

Soaps and detergents

1 Common fatty acids

Name	Formula	Found in
palmitic acid	$CH_3(CH_2)_{14}COOH$	animal and vegetable fats
stearic acid	$CH_3(CH_2)_{16}COOH$	animal and vegetable fats
oleic acid	$CH_3(CH_2)_7CH=CH(CH_2)_7COOH$	most fats and oils
linoleic acid	$CH_3(CH_2)_4CH=CHCH_2CH=CH(CH_2)_7COOH$	soya-bean oil and nut oil

2 Making soap

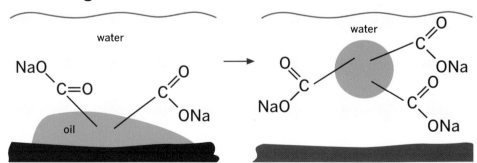

$$CH_2-O-\overset{\overset{\displaystyle O}{\|}}{C}-R'$$
$$CH-O-\overset{\overset{\displaystyle O}{\|}}{C}-R'' \quad + 3NaOH$$
$$CH_2-O-\overset{\overset{\displaystyle O}{\|}}{C}-R'''$$

$$CH_2-OH + R'-\overset{\overset{\displaystyle O}{\|}}{C}-O^-Na^+$$
$$CH-OH + R''-\overset{\overset{\displaystyle O}{\|}}{C}-O^-Na^+$$
$$CH_2-OH + R'''-\overset{\overset{\displaystyle O}{\|}}{C}-O^-Na^+$$

3 Soap molecule

4 Cleaning action

5 Detergent molecule

Organic compounds: states

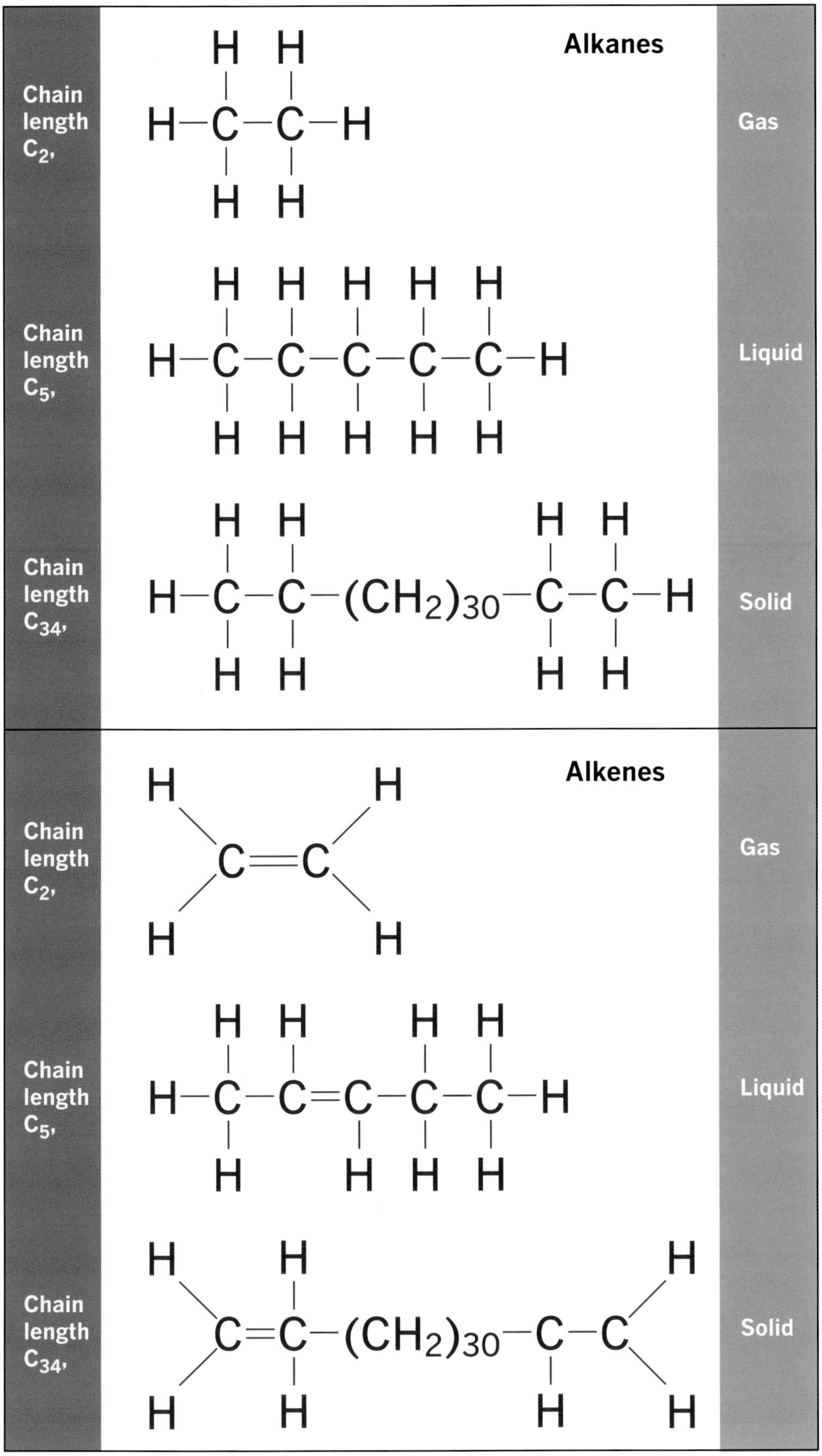

Alkanes

Chain length C_2, — Gas

Chain length C_5, — Liquid

Chain length C_{34}, — Solid

Alkenes

Chain length C_2, — Gas

Chain length C_5, — Liquid

Chain length C_{34}, — Solid

Key words

alkane
alkene
homologous
  series

Physical properties

- All *homologous series* of compounds show a gradation of physical properties as the carbon chain length increases.

Alkanes

- The simplest *alkane* is CH_4, methane. The next simplest alkane is the two carbon alkane, ethane (C_2H_6). Both of these are gases.
- The five carbon alkane, pentane (C_5H_{12}), is a liquid.
- The 34 carbon compound, butadecane is a solid.

Alkenes

- The simplest *alkene* is the two carbon alkene, ethene (C_2H_4), which is a gas.
- 2-pentene (C_5H_{10}), which is a five carbon alkene, is a liquid.
- 2-butedecane, which is a 34 carbon alkene, is a solid.

© Diagram Visual Information Ltd.

© Diagram Visual Information Ltd.

Key words

alcohol	functional group
aldehyde	homologous
alkene	series
carboxylic acid	ketone
ester	polymer

Functional groups and properties

- All members of an *homologous series* of compounds has the same *functional group*. Because the functional group determines most of the chemistry of a compound, members of a particular homologous series will have similar chemical reactions.

- *Alkenes* are unsaturated compounds because they all contain a carbon–carbon double bond that makes them very reactive. Typically, they will undergo addition reactions with hydrogen, halogens, and water. They also form a variety of *polymers*.

- *Alcohols* with a small relative molecular mass are flammable liquids and readily dissolve in water. Primary alcohols are readily oxidized: first to *aldehydes* and then to *carboxylic acids*. Secondary alcohols are oxidized to *ketones*:

$$R\text{-}CH_2\text{-}OH \xrightarrow{[O]} R\text{-}CHO \xrightarrow{[O]} R\text{-}COOH$$

primary alcohol → aldehyde → carboxylic acid

$$R\text{-}CHOH\text{-}R \xrightarrow{[O]} R\text{-}CO\text{-}R$$

secondary alcohol → ketone

- Carboxylic acids are weak acids since they only partially ionize. They have similar reactions to fully ionized mineral acids but they react with less vigor. Sodium salts of carboxylic acids are ionic compounds. Those with short carbon chains are readily soluble in water.

- *Esters* are volatile liquids or low-melting solids. They are usually insoluble in water but soluble in ethanol and diethyl ether. Esters have sweet fruity smells and are used in perfumes, flavorings, and essences.

Functional groups and properties

Class of compound	Example	Functional group
Alkene	 Ethene	
Alcohol	 Ethanole	
Carboxylic acid	 Ethanoic acid	
Ester	 Methyl methanoate	

Class of compound	Typical chemical property
Alkene	 Decolorizes bromine water
Alcohol	 Decolorizes bromine water
Carboxylic acid	$2CH_3COOH + Na_2CO_3 \longrightarrow 2CH_3COO^-Na^+ + CO_2\uparrow + H_2O$ Reacts with sodium carbonate solution
Ester	$HCOOH_3 + NaOH \longrightarrow HCOO^-Na^+ + CO_3OH$ Can be hydrolized by alkali

Reaction summary: alkanes and alkenes

Key words

addition
  polymerization
alkane
alkene
solvent

Alkanes

Combustion

$$C_3H_8 + 5O_2 \longrightarrow 3CO_2 + 4H_2O$$

Substitution

$$CH_4 + Cl_2 \longrightarrow CH_3Cl + HCl$$

Cracking

$$C_8H_{18} \longrightarrow H_2C = CH_2 + C_6H_{14}$$

Alkenes

Hydrogenation

$$H_2C = CH_2 + H_2 \longrightarrow H_3C - CH_3$$

Substitution

$$H_2C = CH_2 + Br_2 \longrightarrow \begin{array}{c} H_2C - CH_2 \\ | \quad\quad | \\ Br \quad Br \end{array}$$

General reaction alkene to alkane

$$nCH_2 = CH_2 \longrightarrow (CH_2 - CH_2)n-$$

Reaction of alkanes and alkenes

- Both *alkanes* and *alkenes* burn readily in a good supply of air to produce carbon dioxide and water.
- Crude oil is a complex mixture of alkanes, which are separated into fractions (components) on the basis of boiling point during the refining process. Some of these fractions provide gasoline, diesel, aviation fuel, and fuel oil.
- The quality of gasoline (how smoothly it burns) in indicated by its octane number, which ranges from 0–100: the higher the octane number the smoother burning the gasoline. The octane number is the percentage by volume of 2,2,4-trimethylpentane (also known as iso-octane) in a mixture of 2,2,4-trimethylpentane and heptane, which has the same knocking characteristics as the gasoline being tested.
- Historically, tetraethyllead(IV) $Pb(C_2H_5)_4$ was added to gasoline as an anti-knock additive to make it burn more smoothly. A growing knowledge of the poisonous nature of lead has resulted in the development of lead-free fuels in which other anti-knock additives, such as MTBE (methyltert-butyl ether), are used.
- Crude oil contains no alkenes, but they are produced in cracking and other refining processes. Alkenes are important feedstock for *addition polymerization* but are also used in gasoline blending, making plasticizers, and as *solvents*.
- Much of the chemistry of the alkenes is the result of the reactive nature of the carbon–carbon double bond. Alkenes undergo addition reactions with a variety of substances.

Key words

alcohol	ethene
aldehyde	oxidizing agent
carboxylic acid	
ester	
ethanol	

1 Alcohols

- The majority of the world's annual production of *ethanol* is made by the catalytic hydration of *ethene*. A mixture of ethene and steam at 300°C and 70 atmospheres is passed over a phosphoric acid catalyst.
- Ethanol is also made industrially by the fermentation of carbohydrates.
- It can also be prepared in the laboratory using concentrated sulfuric acid and heat.
- Ethanol burns readily in air. In some countries it is used as a blending agent in motor fuels.
- *Alcohols* can be oxidized to *carboxylic acids* by heating with a suitable *oxidizing agent* such as acidified potassium dichromate. The oxidation involves two stages and goes via a group of compounds called *aldehydes*. Under suitable conditions, the ethanal can be removed from the reaction mixture before it is further oxidized to ethanoic acid.

2 Acids

- Salts of short-chain carboxylic acids, like sodium ethanoate, are ionic compounds and are soluble in water.
- Ethanoic acid and ethanol react in the presence of a concentrated sulfuric acid catalyst to form the *ester* ethyl ethanoate. This reaction is reversed by heating ethyl ethanoate with an alkali such as sodium hydroxide solution. The sodium salt formed, sodium ethanoate, can be neutralized by dilute mineral acid to regenerate ethanoic acid.

esterification

ethanoic acid + ethanol →
  ethyl ethanoate

hydrolysis

ethyl ethanoate →
  ethanoic acid + ethanol

Reaction summary: alcohols and acids

Alcohols

Preparation in industry

$$CH_2 = CH_2 + H_2O \xrightarrow[\text{+70 Atmospheres}]{\text{H}_3\text{PO}_4 \text{ at } 300°C} CH_3CH_2OH$$

Fermentation

$$C_{12}H_{22}O_{11} + H_2O \xrightarrow[\text{catalyst}]{\text{enzyme}} 2C_6H_{12}O_6 \xrightarrow[\text{catalyst}]{\text{enzyme}} 4CH_3CH_2OH + 4CO_2$$

Preparation in the laboratory

$$CH_2 = CH_2 + H_2O \xrightarrow[\text{+ heat}]{\text{conc H}_2\text{SO}_4} CH_3CH_2OH$$

Oxidation by burning

$$CH_3CH_2OH + 3O_2 \longrightarrow 2CO_2 + 3H_2O$$

Oxidation by oxidizing agent

$$CH_3CH_2OH \xrightarrow{\text{K}_2\text{CR}_2\text{O}_7 + \text{dil H}_2\text{SO}_4} CH_3 + COOH$$

Reaction to produce an ester

$$CH_3CH_2OH + CH_3CO_2H \xrightarrow[\text{H}_2\text{SO}_4]{\text{conc}} H_2O + CH_3CO_2CH_2CH_3$$

Organic acids

Reaction giving ionic salt

$$CH_3CO_2 + NaOH \longrightarrow CH_3COO^-Na^+ + H_2O$$

Reaction giving covalent ester

$$CH_3CO_2 + CH_3CH_2OH \longrightarrow CH_3COOCH_2CH_3 + H_2O$$

Reaction giving hydrolysis of an ester

$$CH_3COOCH_2CH_3 + NaOH \longrightarrow CH_3COO^-Na^+ + CH_3CH_2OH$$

Optical isomerism

1 Chiral molecule

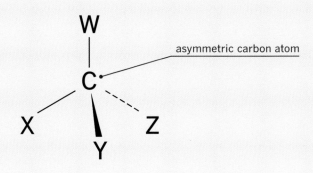

asymmetric carbon atom

2 Enantioners

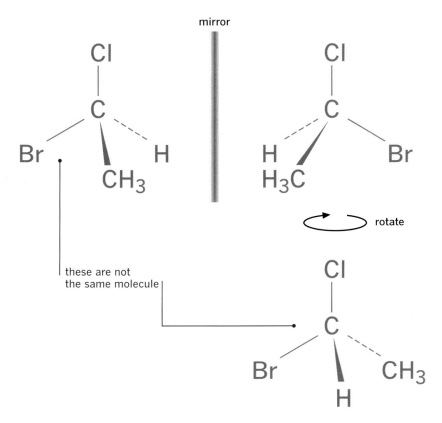

mirror

these are not
the same molecule

rotate

3 Optical activity

Polarized	→	dextro-rotatory or (+) rotatory
light	←	laevo-rotatory or (−) rotatory

Key words

chiral
enantiomer
optical isomerism
racemate

Optical isomerism

- *Optical isomerism* is a form of isomerism in which two isomers are the same in every way except that they are mirror images that cannot be superimposed on each other.

1 Chiral molecule

- When four different groups are attached to a carbon atom, the resulting molecule has no symmetry. The molecule is said to be *chiral*, and the carbon atom at the center is described as asymmetric.

2 Enantiomers

- 1-bromo-1-chloroethane is a chiral molecule. It exists in two forms, called *enantiomers*, that differ only in the way that the bonds are arranged in space.
- The enatiomers of a chiral molecule are mirror images of each other and cannot be superimposed on each other.

3 Optical activity

- Chiral molecules are said to be optically active since they rotate the plane of polarized light. If polarized light is passed through a solution containing only one of the enantiomers, the plane of the light will be rotated either to the right (dextro-rotatory) or to the left (laevo-rotatory). A similar solution containing only the other enantiomer will rotate the plane of the light by the same amount in the opposite direction.
- A solution containing equal amounts of the enantiomers is called a racemic mixture or *racemate*. It is optically inactive since the two effects cancel each other out.

Key words

amine	protein
amino acid	zwitterion
carboxylic acid	
functional group	
optical isomerism	

1 Amino acids

- *Amino acids* are compounds that contain both *amine* (-NH$_2$) and a *carboxylic acid* (-COOH) *functional groups*.
- Amino acids are generally crystalline solids that decompose on melting. They are soluble in water and insoluble in organic solvents such as ethanol.

2 Alanine

- Like most α-amino acids, alanine contains an asymmetric carbon atom and exhibits *optical isomerism*. There are two forms of alanine; L-alanine and D-alanine (L=laevo-[left] rotatory; D=dextro-[right] rotatory.)

3 Zwitterions

- In aqueous solution, amino acids are able to form ions that carry both positive and negative charge. Such ions are called *zwitterions*. They form by the loss of a proton from the carboxylic acid group and the gain of a proton on the amine group.

4 Proteins

- *Proteins* are polymers consisting of long chains of amino acids. The amino acids join together forming peptide bonds by the loss of water:

$$H_2N\text{-}CHR\text{-}COOH + H_2N\text{-}CHR\text{-}COOH \xrightarrow{-H_2O}$$
$$H_2N\text{-}CHR\text{-}CONH\text{-}CHR\text{-}COOH$$

- All of the amino acids in proteins are the L-isomers.

Amino acids and proteins

1 Amino acids

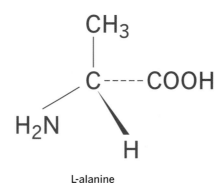

$$\underset{\text{alanine}}{H_2N\text{-}\overset{\overset{\displaystyle CH_2}{|}}{CH}\text{-}COOH}$$

$$\underset{\text{glycine}}{H_2N\text{-}\overset{\overset{\displaystyle H}{|}}{CH}\text{-}COOH}$$

$$\underset{\text{aspartic acid}}{H_2N\text{-}\overset{\overset{\displaystyle COOH}{\overset{|}{\underset{|}{CH_2}}}}{CH}\text{-}COOH}$$

$$\underset{\text{asparagine}}{H_2N\text{-}\overset{\overset{\displaystyle NH_2}{\overset{|}{\underset{|}{\overset{\displaystyle C=O}{\underset{|}{CH_2}}}}}}{CH}\text{-}COOH}$$

2 Alanine

L-alanine

D-alanine

3 Zwitterions

$$\underset{}{H_2N\text{-}\overset{\overset{\displaystyle R}{|}}{CH}\text{-}COOH} \rightleftharpoons \overset{+}{H_2N}\text{-}\overset{\overset{\displaystyle R}{|}}{CH}\text{-}COO^-$$

4 Proteins

peptide link

Monosaccharides

1 Chain structure

$$^1CHO$$
$$H-^2C-OH$$
$$HO-^3C-H$$
$$H-^4C-OH$$
$$H-^5C-OH$$
$$^6CH_2OH$$

D-glucose

$$^1CHO$$
$$HO-^2C-H$$
$$H-^3C-OH$$
$$HO-^4C-H$$
$$HO-^5C-H$$
$$^6CH_2OH$$

L-glucose

2 Ring structure

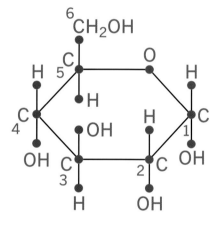

α-D-glucose

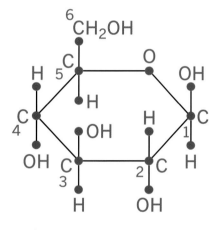

β-D-glucose

3 Hexagonal ring

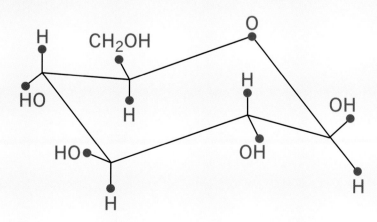

Key words

aldehyde	hexose
aldohexose	monosaccharide
aldose	
anomer	
glucose	

Monosaccharides

- *Monosaccharides* are simple sugars that have between three and six carbon atoms. Those with six carbon atoms are known as the *hexoses* and have the general formula $C_6H_{12}O_6$.
- Monosaccharides with an *aldehyde* group (**-CHO**) are called *aldoses*.
- *Glucose* has both an aldehyde group and six carbon atoms and is therefore an *aldohexose*.

1 Chain structure

- For simplicity, monosaccharides are sometimes displayed as vertical open chain structures to which the **-H** and **-OH** groups are attached.
- Aldohexoses contain four asymmetrical carbon atoms: **C-2**, **C-3**, **C-4**, and **C-5**. There are 8 different possible ways of arranging the **-H** and **-OH** groups on these carbon atoms, and each of these has two optical isomers, making a total of 16.
- The most important of these are the two optical isomers of glucose.
- For glucose the **D-** and **L-** indicate the configuration of the **-H** and **-OH** groups on **C-5**.

2 Ring structure

- In reality, solid monsaccharides do not exist as open chain structures but as ring structures.
- In Howarth projections of monosaccharides, groups are shown on vertical bonds above and below a flat hexagonal ring.
- D-glucose can exist in two separate crystalline forms known and α-D-glucose and β-D-glucose. These forms are known as *anomers*.

3 Hexagonal ring

- The hexagonal ring in a monosaccharide is not flat but in the form of a chair.

© Diagram Visual Information Ltd.

Key words

cellulose	polysaccharide
disaccharide	starch
glycogen	sucrose
monosaccharide	

Di-and polysaccharides

- A *disaccharide* is formed when two *monosaccharides* join together. A molecule of water is lost and a glycosidic link is formed.
- A *polysaccharide* is a polymer formed by the joining of many monosaccharide units.

1 Sucrose

- *Sucrose*, the sugar widely used on foods, is a disaccharide.

2 Cellulose

- *Cellulose*, a polysaccharide, provides plant cells with a rigid structure.

3 Starch

- *Glycogen* is the storage polysaccharide of animals.
- *Starch* is the storage polysaccharide of plants.

Disaccharides and polysaccharides

1 Sucrose

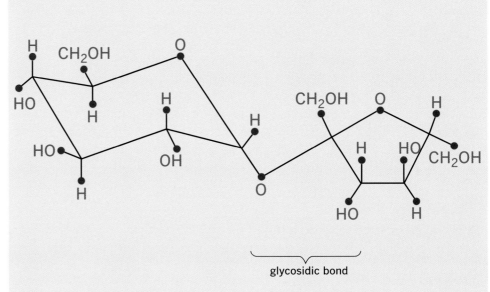

glycosidic bond

2 Cellulose

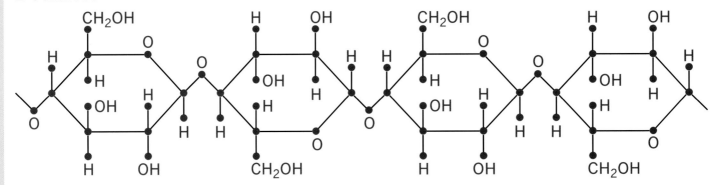

3 Starch

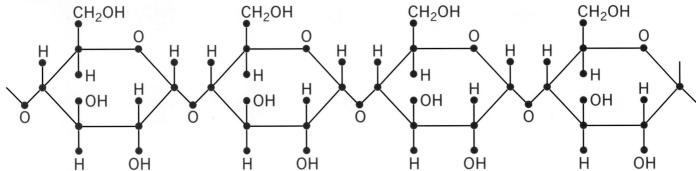

Ionizing radiation

Key words

alpha particle
beta particle
gamma radiation
ionizing radiation

1 Alpha particles

α-radiation consists of a stream of α particles

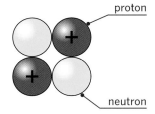

proton

neutron

Produces intense ionization in a gas

2 Beta particles

β-radiation consists of a stream of β particles

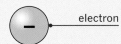

electron

Produces less intense ionization in a gas than a particles

3 Gamma radiation

γ-radiation is a form of electromagnetic radiation

Wavelength $<10^{-12}$ m
Frequency $>10^{21}$ Hz

Only weakly ionizes a gas

4 Radiation in laboratories

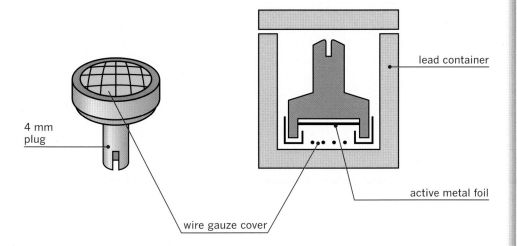

4 mm plug

lead container

active metal foil

wire gauze cover

Ionizing radiation

- *Ionizing radiation* is any radiation capable of displacing electrons from atoms or molecules and so producing ions. Examples include *alpha particles*, *beta particles*, and *gamma radiation*.

1 Alpha particles

- An alpha (α) particle has the same structure as a helium nucleus (two protons and two neutrons).
- Alpha particles are relatively heavy, high-energy particles with a positive charge.
- Alpha particles produce intense ionization in a gas.
- Emission speeds are typically of the order of 5–7 percent of the speed of light.

2 Beta particles

- A beta (β) particle is a fast-moving electron with a negative charge.
- Beta particles produce less ionization in a gas than alpha particles and on average produce only 1/1000th as many ions per unit length.
- Emission speeds can be as high as 99 percent of the speed of light.

3 Gamma radiation

- Gamma (γ) rays ionize gas only weakly and on average produce only 1/1000th as many ions per unit length as beta particles.

4 Radiation in laboratories

- Sources of radiation used for laboratory experiments are usually supplied mounted in a holder. The active material is sealed in metal foil, which is protected by a wire gauze cover. When not in use, the material is stored in a small lead container.

Key words

ionizing radiation
radiation
radioactivity

Detectors

- *Radioactivity* is invisible, but because it affects the atoms that it passes, scientists can easily detect it using a variety of methods.

1 Spark counter

- High voltage is applied between the stiff wire (anode) and the gauze (cathode) and reduced until it just stops sparking.
- When a radium source is brought near the gauze, the air between the wire and the gauze is ionized, and sparks are seen and heard at irregular intervals.

2 Cloud chamber

- When air containing ethanol vapor is cooled, it becomes saturated. If *ionizing radiation* passes through this air, further cooling causes the vapor to condense on the ions created in the air. The result is a white line of tiny liquid droplets that shows up as a track when illuminated.

3 GM tube

- When *radiation* enters the metal tube, either through the mica window or through the tube wall, it creates argon ions and electrons. These are accelerated toward the electrodes and collide with other argon atoms. On reaching the electrodes, the ions produce a current pulse, which is amplified before being fed to a pulse counter.

4 Testing absorption

- The ability of materials to absorb alpha, beta, and gamma radiation can be tested by placing the material between a radioactive source and a GM tube and comparing the count per minute with the count over the same period when the material is removed.

Radiation detectors

1 Spark counter

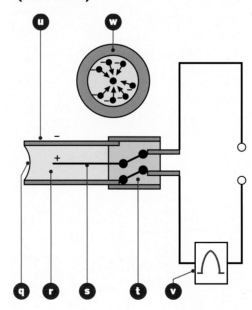

2 Cloud chamber

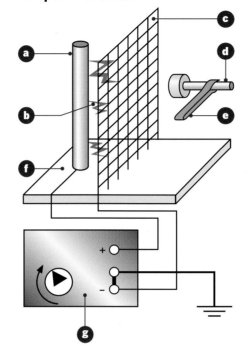

3 Geiger-Muller tube (GM tube)

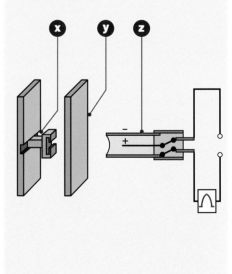

4 Testing absorbtion of alpha, beta, and gamma radiation

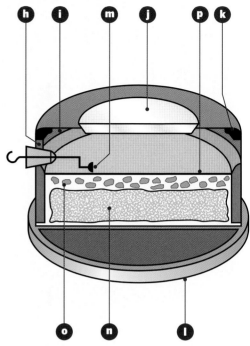

a stiff wire (anode)
b sparks
c wire gauze (cathode)
d radium source
e forceps
f insulating base
g E.h.t. supply
h circular transparent plastic chamber
i super-cooled vapor

j transparent lid
k felt strip soaked with alcohol and water
l base
m radioactive source
n foam sponge
o crushed dry ice
p black metal base plate
q mica window
r argon gas at low pressure

s anode wire
t insulator
u cathode metal tube
v pulse counter
w electrons are pulled toward the anode wire in an avalanche
x source
y absorbing material
z GM tube

Properties of radiations: penetration and range

Key words

alpha particle
beta particle
gamma radiation
radiation

1 Penetration of radiation

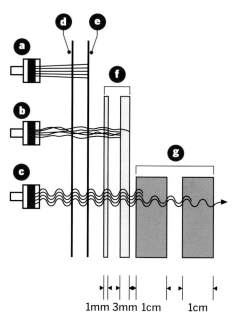

|1mm|3mm|1cm| |1cm|

a α – source
b β – source
c γ – source
d metal foil

e paper
f aluminum
g lead

2 Range of radiation in air

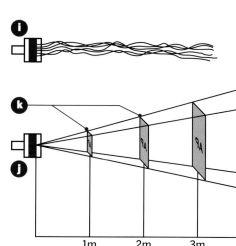

|1m|2m|3m|

h α – a few centimeters
i β – a few meters
j γ – many meters
k area covered by γ radiation at 1m distances

3 The inverse square law for gamma radiation penetration

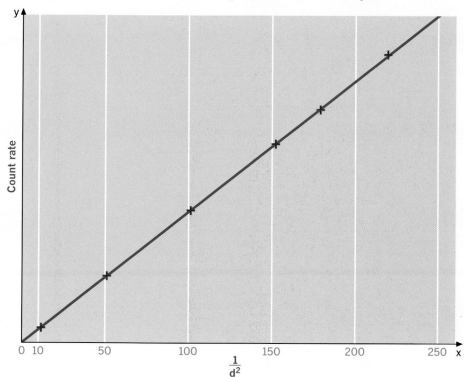

Count rate (y-axis)

$\frac{1}{d^2}$ (x-axis): 0 10   50   100   150   200   250

1 Penetration

- Alpha, beta, and *gamma radiation* penetrate by different amounts.
- Alpha radiation is the least penetrating and is stopped by a sheet of paper or very thin metal foil.
- Beta radiation is stopped by aluminum a few millimeters thick.
- Gamma radiation is most penetrating, and is only stopped by a thick block of lead.

2 Range

- The penetrating power of alpha, beta, and gamma radiation is reflected in the distance that they can travel through air. *Alpha particles* can only travel a few centimeters before colliding with air particles. *Beta particles* travels a few meters, while gamma radiation can travel many meters.

3 Gamma penetration

- Gamma rays are highly penetrating because they have relatively little interaction with matter. There is very little absorption or scattering as they pass through air.
- The intensity falls off with distance according to the inverse square law:

$$I = \frac{k}{d^2}$$

where I is intensity, d is the distance from the source, and k is a constant. At a distance x, the intensity of the gamma radiation:

$$I_x = \frac{k}{x^2}$$

At a distance 2x, the intensity of the gamma radiation:

$$I_{2x} = \frac{k}{(2x)^2} = \frac{k}{4x^2}$$

As the distance increases by a factor of 2, the intensity of the gamma radiation decreases by a factor of 4.

Key words

alpha particle
beta particle
electric field
gamma radiation

Properties of radiations: in fields

Electric and magnetic fields

- An *electric field* is a field extending outward in all directions from a charged particle.
- A magnetic field is an area of force that exists around a magnetic body or a current-carrying conductor. Alpha, beta, and gamma radiation behave differently in both.

1 Electric field

- Alpha radiation is composed of positively charged particles. A stream of *alpha particles* is deflected when passing through the electric field between two oppositely charged plates. The particles are repelled from the positively charged plate and attracted toward the negatively charged plate.
- Beta radiation is composed of negatively charged particles. A stream of *beta particles* is deflected by an electric field in the opposite direction to alpha particles. The deflection is greater because the beta particles have a much smaller mass.
- *Gamma radiation* is not deflected by an electric field. This is evidence that gamma radiation carries no charge.

2 Magnetic field

- Alpha radiation is deflected by a strong magnetic field. Weak magnetic fields have no noticeable effect due to the greater mass of alpha particles compared to beta particles.
- Beta radiation is deflected by a relatively weak magnetic field. Beta radiation is deflected in the opposite direction to alpha radiation, indicating its particles carry an opposite charge.
- Gamma radiation is not deflected by a magnetic field, indicating that gamma radiation carries no charge.

Radiation	1 Electric field	2 Magnetic field
Alpha	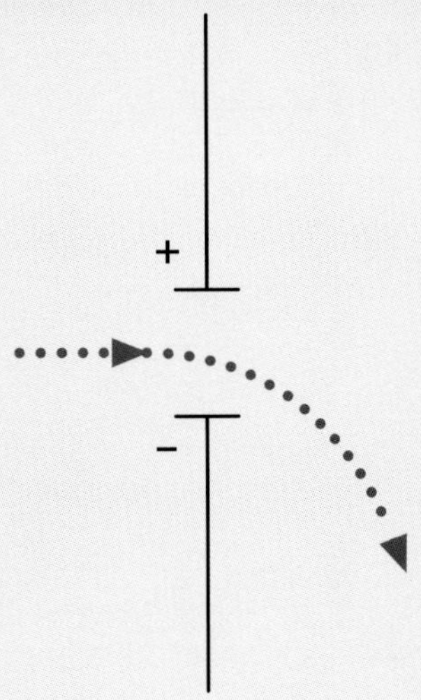	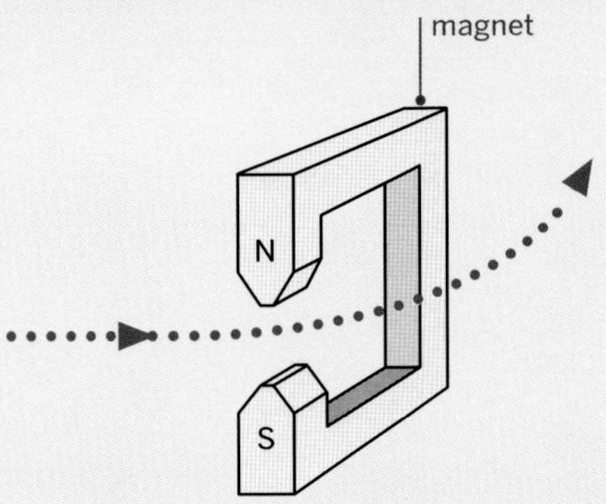
Beta	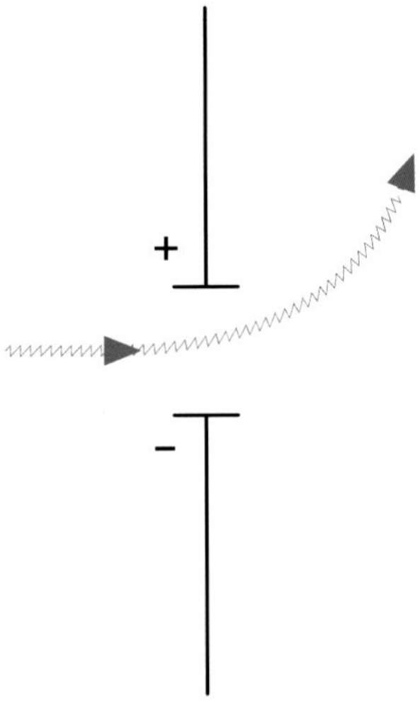	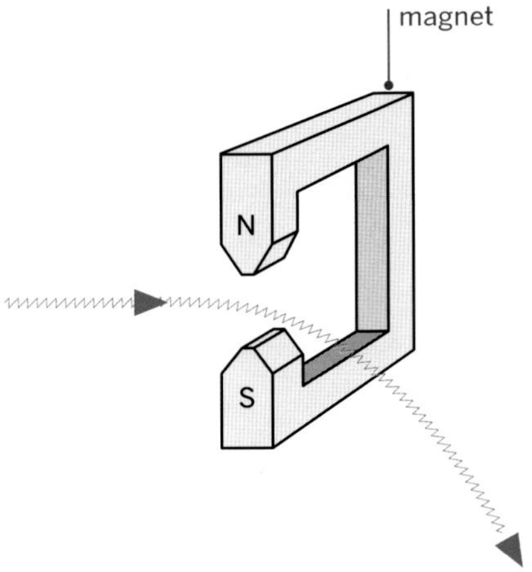
Gamma	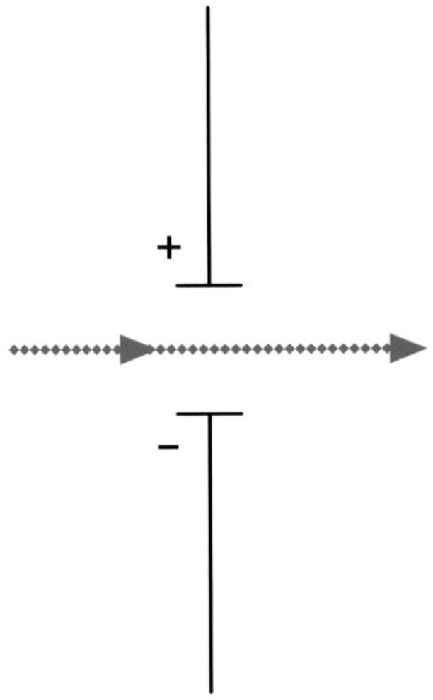	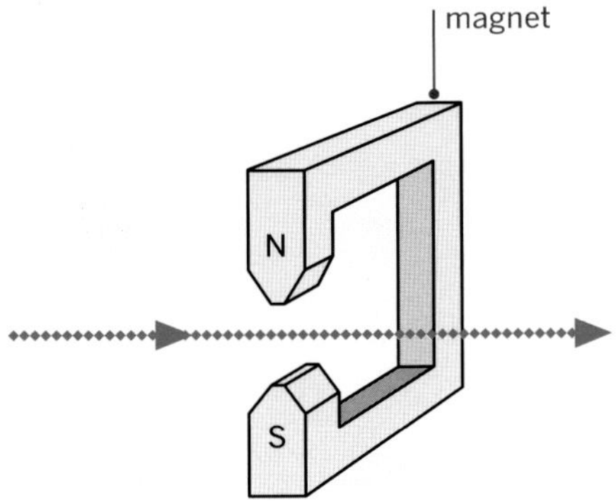

Stable and unstable isotopes

Key words

isotope
nucleon
nuclide

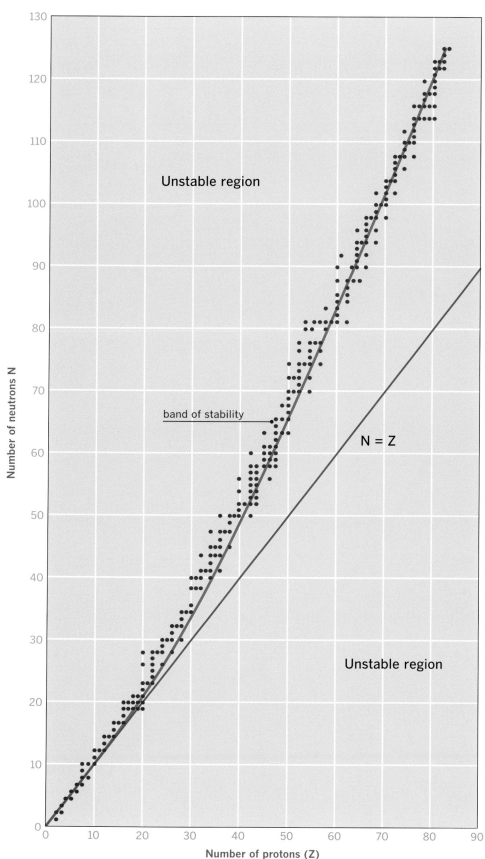

Stability

- The stability of *isotopes* is based on the ratio of neutrons and protons in their nucleus. Although most nuclei are stable, some are not and spontaneously decay, emitting radiation.
- The lightest stable *nuclides* (particular isotopes of an element) have almost equal numbers of protons and neutrons. The heavier stable nuclides require more neutrons than protons. The heaviest stable nuclides have approximately 50 percent more neutrons than protons.

Odd-even rule

- Isotopes tend to be more stable when they have even numbers of protons and neutrons than when they have odd. This is the result of the spins of the *nucleons* (the constituents of the atomic nucleus). When two protons or neutrons have paired spins (spins in opposite directions), their combined energy is less than when they are unpaired.

Decay

- When unstable nuclides disintegrate, they tend to produce new nuclides that are nearer to the stability line. This will continue until a stable nuclide is formed.
- An unstable nuclide above the band of stability decays by beta emission. This increases the proton number and decreases the neutron number. Thus, the neutron to proton ratio is decreased.
- An unstable nuclide below the band of stability disintegrates so as to decrease the proton number and increase the neutron to proton ratio. In heavy nuclides this can occur by alpha emission.

Key words

alpha particle
half-life
isotope
nuclide

1 Half-life

- *Half-life* is the time required for half the nuclei in a sample of an *isotope* to undergo *radioactive decay*.
- Radioactive decay is a completely random process in which nuclei disintegrate independently of each other or external factors such as temperature and pressure.

2 Rate of decay

- There are always very large numbers of active *nuclides* even in small amounts of radioactive material, so statistical methods can be employed to predict the fraction that will have decayed, on average, over a given period of time.
- The rate of decay of a nuclide at any time is directly proportional to the number of nuclei, N, of the nuclide:

$$-\frac{dN}{dt} \propto N \text{ or } \frac{dN}{dt} = -\lambda N$$

where N is the number of undecayed nuclei and λ is the decay constant. The minus sign indicates that the number of undecayed nuclei falls with time. Integrating this gives the exponential law equation:

$$N_t = N_0 e^{-\lambda t}$$

where N_0 is the number of undecayed atoms at time $t = 0$ and N_t the number of undecayed atoms after time t.

- After one half life ($t_{1/2}$) has passed, the number of undecayed atoms remaining in the sample will be $N_0/2$. Substituting this into the exponential law equation for N_t and taking natural logs of both sides provides a mathematical relationship between the decay constant and the half life of a radioactive atom:

$$t_{(1/2)} = \frac{0.693}{\lambda}$$

Half-life

1 Half-life

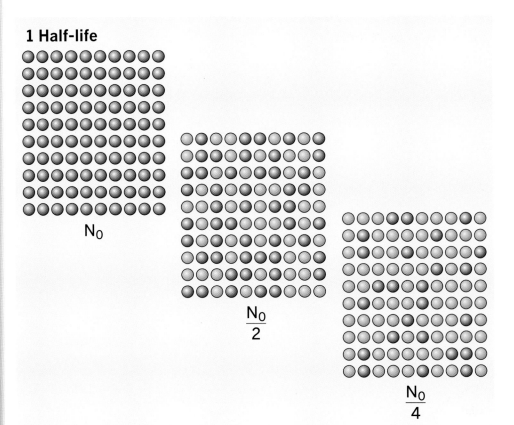

2 Rate of decay

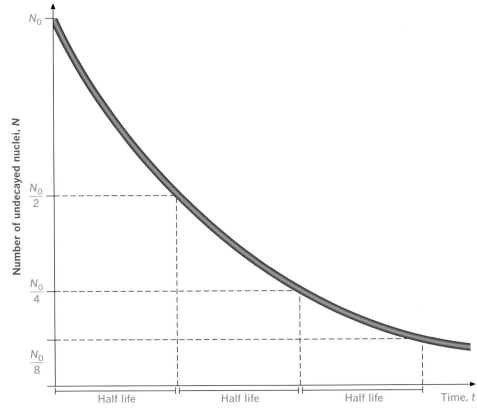

Typical radioactive decay curve

Measuring half-life

Key words

alpha particle
half-life
isotope

1 Half-life of radon

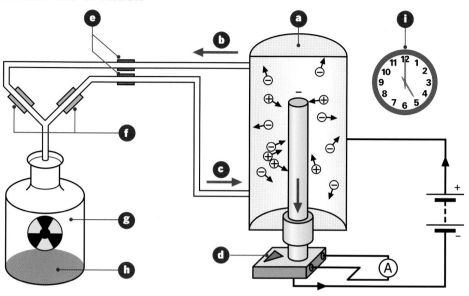

a ionization chamber
b air
c radon
d d.c. amplifier
e clips

f valves
g squeezable polyethylene
   bottle
h thorium hydroxide powder
i clock

1 Half-life of radon

- Thorium decays to produce the radioactive *isotope* radon-220. This isotope is sometimes referred to as thoron.
- The bottle containing thorium hydroxide powder is squeezed a few times to transfer some radon-220 to the flask. The clips are then closed.
- As the radon decays, the ionization current decreases. It is always a measure of the number of *alpha particles* present and, therefore, the proportion of radon-220 remaining.
- The current is noted every 15 seconds for 2 minutes and then every 60 seconds for several minutes.

2 Exponential decay

- A graph of current against time is plotted.
- In this experiment, the *half-life* is indicated by the amount of time taken for the current to fall to half of its original value.
- The half-life of radon-220 is approximately 55 seconds.

3 Radon decay

- Radon-220 decays with the loss of an alpha particle to form polonium-216, which decays to form lead-212. The half life of polonium-216 is 0.145 seconds, and the half life of lead-212 is 10.64 hours.

2 Exponential decay: decay curve for radon gas

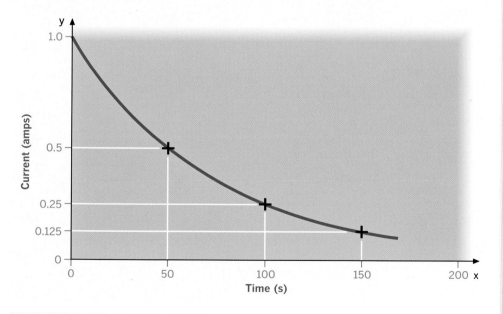

3 Radon decay

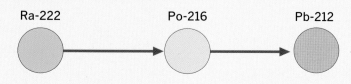

Ra-222   Po-216   Pb-212

1 Tracers

- Radioactive *isotopes* are used as tracers to monitor the movement of substances in plants and animals. A solution containing radioactive phosphorus-32 is introduced into the stem of a plant. A Geiger counter is used to detect the movement of the isotope through the plant.

2 Thyroid monitor

- A solution containing iodine-131 is introduced to the bloodstream of a patient with a defective thyroid. A Geiger counter is used to detect the isotope and monitor thyroid activity.

3 Food preservation

- Food is irradiated by exposing it to *gamma radiation. Irradiation* destroys disease-causing bacteria as well as those that spoil food, so the shelf life of food is extended.

4 Sterilization

- Gamma radiation is used to sterilize medical equipment.

5 Smoke detectors

- Americium-241, a source of alpha radiation, is widely used in smoke detectors. The *alpha particles* ionize the air in the sensing circuit. Any smoke particles interfere with this and cause a change in the current, which triggers an alarm.

6 Duration of death

- All organisms contain a specific ratio of radioactive carbon-14 to carbon-12. When an organism dies, no carbon-14 is added. After death, carbon-14 decays at a predictable rate: the half-life is 5,700 years. By comparing the ratio of carbon-14 to carbon-12, it is possible to say when an organism died.

Radioactive isotopes

1 Tracers

2 Thyroid monitor

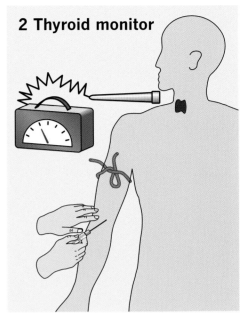

3 Food preservation

gamma rays

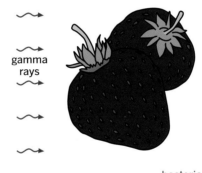

bacteria dying

4 Sterilization

gamma rays

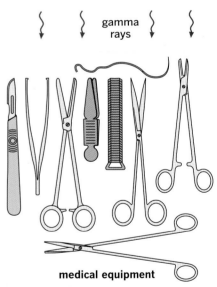

medical equipment

5 Smoke detectors

current-sensing circuit

battery

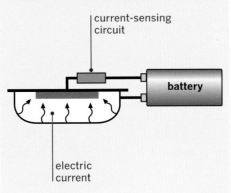

electric current

6 Duration of death

Carbon-12 constant

Carbon-14 decreases

Dead organism

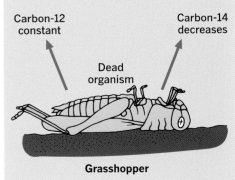

Grasshopper

Nuclear fusion

1 Nuclear fusion

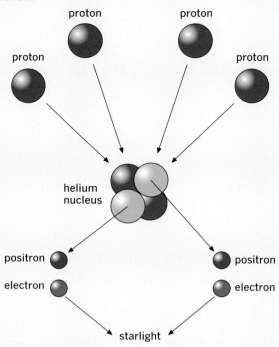

helium
nucleus

proton   proton

proton   proton

positron   positron

electron   electron

starlight

2 Fusion of deuterium

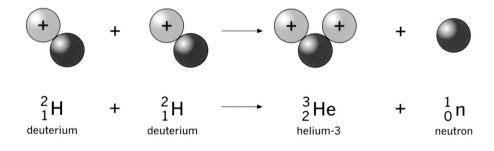

$$^{2}_{1}H \quad + \quad ^{2}_{1}H \quad \longrightarrow \quad ^{3}_{2}He \quad + \quad ^{1}_{0}n$$

deuterium   deuterium   helium-3   neutron

3 Fusion of deuterium and tritium

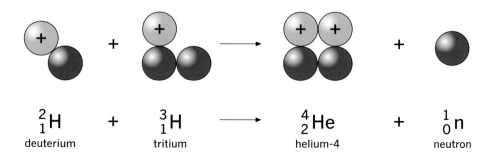

$$^{2}_{1}H \quad + \quad ^{3}_{1}H \quad \longrightarrow \quad ^{4}_{2}He \quad + \quad ^{1}_{0}n$$

deuterium   tritium   helium-4   neutron

Key words

fusion
isotope

1 Nuclear fusion

- In nuclear *fusion*, two or more light atomic nuclei join to make a more massive one. During the process, some of the mass of the nuclei is converted into energy. Nuclear fusion, which first occurred during the Big Bang, powers stars. It also occurs in hydrogen bombs. Currently scientists are working to control fusion so it can be used in nuclear reactors.

2 Deuterium

- Deuterium is an *isotope* of hydrogen known as heavy hydrogen. The nucleus of a deuterium atom consists of one neutron and one proton.
- The fusion of two deuterium nuclei results in the formation of a helium-3 nucleus. A small amount of mass is converted into energy:
  Mass of two deuterium nuclei =
  $2 \times 2.014 = 4.028$ u
  Mass of helium-3 nucleus plus a neutron =
  $3.016 + 1.009 = 4.025$ u
  Mass converted to energy by fusion =
  $4.028 - 4.025 = 0.003$ u
  Energy released by the fusion reaction $= 4.5 \times 10^{-13}$ J
  Energy released per kilogram of deuterium is approximately 9×10^{13} J.

3 Tritium

- Tritium is another isotope of hydrogen. The nucleus of a tritium atom consists of two neutrons and one proton.
- The fusion of a deuterium nucleus and a tritium nucleus results in the formation of a helium-4 nucleus and the release of energy. The energy released per kilogram of deuterium and tritium is approximately 30×10^{13} J.
- This reaction produces more energy, and the fusion takes place at a lower temperature.

Key words

chain reaction
fission

Nuclear fission

- In nuclear *fission*, a heavy atomic nucleus divides to make two smaller ones. Some of the mass of the nuclei is converted into energy during the process.

1 Reaction with uranium

- In a nuclear reaction with uranium and slow-moving neutrons, the nucleus of the uranium-235 atom undergoes fission and forms two smaller nuclei (lanthanum-148 and bromine-85) plus three neutrons. A small amount of mass is converted to energy.

2 Chain reaction

- A nuclear *chain reaction* is a series of self-sustaining reactions in which the particles released by one nucleus trigger the fission of at least as many other nuclei.
- Under normal circumstances, only a very small proportion of fission neutrons act in this way. However, if there is a sufficient amount of a radioactive isotope, a chain reaction can start.
- In an atomic bomb, an increasing uncontrolled chain reaction occurs in a very short time when two pieces of uranium-235 (or plutonium-239) are rapidly brought together.
- In a nuclear power station, the chain reaction is steady and controlled, so only a limited number of fission neutrons bring about further fission reactions.

Nuclear fission

1 Reaction with uranium

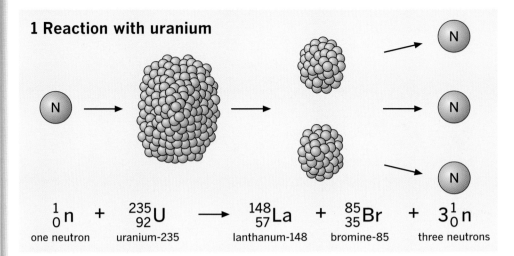

$$^{1}_{0}n \; + \; ^{235}_{92}U \; \longrightarrow \; ^{148}_{57}La \; + \; ^{85}_{35}Br \; + \; 3^{1}_{0}n$$

one neutron   uranium-235   lanthanum-148   bromine-85   three neutrons

2 Chain reaction

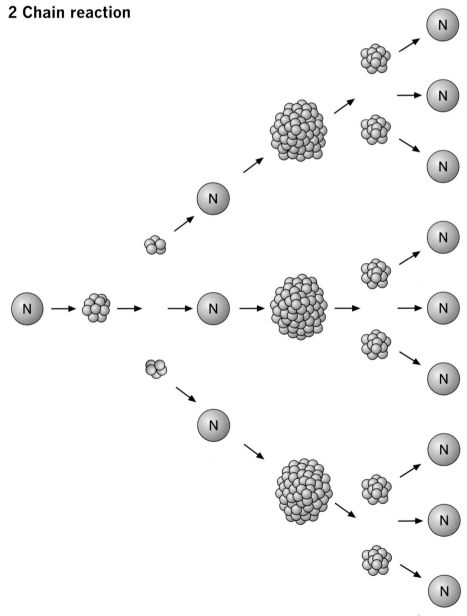

1 neutron   3 neutrons   9 neutrons

Nuclear reactor

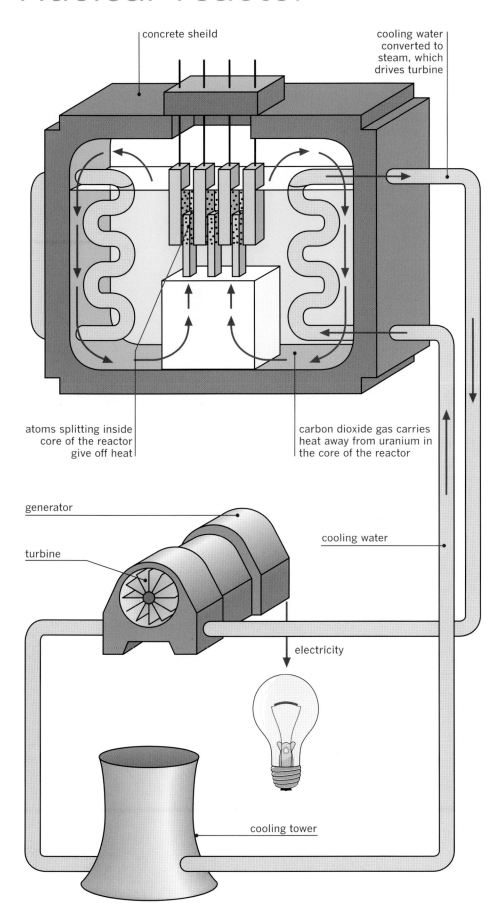

concrete sheild

cooling water converted to steam, which drives turbine

atoms splitting inside core of the reactor give off heat

carbon dioxide gas carries heat away from uranium in the core of the reactor

generator

turbine

cooling water

electricity

cooling tower

Key words

fission
isotope
uranium

Nuclear reactor

● *Uranium*, either the metal or the metal oxide, is used as fuel in nuclear reactors. The fuel is in the form of fuel rods, which are suspended in the reactor.

● Naturally occurring uranium contains 99.3 percent uranium-238 and only 0.7 percent of the radioactive *isotope* uranium-235. The uranium-235 content must be increased to approximately 3 percent before the uranium can be use as a fuel.

● Uranium-235 undergoes spontaneous *fission*. However, in a nuclear power station, the fission is brought about by bombarding the uranium nuclei with neutrons.

● The fission of one atom of uranium-235 absorbs one neutron and releases three others. In order to increase the chances that these neutrons will strike other uranium-235 atoms, they are slowed down by a moderator.

● Control rods are suspended between the fuel rods. These can be raised or lowered as needed to control the nuclear reaction. The control rods are made of alloys that absorb neutrons. When they are lowered, more neutrons are absorbed.

● The heat produced by the fission reaction is removed through a heat exchanger. The loop between the nuclear reactor and the heat exchanger is sealed so there is no danger of radioactive material escaping into the environment.

● The heat is used to convert water into pressurized steam. The high pressure steam drives a turbine connected to a generator, which produces electricity.

Key words

alpha particle	mass number
atomic number	nuclide
beta particle	radioactive decay
daughter nucleus	uranium
half-life	uranium series

Radioactive decay

- Radioactive nuclei break down by a process known as *radioactive decay* in order to become more stable. In a radioactive decay series, each member of the series is formed by the decay of the *nuclide* before it until a stable nuclide is produced. As the nuclei disintegrate, they emit *alpha* (α) or *beta* (β) *particles*.

- There are three naturally occurring radioactive decay series: the *uranium series*, the actinium series, and the thorium series. Each ends with a stable isotope of lead.

The uranium series

- The uranium series involves the radioactive decay of U-238 to stable Pb-206. It is also known as the **4n+2** series (where **n** is an integer), because each member of the series has a mass equivalent to **4n+2**.

- The graph indicates how the decay occurs. *Atomic numbers* are plotted on the x-axis. The *mass numbers* are on the y-axis. The symbol for the element is at the top of the graph. Each diagonal line represents an alpha (α) decay; each horizontal line a beta (β) decay. A circle indicates the *daughter nucleus* (the nucleus produced by the decay of the previous nucleus). *Half-life* is indicated in years (a), days (d), hours (h), minutes (m), and seconds (s).

Decay chain

U-238 → Th-234 → Pa-234 → U-234 →
Th-230 → Ra-226 → Rn-222 → Po-218 →
At-218 → Pb-214 → Bi-214 → Po-214 →
Ti-210 → Pb-210 → Bi-210 → Po-210 →
Pb-206 (stable)

The uranium series

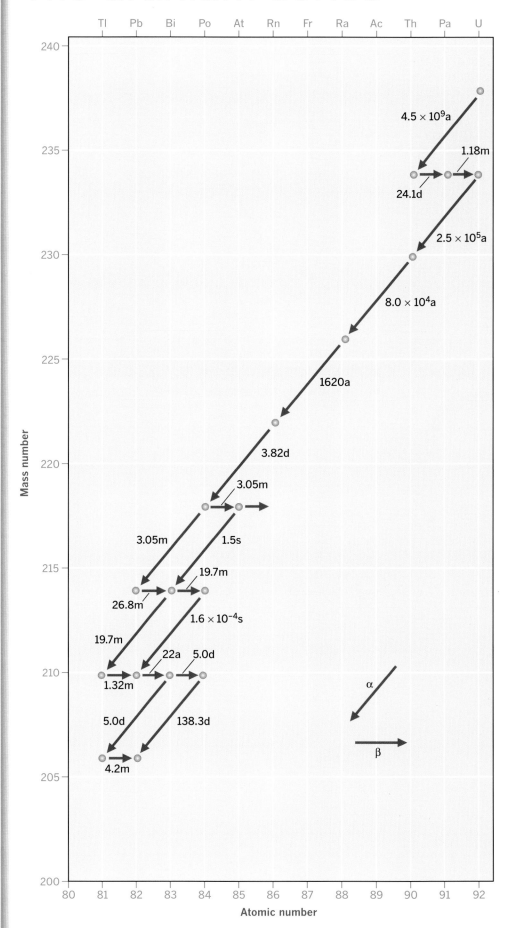

The actinium series

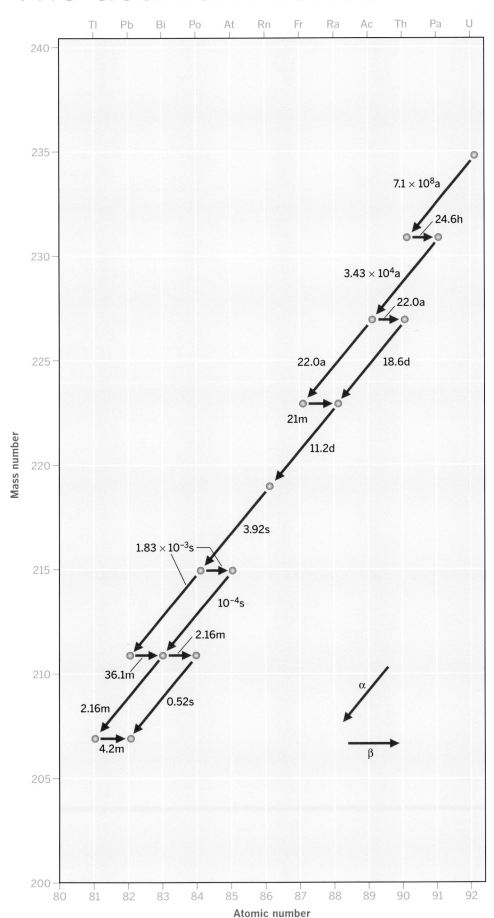

Key words

actinium	daughter nucleus
actinium series	half-life
alpha particle	mass number
atomic number	nuclide
beta particle	radioactive decay

Radioactive decay

- Radioactive nuclei break down by a process known as *radioactive decay* in order to become more stable. In a radioactive decay series, each member of the series is formed by the decay of the *nuclide* before it until a stable nuclide is produced. As the nuclei disintegrate, they emit *alpha* (α) or *beta* (β) *particles*.
- There are three naturally occurring radioactive decay series: the uranium series, the *actinium series*, and the thorium series. Each ends with a stable isotope of lead.

The actinium series

- The actinium series involves the radioactive decay of U-235 to stable Pb-207. It is also known as the **4n+3** series (where **n** is an integer), because each member of the series has a mass equivalent to **4n+3**.
- The graph indicates how the decay occurs. *Atomic numbers* are plotted on the x-axis. The *mass numbers* are on the y-axis. The symbol for the element is at the top of the graph. Each diagonal line represents an alpha (α) decay; each horizontal line a beta (β) decay. A circle indicates the *daughter nucleus* (the nucleus produced by the decay of the previous nucleus). *Half-life* is indicated in years (a), days (d), hours (h), minutes (m), and seconds (s).

Decay chain

U-235 → Th-231 → Pa-231 → Ac-227 → Th-227 → Fr-223 → Ra-223 → Rn-219 → Po-215 → At-215 → Pb-211 → Bi-211 → Po-211 → Tl-207 → Pb-207 (stable)

RADIOACTIVITY

Key words

alpha particle	mass number
atomic number	nuclide
beta particle	radioactive decay
daughter nucleus	thorium
half-life	thorium series

Radioactive decay

- Radioactive nuclei break down by a process known as *radioactive decay* in order to become more stable. In a radioactive decay series, each member of the series is formed by the decay of the *nuclide* before it until a stable nuclide is produced. As the nuclei disintegrate, they emit *alpha* (α) or *beta* (β) *particles*.
- There are three naturally occurring radioactive decay series: the uranium series, the actinium series, and the *thorium series*. Each ends with a stable isotope of lead.

The thorium series

- The thorium series involves the radioactive decay of Th-232 to stable Pb-208. It is also known as the (**4n**) series (where **n** is an integer) because each member of the series has a mass equivalent to **4n**.
- The graph indicates how the decay occurs. *Atomic numbers* are plotted on the x-axis. The *mass numbers* are on the y-axis. The symbol for the element is at the top of the graph. Each diagonal line represents an alpha (α) decay; each horizontal line a beta (β) decay. A circle indicates the *daughter nucleus* (the nucleus produced by the decay of the previous nucleus). *Half-life* is indicated in years (a), days (d), hours (h), minutes (m), and seconds (s).

Decay chain

Th-232 → Ra-228 → Ac-228 → Th-228 →
Ra-224 → Rn-220 → Po-216 → Pb-212 →
Bi-212 → Po-212 → Tl-208 →
Pb-208 (stable)

The thorium series

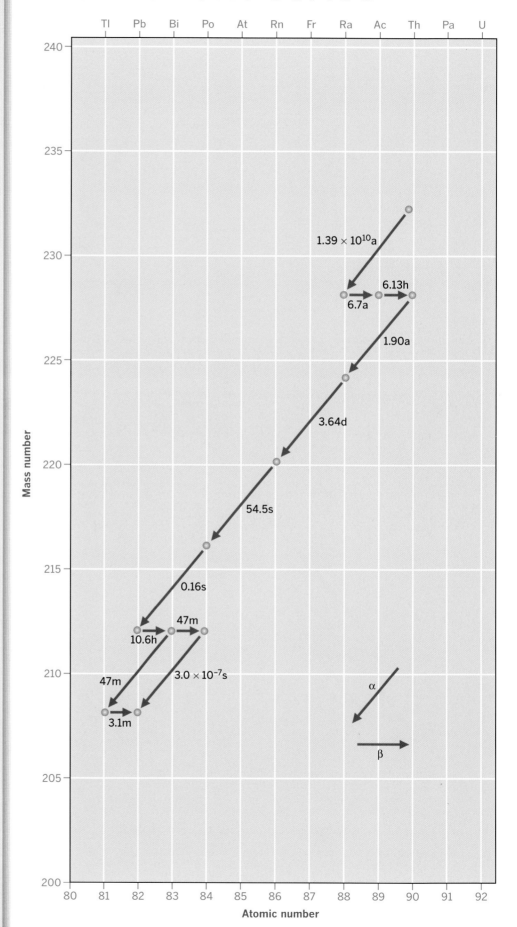

The neptunium series

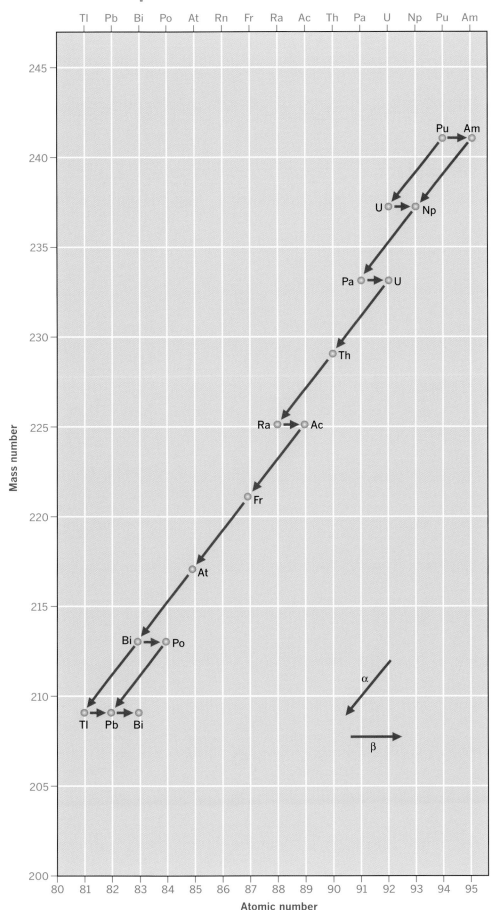

© Diagram Visual Information Ltd.

Key words

alpha particle	mass number
atomic number	neptunium
beta particle	neptunium series
daughter nucleus	nuclide
half-life	radioactive decay

Radioactive decay

- Radioactive nuclei break down by a process known as *radioactive decay* in order to become more stable. In a radioactive decay series, each member of the series is formed by the decay of the *nuclide* before it until a stable nuclide is produced. As the nuclei disintegrate, they emit *alpha* (α) or *beta* (β) *particles*.
- The *neptunium* series is composed of isotopes that do not occur in nature.

The neptunium series

- The neptunium series starts with the artificial isotope plutonium-241 and ends with bismuth-209. Each member of the series has a mass equivalent to **4n+1** (where **n** is an integer).
- The graph indicates how the decay occurs. *Atomic numbers* are plotted on the x-axis. The *mass numbers* are on the y-axis. The symbol of the element is at the top of the graph. Each diagonal line represents an alpha (α) decay; each horizontal line a beta (β) decay. A circle indicates the *daughter nucleus* (the nucleus produced by the decay of the previous nucleus).

Decay chain

Pu-241 → Am-241 → Np-237 → Pa-233 → U-233 → Th-229 → Ra-225 → Ac-225 → Fr-221 → At-217 → Bi-213 → Po-213 → Pb-209 → Bi-209 (stable)

1 Alpha decay

- *Alpha decay* is the process in which the nucleus of an atom emits an *alpha particle* (which has the same structure as the helium-4 nucleus: $_2^4\text{He}$).
- The new atom's atomic *mass number* (**A**) is reduced by 4 and its *atomic number* (**Z**) is decreased by 2.
- Uranium-238 decays to thorium-234 by the loss of an alpha particle.
- Energy is also released as *gamma* (γ) *radiation*.

2 Alpha particle spectrum

- The *ground state* of the uranium nucleus (the natural state of the lowest energy of the nucleus) is at a higher energy than the ground state of the thorium nucleus.
- Some energy is released in the form of *kinetic energy*, which is carried by the alpha particle.
- The remaining energy is released as gamma radiation.

3 Beta decay

- *Beta decay* is the process in which the nucleus of an atom emits a *beta particle* (an electron).
- The new atom's atomic number (**Z**) is increased by 1, while the atomic mass number (**A**) remains unchanged.
- Thorium-234 decays to protactinium-234 by the loss of a beta particle. The half-life for this decay is 6.75 hours.

4 Beta particle spectrum

- The ground state of the thorium *nuclide* is at a higher energy than the ground state of the protactinium nucleus.
- Some energy is released in the form of kinetic energy, which is carried by the beta particle.
- The remaining energy is released as gamma radiation.

Radioactivity of decay sequences

1 Alpha decay

$$_Z^A\text{X} \xrightarrow{\alpha} {}_{Z-2}^{A-4}\text{Y} + {}_2^4\text{He} + \gamma$$

General sequence of alpha decay

$$_{92}^{238}\text{U} \xrightarrow{\alpha} {}_{90}^{234}\text{Th} + {}_2^4\text{He} + \gamma$$

Example of alpha decay: uranium decay to thorium

2 Alpha particle spectrum

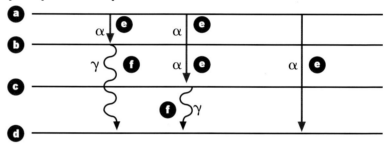

3 Beta decay

$$_Z^A\text{X} \xrightarrow{\beta} {}_{Z+1}^A\text{Y} + e^- + \tilde{\nu}$$

General sequence of beta decay

$$_{90}^{234}\text{Th} \xrightarrow{\beta} {}_{91}^A\text{Pa} + e^- + \tilde{\nu}$$

Example of beta decay: thorium decay to protactinium

4 Beta particle spectrum

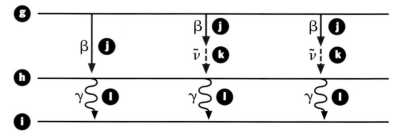

a nuclide z
b excited states of $Z - 2$
c excited states of $Z - 2$
d ground state of $Z - 2$

e alpha particle energy
f gamma radiation
g nuclide Z
h excited state of $Z + 1$

i ground state of $Z + 1$
j beta particle energy
k neutrino energy
l gamma radiation

Table of naturally occurring isotopes 1

Table of masses and abundance of naturally occurring isotopes

Atomic number (Z)	Element	Symbol	Mass number (A)	Percentage	Atomic mass
0	Neutron	n	1	—	1.008665
1	Hydrogen	H	1	99.99	1.007825
			2	0.01	2.014102
2	Helium	He	3	1.3×10^{-1}	3.016030
			4	100	4.002604
3	Lithium	Li	6	7.4	6.015126
			7	92.6	7.016005
4	Beryllium	Be	9	100	9.012186
5	Boron	B	10	19.6	10.012939
			11	80.4	11.009305
6	Carbon	C	12	98.9	12.000000
			13	1.1	13.003354
7	Nitrogen	N	14	99.6	14.003074
			15	0.4	15.000108
8	Oxygen	O	16	99.76	15.994915
			17	0.04	16.999133
			18	0.20	17.999160
9	Fluorine	F	19	100	18.998405
10	Neon	Ne	20	90.9	19.992440
			21	0.3	20.993849
			22	8.8	21.991384
11	Sodium	Na	23	100	22.989773
12	Magnesium	Mg	24	78.8	23.985045
			25	10.2	24.985840
			26	11.1	25.982591
13	Aluminum	Al	27	199	26.981535
14	Silicon	Si	28	92.2	27.976927
			29	4.7	28.976491
			30	3.1	29.973761
15	Phosphorus	P	31	100	30.973763
16	Sulfur	S	32	95.0	31.972074
			33	0.8	32.971460
			34	4.2	33.967864
			36	0.01	35.967091
17	Chlorine	Cl	35	75.5	34.968854
			37	24.5	36.965895
18	Argon	Ar	36	0.34	35.967548
			38	0.06	37.962724
			40*	99.6	30.962384
19	Potassium	K	39	93.1	38.963714
			40	0.012	39.964008
			41	6.9	49.961835
20	Calcium	Ca	40	97.0	39.962589
			42	0.6	41.958628
			43	0.1	42.958780
			44	2.1	43.955490
			46	0.003	45.953689
			48	0.2	47.952519
21	Scandium	Sc	45	100	44.955919

*denotes radioactive isotope

Atomic number

- The *atomic number* (Z) of an element is the number of protons in the nucleus of one atom of that element. All atoms of the same element have the same atomic number.

Element

- "Element" refers to the common name of the element. This list is restricted to the 89 naturally occurring elements.

Symbol

- "Symbol" refers to the shorthand form of the element's name used in chemical equations.

Mass number

- The *mass number* (A) represents the number of protons or neutrons in the nucleus of one atom of that element. Not all atoms of the same element have the same mass number. Atoms of an element that have different mass numbers are called *isotopes*.

Percentage

- "Percentage" refers to isotopic abundance. For example, 99.99 percent of naturally-occurring hydrogen has the mass number 1. Only 0.01 percent has the mass number 2.

Atomic mass

- "*Atomic mass*" refers to the average atomic mass of that element's isotope weighted by isotopic abundance.

Atomic number

- The *atomic number* (Z) of an element is the number of protons in the nucleus of one atom of that element. All atoms of the same element have the same atomic number.

Element

- "Element" refers to the common name of the element. This list is restricted to the 89 naturally occurring elements.

Symbol

- "Symbol" refers to the shorthand form of the element's name used in chemical equations.

Mass number

- The *mass number* (A) represents the number of protons or neutrons in the nucleus of one atom of that element. Not all atoms of the same element have the same mass number. Atoms of an element that have different mass numbers are called *isotopes*.

Percentage

- "Percentage" refers to isotopic abundance. For example, 99.99 percent of naturally-occurring hydrogen has the mass number 1. Only 0.01 percent has the mass number 2.

Atomic mass

- "*Atomic mass*" refers to the average atomic mass of that element's isotope weighted by isotopic abundance.

Table of naturally occurring isotopes 2

Table of masses and abundance of naturally occurring isotopes

Atomic number (Z)	Element	Symbol	Mass number (A)	Percentage	Atomic mass
22	Titanium	Ti	46	8.0	45.952633
			47	7.3	46.95176
			48	74.0	47.947948
			49	5.5	48.947867
			50*	5.2	49.944789
23	Vanadium	V	50	0.25	49.947165
			51	99.75	50.943978
24	Chromium	Cr	50	4.3	49.946051
			52	83.8	51.940514
			53	9.5	52.940651
			54	2.4	53.938879
25	Manganese	M	55	100	54.938054
26	Iron	Fe	54	5.8	53.93962
			56	91.7	55.93493
			57	2.2	56.93539
			58	0.3	57.93327
27	Cobalt	Co	59	100	58.933189
28	Nickel	Ni	58	67.8	57.93534
			60	26.2	59.93078
			61	1.2	60.93105
			62	3.7	61.92834
			64	1.1	63.92796
29	Copper	Cu	63	69.1	62.92959
			65	30.9	64.92779
30	Zinc	Zn	64	48.9	63.929145
			66	27.8	65.92605
			67	4.1	66.92715
			68	18.6	67.92486
			70	0.6	69.92535
31	Gallium	Ga	69	60.5	68.92568
			71	39.5	70.92484
32	Germanium	Ge	70	20.5	69.92428
			72	27.4	71.92174
			73	7.7	72.9234
			74	36.7	73.9211
			76	7.7	75.9214
33	Arsenic	As	75	100	74.92158
34	Selenium	Se	74	0.9	73.9224
			76	9.0	75.91923
			77	7.6	76.91993
			78	23.5	77.91735
			80	49.8	79.91651
			82	9.2	81.9167
35	Bromine	Br	79	50.6	78.91835
			81	49.4	80.91634
36	Krypton	Kr	78	0.3	77.920368
			80	2.3	79.91639
			82	11.6	81.91348
			83	11.5	82.91413
			84	56.9	83.911504
			86	17.4	85.91062

*denotes radioactive isotope

Table of naturally occurring isotopes 3

© Diagram Visual Information Ltd.

Table of masses and abundance of naturally occurring isotopes

Atomic number (Z)	Element	Symbol	Mass number (A)	Percentage	Atomic mass
37	Rubidium	Rb	85	72.1	84.9117
			87*	27.9	86.9092
38	Strontium	Sr	84	0.6	83.91338
			86	9.9	85.9093
			87	7.0	86.9089
			88	82.5	87.9056
39	Yttrium	Y	89*	100	88.9054
40	Zirconium	Zr	90	51.5	89.9043
			91	11.2	90.9052
			92	17.1	91.9046
			94	17.4	93.9061
			96	2.8	95.9082
41	Niobium	Nb	93	100	92.9060
42	Molybdenum	Mo	92	15.9	91.9063
			94	9.1	93.9047
			95	15.7	94.9057
			96	16.5	95.9045
			97	9.4	96.9057
			98	23.8	97.9055
			100	9.6	99.9076
43	Technetium	Tc	has no stable or naturally-occuring isotopes		
44	Ruthenium	Ru	96	5.6	95.9076
			98	1.9	97.905
			99	12.7	98.9061
			100	12.6	
			101	17.1	
			102	31.6	101.9037
			104	18.5	103.9055
45	Rhodium	Rh	103	100	102.9048
46	Palladium	Pd	102	1.0	101.9049
			104	11.0	103.9036
			105	22.2	104.9046
			106	27.3	105.9032
			108	26.7	107.9039
			110	11.8	109.9045
47	Silver	Ag	107	51.4	106.9050
			109	48.6	108.9047
48	Cadmium	Cd	106	1.2	105.9059
			108	0.9	107.9040
			110	12.4	109.9030
			111	12.7	110.9041
			112	24.1	111.9028
			113	12.3	112.9046
			114	28.8	113.9036
			116	7.6	115.9050
49	Indium	In	113	4.3	112.9043
			115*	95.7	114.9041

*denotes radioactive isotope

Atomic number
- The *atomic number* (Z) of an element is the number of protons in the nucleus of one atom of that element. All atoms of the same element have the same atomic number.

Element
- "Element" refers to the common name of the element. This list is restricted to the 89 naturally occurring elements.

Symbol
- "Symbol" refers to the shorthand form of the element's name used in chemical equations.

Mass number
- The *mass number* (A) represents the number of protons or neutrons in the nucleus of one atom of that element. Not all atoms of the same element have the same mass number. Atoms of an element that have different mass numbers are called *isotopes*.

Percentage
- "Percentage" refers to isotopic abundance. For example, 99.99 percent of naturally-occurring hydrogen has the mass number 1. Only 0.01 percent has the mass number 2.

Atomic mass
- "*Atomic mass*" refers to the average atomic mass of that element's isotope weighted by isotopic abundance.

Atomic number

- The *atomic number* (Z) of an element is the number of protons in the nucleus of one atom of that element. All atoms of the same element have the same atomic number.

Element

- "Element" refers to the common name of the element. This list is restricted to the 89 naturally occurring elements.

Symbol

- "Symbol" refers to the shorthand form of the element's name used in chemical equations.

Mass number

- The *mass number* (A) represents the number of protons or neutrons in the nucleus of one atom of that element. Not all atoms of the same element have the same mass number. Atoms of an element that have different mass numbers are called *isotopes*.

Percentage

- "Percentage" refers to isotopic abundance. For example, 99.99 percent of naturally-occurring hydrogen has the mass number 1. Only 0.01 percent has the mass number 2.

Atomic mass

- "*Atomic mass*" refers to the average atomic mass of that element's isotope weighted by isotopic abundance.

Table of naturally occurring isotopes 4

Table of masses and abundance of naturally occurring isotopes

Atomic number (Z)	Element	Symbol	Mass number (A)	Percentage	Atomic mass
50	Tin	Sn	112	1.0	111.9049
			114	0.6	113.9030
			115	0.3	114.9035
			116	14.2	115.9021
			117	7.6	116.9031
			118	24.0	117.9018
			119	8.8	118.9034
			120	33.0	119.9021
			122	4.7	121.9034
			124	6.0	123.9052
51	Antimony	Sb	121	57.3	120.9037
			123	42.7	122.9041
52	Tellurium	Te	120	0.1	119.9045
			122	2.4	121.9030
			123	0.9	122.9042
			124	4.6	123.9028
			125	7.0	124.9044
			126	18.7	125.90324
			128	31.8	127.9047
			130	34.5	129.9067
53	Iodine	I	127	100	126.90435
54	Xenon	Xe	124	0.1	123.9061
			126	0.1	125.90417
			128	1.9	127.90354
			129	26.4	128.90478
			130	4.1	129.90351
			131	21.2	130.90509
			132	26.9	131.90416
			134	10.4	133.90540
			136	8.9	135.90722
55	Cesium	Ca	133	100	132.9051
56	Barium	Ba	130	0.1	129.90625
			132	0.2	131.9051
			134	2.6	133.9043
			135	6.7	134.9056
			136	8.1	135.9044
			137	11.9	136.9056
			138	70.4	137.9050
57	Lanthanum	La	138*	0.1	137.9068
			139	99.9	138.9061
58	Cerium	Ce	136	0.2	135.9071
			138	0.2	137.9057
			140	88.5	139.90528
			142*	11.1	141.9090
59	Praseodymium	Pr	141	100	140.90739

*denotes radioactive isotope

Table of naturally occurring isotopes 5

Table of masses and abundance of naturally occurring isotopes

Atomic number (Z)	Element	Symbol	Mass number (A)	Percentage	Atomic mass
60	Neodymium	Nd	142	27.3	141.90748
			143	12.3	142.90962
			144*	23.8	143.90990
			145	8.3	144.9122
			146	17.1	145.9127
			148	5.7	147.9165
			150	5.5	149.9207
61	Promethium	Pm	has no naturally occuring isotope		
62	Samarium	Sm	144	3.1	143.9116
			147*	15.1	146.91462
			148	11.3	146.9146
			149	14.0	148.9169
			150	7.5	149.9170
			152	26.6	151.9193
			154	22.4	153.9217
63	Europium	Eu	151	47.8	150.9196
			153	52.2	152.9207
64	Gadolinium	Gd	152	0.2	151.9194
			154	2.2	153.9202
			155	15.1	154.9220
			156	20.6	155.9222
			157	15.7	156.9240
			158	24.5	157.9242
			160	21.7	159.9273
65	Terbium	Tb	159	100	158.924
66	Dysprosium	Dy	156	0.1	
			158	0.1	
			160	2.3	159.924
			161	19.0	160.926
			162	25.5	161.926
			163	24.9	162.928
			164	28.1	163.928
67	Holmium	Ho	165	100	164.930
68	Erbium	Er	162	0.1	
			164	1.6	163.929
			166	33.4	165.929
			167	22.9	166.931
			168	27.1	167.931
			170	14.9	169.935
69	Thulium	Tm	169	100	
70	Ytterbium	Yb	168	0.1	
			170	3.1	
			171	14.4	
			172	21.9	171.929
			173	16.2	
			174	31.7	173.926
			176	12.6	
71	Lutetium	Lu	175	97.4	
			176*	2.6	175.9414

*denotes radioactive isotope

Atomic number
- The *atomic number* (Z) of an element is the number of protons in the nucleus of one atom of that element. All atoms of the same element have the same atomic number.

Element
- "Element" refers to the common name of the element. This list is restricted to the 89 naturally occurring elements.

Symbol
- "Symbol" refers to the shorthand form of the element's name used in chemical equations.

Mass number
- The *mass number* (A) represents the number of protons or neutrons in the nucleus of one atom of that element. Not all atoms of the same element have the same mass number. Atoms of an element that have different mass numbers are called *isotopes*.

Percentage
- "Percentage" refers to isotopic abundance. For example, 99.99 percent of naturally-occurring hydrogen has the mass number 1. Only 0.01 percent has the mass number 2.

Atomic mass
- "*Atomic mass*" refers to the average atomic mass of that element's isotope weighted by isotopic abundance.

Atomic number

● The *atomic number* (Z) of an element is the number of protons in the nucleus of one atom of that element. All atoms of the same element have the same atomic number.

Element

● "Element" refers to the common name of the element. This list is restricted to the 89 naturally occurring elements.

Symbol

● "Symbol" refers to the shorthand form of the element's name used in chemical equations.

Mass number

● The *mass number* (A) represents the number of protons or neutrons in the nucleus of one atom of that element. Not all atoms of the same element have the same mass number. Atoms of an element that have different mass numbers are called *isotopes*.

Percentage

● "Percentage" refers to isotopic abundance. For example, 99.99 percent of naturally-occurring hydrogen has the mass number 1. Only 0.01 percent has the mass number 2.

Atomic mass

● *"Atomic mass"* refers to the average atomic mass of that element's isotope weighted by isotopic abundance.

Table of naturally occurring isotopes 6

Table of masses and abundance of naturally occurring isotopes

Atomic number (Z)	Element	Symbol	Mass number (A)	Percentage	Atomic mass
72	Hafnium	Hf	174	0.2	
			176	5.2	175.9403
			177	18.6	176.9419
			178	27.1	177.9425
			179	13.7	178.9444
			180	35.2	179.9451
73	Tantalum	Ta	180	0.01	179.9457
			181	99.99	180.9462
74	Tungsten	W	180	0.2	179.9450
			182	26.4	181.9465
			183	14.4	182.9485
			184	30.6	183.9491
			186	28.4	185.951
75	Rhenium	Re	185	37.1	184.950
			187*	62.9	186.9550
76	Osmium	Os	184	0.02	
			186	1.6	185.9529
			187	1.6	186.9550
			188	13.3	187.9550
			189	16.1	188.9572
			190*		189.9574
			192*		191.9605
77	Iridium	Ir	191	38.5	190.9599
			193	61.5	192.9623
78	Platinum	Pt	190		189.9592
			192	0.8	191.9605
			194	32.9	193.9624
			195		194.9645
			196		195.9646
			198	7.2	197.9675
79	Gold	Au	197	100	196.96655
80	Mercury	Hg	196	0.1	195.96582
			198	10.0	197.96677
			199	16.9	198.96826
			200	23.1	199.96834
			201	13.2	200.97031
			202	29.8	201.97063
			204	6.9	203.97348
81	Thallium	Tl	203	29.5	202.97233
			205	70.5	204.97446
			206*	—	205.97608
			207*	—	206.97745
			208*	—	207.98201
			210*	—	209.99000

*denotes radioactive isotope

Table of naturally occurring isotopes 7

Table of masses and abundance of naturally occurring isotopes

Atomic number (Z)	Element	Symbol	Mass number (A)	Percentage	Atomic mass
82	Lead	Pb	204	1.4	203.97307
			206	25.2	205.97446
			207	21.7	206.97590
			208	51.7	207.97664
			210*	—	209.98418
			211*	—	210.98880
			212*	—	211.99190
			214*	—	213.99976
83	Bismuth	Bi	209	100	208.98042
			210*	—	209.98411
			211*	—	210.98729
			212*	—	211.99127
			214*	—	213.99863
84	Polonium	Po	210*	—	209.98287
			211*	—	210.98665
			212*	—	211.98886
			214*	—	213.99519
			215*	—	214.99947
			216*	—	216.00192
			218*	—	218.0089
85	Astatine	At	215*	—	214.99866
			218*	—	218.00855
86	Emanation	Em	219*	—	219.00952
			220*	—	220.01140
			222*	—	222.0175
87	Francium	Fr	223*	—	223.01980
88	Radium	Ra	223*	—	223.01857
			224*	—	224.02022
			226*	—	226.0254
			228*	—	228.03123
89	Actinium	Ac	227*	—	227.02781
			228*	—	228.03117
			230*	—	230.0331
			231*	—	231.03635
			232*	100	232.03821
			234*	—	234.0436
91	Protactinium	Pa	231*	—	231.03594
			234*	—	234.0434
92	Uranium	U	234*	0.006	234.04090
			235*	0.718	235.04393
			238*	99.276	238.0508

*denotes radioactive isotope

Atomic number

- The *atomic number* (Z) of an element is the number of protons in the nucleus of one atom of that element. All atoms of the same element have the same atomic number.

Element

- "Element" refers to the common name of the element. This list is restricted to the 89 naturally occurring elements.

Symbol

- "Symbol" refers to the shorthand form of the element's name used in chemical equations.

Mass number

- The *mass number* (A) represents the number of protons or neutrons in the nucleus of one atom of that element. Not all atoms of the same element have the same mass number. Atoms of an element that have different mass numbers are called *isotopes*.

Percentage

- "Percentage" refers to isotopic abundance. For example, 99.99 percent of naturally-occurring hydrogen has the mass number 1. Only 0.01 percent has the mass number 2.

Atomic mass

- "*Atomic mass*" refers to the average atomic mass of that element's isotope weighted by isotopic abundance.

Key words

accelerator A chemical that increases the rate of a chemical reaction.

acid Any substance that releases hydrogen ions when added to water. It has a pH of less than 7.

acid-base indicator A chemical compound that changes color when going from acidic to basic solutions. An example is Methyl orange.

acidity The level of hydrogen ion concentration in a solution.

actinides The name of the radioactive group of elements with atomic numbers from 89 (actinium) to 103 (lawrencium).

actinium (Ac) A silvery radioactive metallic element that occurs naturally in pitchblende and can be synthesized by bombarding radium with neutrons.

actinium series One of the naturally occurring radioactive series.

activation energy The energy barrier to be overcome in order for a reaction to occur.

active site The part of an enzyme where the chemical reaction occurs.

addition polymerization A chemical reaction in which simple molecules are added to each other to form long-chain molecules without by-products.

addition reaction A reaction in which a molecule of a substance reacts with another molecule to form a single compound.

adsorption The process by which molecules of gases or liquids become attached to the surface of another substance.

aerosol Extremely small liquid or solid particles suspended in air or another gas.

alcohol A member of a family of organic compounds whose structure contains the $-OH$ functional group.

aldehyde One of a group of organic compounds containing the aldehyde group ($-CHO$). Names have the suffix -al.

aldohexose A monosaccharide having six carbon atoms and an aldehyde group.

aldose A sugar containing one aldehyde group per molecule

alkali A solution of a substance in water that has a pH of more than 7 and has an excess of hydroxide ions in the solution.

alkali metals Metallic elements found in group 1 of the periodic table. They are very reactive, electropositive, and react with water to form alkaline solutions.

alkaline earth metals Metallic elements found in group 2 of the periodic table.

alkalinity Having a pH greater than 7.

alkane A member of the hydrocarbon group whose general formula is C_nH_{2n+2}. They have single bonds between the carbon atoms and are not very reactive.

alkanol See alcohol

alkene A member of the hydrocarbon group whose general formula is C_nH_{2n}. They have a double bond between a pair of carbon atoms and are thus reactive.

alkyl A member of the hydrocarbon group whose general formula is CnH_{2n+1}.

alkyne A member of the hydrocarbon group with the general formula CnH_{2n-1}. They have a triple bond between a pair of carbon atoms in each molecule and are thus reactive.

allotrope An element that can exist in more than one physical form while in the same state.

alloy A metallic material made of two or more metals or of a metal and non-metal.

alpha decay The process of radioactive decay in which the nucleus of an atom emits an alpha particle.

alpha particle A particle released during radioactive decay that consists of two neutrons and two protons.

aluminum (Al) A silvery-white. metallic element that is non-magnetic and oxidizes easily.

amine A member of a group of organic compounds containing the amino functional group $-NH_2$.

amino acid An organic compound containing both the carboxyl group ($-COOH$) and the amino group ($-NH_2$).

ammonia (NH_3) A colorless, strong-smelling poisonous gas that is very soluble in water.

ammonium hydroxide (NH_4OH) An aqueous solution of ammonia. It is a corrosive chemical with a strong odor.

ammonium ion (NH_4^+) An ion found in ammonia solution and in ammonium compounds.

amphoteric Exhibiting properties of both an acid and a base.

anhydride The substance remaining when one or more molecules of water have been removed from an acid or a base.

anhydrous Containing no water. Term applied to salts without water of crystallization.

anion An ion having a negative charge.

anode The electrode carrying the positive charge in a solution undergoing electrolysis.

anomer A stereoisometric form of a sugar, involving different arrangements of atoms or molecules around a central atom,

aqueous solution A solution in which water is the solvent.

argon Ar. A colorless, odorless. gaseous element. One of the noble gases.

aryl A member of an aromatic hydrocarbon group formed by the removal of a hydrogen atom from an aromatic hydrocarbon.

association The process by which molecules of a substance combine to form a larger structure.

astatine At. A non-metallic radioactive element that is highly unstable and rare in nature.

atmosphere The layer of gases surrounding Earth.

atom The smallest particle of an element that can exhibit that element's properties.

atomic emission spectrum The amount of electromagnetic radiation an element emits when excited.

atomic mass The ratio of the mass of an average atom of an element to 1/12th of the mass of an atom of the carbon-12 isotope.

atomic number The number of protons in the nucleus of an atom.

atomic volume The volume of one mole of the atoms of an element.

Avogadro's constant The number of particles present in a mole of substance.

azeotropic mixture A mixture of liquids that boils without a change in composition.

bakelite A phenol/methanal resin that has good electrical and heat insulation properties.

base A substance existing as molecules or ions that can take up hydrogen ions.

beta decay The process of radioactive decay in which the nucleus of an atom emits a beta particle.

beta particle A high-speed electron emitted by the nucleus of certain radioactive elements during beta decay.

Big Bang The primeval explosion that most astronomers think gave rise to the Universe.

black hole An object with infinite density.

body-centered cubic packing A crystalline structure in which one atom sits in the center of each cube.

boiling point The point at which a substance changes from the liquid state to the gas state.

bond The chemical connection between atoms within a molecule. Bonds are forces and are caused by electrons.

bond angle In a molecule, the angle between the two straight lines joining the centers of the atoms concerned.

bromine (Br) A non-metallic element that is isolated as a dark red liquid. It is a very reactive oxidizing agent.

brown dwarf A ball of gas like a star but whose mass is too small to have nuclear fusion occur at its core.

Brownian motion The random movement of particles through a liquid or gas.

buckminsterfullerene See buckyball.

buckyball The nickname for buckminsterfullerene. An allotropic form of carbon. It has a cage-like structure and has the formula C_{50}, C_{60}, or C_{70}.

burette A long, graduated glass tube with a tap at the lower end. It is used to measure a volume of liquid accurately.

calcium (Ca) A soft, slivery-white metal.

calcium carbonate A white solid, occurring naturally in marble and limestone, that dissolves in dilute acids.

carbide A compound that contains carbon and an element with lower electronegativity.

carbon (C) A non-metallic element whose compounds occur widely in nature.

carbonate A salt of carbonic acid (containing the ion CO_3^{2-}).

carbon cycle The circulation of carbon through the biosphere.

carbon dioxide (CO_2) A dense, colorless, odorless gas that does not support combustion. It exists in the atmosphere and is instrumental in the carbon cycle.

carbonic acid (H_2CO_3) A very weak acid formed by dissolving carbon dioxide in water.

carbon monoxide(CO) A colorless, odorless, very poisonous gas. It is sparingly soluble in water.

carboxyl group The organic radical $-CO.OH$.

carboxylic acid An organic acid that contains one or more carboxyl groups.

catalyst A substance that alters the rate of a chemical reaction but remains chemically unchanged by it.

catalytic cracking The process used in the petroleum industry to convert large-chain hydrocarbon molecules to smaller ones.

catenation The formation of chains of bonded atoms.

cathode The electrode carrying the negative charge in a solution undergoing electrolysis.

cathode rays A stream of electrons emitted from the cathode in a vacuum tube.

cation An ion having a positive charge.

cellulose A complex carbohydrate that is the main component of the cell walls of plants.

centrifuge A machine that rotates an object at high speed.

chain reaction A self-sustaining nuclear reaction yielding energy and electrons emitted by the fission of an atomic nucleus, which proceeds to cause further fissions.

chemical compound A substance composed of two or more elements linked by chemical bonds that may be ionic or covalent.

chemical energy The energy stored in the bonds between atoms and molecules that is released during a chemical reaction.

chemical reaction The process in which one or more substances reacts to form new substances.

chiral An object or a system that differs from its mirror image.

chloride A compound containing chlorine and another element.

chlorine (Cl) A poisonous, greenish, gaseous element that is a powerful oxidizing agent.

chlorophyll A green pigment found in most plants. It absorbs light energy during photosynthesis.

chromatography A technique for separating and identifying mixtures of solutes in a solution.

chromium (Cr) A hard, brittle, gray-white metallic element that is very resistant to corrosion and takes a high polish.

cobalt (Co) A hard, lustrous, silvery-white metallic element found in ores,

colloid A substance made of very small particles whose size (1–100 nm) is between those of a suspension and those in solution.

compound See chemical compound

concentration A measure of the quantity of solute dissolved in a solution at a given temperature.

conductor A material that is able to conduct heat and electricity.

convection current A circular current in a fluid such as air.

coordinate bonding A type of covalent bond in which one of the atoms supplies both electrons.

coordination number The number of atoms, ions, or molecules to which bonds can be formed.

copper (Cu) A pinkish metallic element used widely in alloys and electrical wires.

covalent bond A bond formed when two electrons are shared between two atoms (usually between two non-metallic atoms), one contributed by each atom.

covalent compound A compound in which the atoms in the molecules are held together by covalent bonds.

crust The outer layer of Earth.

cryolite A compound of aluminum fluoride and sodium fluoride.

crystal A substance with an orderly arrangement of atoms, ions, or molecules in a regular geometrical shape.

daughter nucleus In radio active decay, the nucleus produced by the decay of the previous nucleus.

dehydrating agent A substance that has an attraction for water and is therefore used as a drying agent.

dehydrogenation The chemical process of removal of hydrogen atoms from a molecule (a form of oxidation), increasing its degree of unsaturation.

density The mass per unit volume of a given substance.

detergent The term for a synthetic soap substitute.

diamond A transparent crystalline allotrope of carbon. It is the hardest naturally occurring substance.

diatomic molecule A molecule that consists of two atoms.

diffusion The process of rapid random movement of the particles of a liquid or gas that eventually form a uniform mixture.

dipole A chemical compound with an unequally distributed electric charge.

disaccharide A sugar molecule formed by a condensation reaction between two monosaccharide molecules.

displacement reaction A reaction in which a more reactive substance displaces the ions of a less reactive substance.

dissociation The breaking down of a molecule into smaller molecules, atoms, or ions.

dissolve To add a solute to a solvent to form a uniform solution.

distillation A process in which a solution is boiled and its vapor then condensed.

double bond A covalent bond formed between two atoms in which two pairs of electrons contribute to the bond..

dry gas A gas from which all water has been removed

ductile Capable of being drawn out, shaped, or bent.

effective collision A collision that brings about a reaction.

electric field A field of force around a charged particle.

electrode A conductor that allows current to flow through an electrolyte, gas, vacuum, or semiconductor.

electrolysis The process by which an electrolyte is decomposed when a direct current is passed through it between electrodes.

electrolyte A substance that forms ions when molten or dissolved in a solvent and that carries an electric current during electrolysis.

electron One of the three basic subatomic particles. Very light and carrying a negative charge, it orbits around the nucleus of an atom.

element A substance that cannot be split into simpler substances using chemical methods.

emulsion A colloidal dispersion of small droplets of one liquid dispersed within another, such as oil in water or water in oil.

enantiomer One of two "mirror images" of a chiral molecule.

end point The point at which a reaction is complete.

endothermic a chemical change during which heat is absorbed.

enthalpy A measure of the stored heat energy of a substance.

enzyme An organic catalyst, made of proteins, that increases the rate of a specific biochemical reaction.

equilibrium The state of a reversible chemical reaction where the forward and backward reactions take place at the same rate.

equivalence point The point at which there are equivalent amounts of acid and alkali.

ester A member of a hydrocarbon group that is formed by a reaction between a carboxylic acid and an alcohol.

ethane (C_2H_6) A colorless, flammable alkane that occurs in natural gas.

ethanol (C_2H_5OH) A volatile, colorless liquid alcohol used in beverages and as a gasoline octane enhancer.

ethene (C_2H_4) A colorless, flammable unsaturated gas, manufactured by cracking petroleum gas, used in ethanol and polyethene production.

evaporation The change in state from liquid to vapor.

exothermic A chemical change resulting in the liberation of heat.

face-centered cubic close packing A crystal structure in which one atom sits in each "face" of the cube.

Faraday constant The amount of electricity needed to liberate one mole of a monovalent ion during electrolysis ($9.648\ 670 \times 10^{-4}$ C mol^{-1}).

fatty acid A hydrocarbon chain with a carboxyl group at one end.

filtrate A clear liquid that has passed through a filter.

filtration The process of removing particulate matter from a liquid by passing the liquid through a porous substance.

fission A process during which a heavy atomic nucleus disintegrates into two lighter atoms and the lost mass is converted to energy.

fluorescence The emission of light from an object that has been irradiated by light or other radiations.

fluorine (F) A gaseous non-metallic element that is poisonous and very reactive gas.

flux A substance that combines with another substance (usually an oxide), forming a compound with a lower melting point than the oxide.

foam A dispersion of gas in a liquid or solid. Small bubbles of gas are separated by thin films of the liquid or solid.

formula mass The relative molecular mass of a compound calculated using its molecular formula. The mass of a mole of the substance.

forward reaction A reaction in which reactants are converted to products.

fractional distillation The separation of a mixture or liquids that have differing but similar boiling points.

fullerenes Allotropes of carbon in the form of a hollow sphere (buckyball) or tube (nanotube).

functional group The atom (or group of atoms) present in a molecule that determines the characteristic properties of that molecule.

fusion The process by which two or more light atomic nuclei join, forming a single heavier nucleus. The products of fusion are lighter than the components. The mass lost is liberated as energy.

galvanizing The coating of iron or steel plates with a layer of zinc to protect against rusting.

gamma radiation Very short-wave electromagnetic radiation emitted as a result of radioactive decay.

gas One of the states of matter. In a gas, the particles can move freely throughout the space in which it is contained. Gas is the least dense of the states of matter.

gas-liquid chromatography A type of chromatography in which the mobile phase is a carrier gas and the stationary phase is a microscopic layer of liquid on an inert solid support.

gel A colloidal solution that has formed a jelly. The solid particles are arranged as a fine network in the liquid phase.

geometric isomerism A form of isomerism that describes the orientation of functional groups at the ends of a bond where no rotation is possible.

glucose In animals and plants, the most widely distributed hexose sugar and the most common energy source in respiration.

glycogen A polysaccharide composed of branched chains of glucose, used to store energy in animals and some fungi..

gold (Au) A shiny, yellow metallic element used in coins, jewelry, and electrical contacts.

grade The concentration of ore in rock.

Graham's law The velocity with which a gas will diffuse is inversely proportional to the square root of its density.

graphite A soft, grayish-black, solid allotrope of carbon.

ground state The lowest allowed energy state of an atom, molecule, or ion.

group The vertical columns of elements in the periodic table. Elements in a group react in a similar way and have similar physical properties.

group 1 elements The alkali metals. The elements lithium, sodium, potassium, rubidium, cesium, and francium. These elements have one electron in their outer shell.

group 2 elements The alkaline earth metals. The elements beryllium, magnesium, calcium, strontium, barium, and radium. These elements have two electrons in their outer shell.

group 3 elements The elements boron, aluminum, gallium, indium, and thallium. These elements have a full s orbital and one electron in a p orbital in their outer shell.

group 4 elements The elements carbon, silicon, germanium, tin, and lead. These elements have a full s orbital and two electrons in two p orbitals in their outer shell.

group 5 elements The elements nitrogen, phosphorus, arsenic, antimony, and bismuth. These elements have a full s orbital and three electrons in three p orbitals in their outer shell.

group 6 elements The chalcogens. The elements oxygen, sulfur, selenium, tellurium, and polonium. These elements have a full s orbital, one full p orbital, and two half-full p orbitals in their outer shell.

group 7 elements The halogens. The elements fluorine, chlorine, bromine, iodine, and astatine. These elements have a full s orbital, two full p orbitals, and one half-full p orbital in their outer shell.

group 8 elements. The noble or inert gases. The elements helium, neon, argon, krypton, xenon, and radon. The outer shell of the atoms in these elements is complete, rendering these elements unreactive.

half-life The time required for half the atoms of a radioactive substance to disintegrate.

halide A compound that a halogen makes with another element. Metal halides are ionic; non-metal halides are formed by covalent bonding.

halogens See Group 7 elements.

helium (He) A colorless, odorless gaseous element that is the second most abundant element on Earth.

hexagonal close packing In crystalline structures, a way of packing atoms so that alternating layers overlie one another in an ABABAB pattern.

hexose A monosaccharide with six carbon atoms.

homologous series A series of related organic compounds. The formula of each member differs from the preceding member by the addition of a $-CH_2-$ group.

hydration The combination of water and another substance to produce a single product.

hydride A compound formed between hydrogen and another element.

hydrocarbon An organic molecule consisting only of carbon and hydrogen.

hydrochloric acid (HCl) A colorless fuming solution of hydrogen chloride.

hydrogen (H) An odorless, easily flammable gaseous element that is the most abundant on Earth.

hydrogen bond A weak bond between hydrogen and another element with partial but opposite electrical charges.

hydrogen chloride (HCl) A colorless gas with a pungent smell that fumes in moist air. It is very soluble in water.

hydrogen peroxide (H_2O_2) A colorless or pale blue viscous liquid. It is a strong oxidizing agent, but it can also act as a reducing agent.

hydrogen sulfide (H_2S) A colorless, poisonous gas smelling of bad eggs that is moderately soluble in water. It is a reducing agent.

hydronium ion The positive ion $(H_3O)^+$. It is the hydrated form of the hydrogen ion (H^+) or proton.

hydrophilic Water-loving. In solution, it refers to a chemical or part of a chemical that is highly attracted to water.

hydrophobic Water-hating. It refers to a chemical or part of a chemical that repels water.

hydroxide A compound containing the hydroxide ion or the hydroxyl group bonded to a metal atom.

hydroxide ion The negative ion (OH^-) present in alkalis.

immiscible Incapable of mixing.

indicator A substance that indicates by a change in its color the degree of acidity or alkalinity of a solution or the presence of a given substance.

inert A substance that is either very or completely unreactive.

inert gases See noble gases.

infrared Electromagnetic radiation with a greater wavelength than the red end of the visible spectrum.

insoluble A substance that does not dissolve in a particular solvent under certain conditions of temperature and pressure.

iodine (I) A grayish-black non-metallic element that is essential in the diet and is used in disinfectants and photography.

ion An electrically charged atom or group of atoms.

ionic bonding A type of bonding that occurs when atoms form ions and electrons are transferred from one atom to another.

ionic compound Compounds consisting of ions held together by strong ionic bonds. Ionic compounds are electrolytes.

KEY WORDS

ionic crystal A type of crystal where ions of two of more elements form a regular three-dimensional arrangement (crystal structure).

ionization energy The energy needed to remove completely an electron from a neutral gaseous atom or ion against the attraction of the nucleus.

ionizing radiation Any radiation capable of displacing electrons from atoms or molecules and so producing ions

iron (Fe) A silvery, malleable and ductile metallic element used in construction.

irradiation The use of radiation to destroy microorganisms in foods.

isomer One of two or more (usually organic) compounds having the same molecular formula and relative molecular mass but different three-dimensional structures.

isomerism The rearrangement atoms in a molecule to make it more efficient.

isomerization The transformation of a molecule into a different isomer.

isotope Atoms of the same element (all chemically identical) having the same atomic number but containing different numbers of neutrons, giving a different mass number.

ketone An organic compound that contain two organic radicals connected to a carbonyl group.

kinetic energy The energy a body has by virtue of its motion.

lanthanide series A series of metallic elements with the atomic numbers 57 to 71. The metals are shiny and are attacked by water and acids.

lattice The orderly three-dimensional arrangements of atoms, molecules, or ions seen in crystals.

lead (Pb) A silvery-white metallic element used in batteries and in water, noise, and radiation shielding.

lead sulfide (PbS) A brownish-black insoluble crystal. It occurs naturally as the mineral galena.

Le Chatelier's principle If a chemical reaction is at equilibrium and a change is made to any of the conditions, further reaction will take place to counteract the changes in order to re-establish equilibrium.

limewater A solution of calcium hydroxide that is used to test for the presence of carbon dioxide.

limiting form The possibilities for the distribution of electrons in a molecule or ion.

liquid A state of matter between solid and gas. Particles are loosely bonded, so can move relatively freely.

lone pair A pair of electrons in the outermost shell of an atom that are not involved in the formation of covalent bonds.

luminescence Light emission from a substance caused by an effect other than heat.

magnesium (Mg) A silvery-white metallic element used in alloys and castings.

magnesium oxide (MgO) A white solid used for reflective coatings and as a component of semiconductors.

manganese (Mn) A soft, gray metallic element used in making steel alloys.

mantle The layer of Earth between the crust and the core.

mass The measure of a body's resistance to acceleration.

mass number The total number of protons and neutrons in the nucleus of an atom.

mass spectrometry A technique for determining the composition of molecules by using the mass of their basic constituents

melting point The point at which a substance changes state from solid to liquid.

methane (CH_4) The simplest alkane. A colorless, tasteless, odorless flammable gas used as a fuel.

mineral A natural inorganic substance with distinct chemical composition and internal structure.

mixture A system consisting of two or more substances that are not chemically combined.

mobile phase The phase that moves along the stationary phase. It is the solvent in paper chromatography.

molarity The concentration of solution giving the number of moles of solute dissolved in 1 kg of solvent.

mole The amount of a substance that contains the same number of entities (atoms, molecules, ions, etc.) as there are atoms in 12 g of the carbon-12 isotope.

molecular mass The sum of the atomic masses of all atoms in a molecule. The mass of a mole of the substance.

molecule The smallest part of an element or chemical compound that can exist independently with all the properties of the element or compound.

monomer A basic unit from which a polymer is made.

monosaccharide A simple sugar such as glucose.

nanotube An isotope of carbon consisting of long thin cylinders closed at either end with caps containing pentagonal rings.

neptunium (Np) A radioactive metallic element that can be synthesized by bombarding U-238 with neutrons.

neptunium series A radioactive series composed of artificial isotopes.

neutral A solution whose pH is 7.

neutralization The reaction of an acid and a base forming a salt and water..

neutron One of the two major components of the atomic nucleus. It has no electric charge.

neutron star The smallest but densest kind of star, apparently resulting from a supernova explosion.

nickel (Ni) A hard, malleable and ductile, silvery-white metallic element that is a component of Earth's core.

nitrate A salt of nitric acid.

nitric acid (HNO_3) A colorless, corrosive, poisonous, fuming liquid that is a strong oxidizing agent.

nitrite A salt of nitrous acid.

nitrogen (N) A colorless gaseous element essential for the growth of plants and animals.

nitrogen cycle The process by which nitrogen is recycled in the ecosystem.

noble gases Group 8 elements: helium, neon, argon, krypton, xenon, and radon. These gases do not combine chemically with other materials.

nucleon A proton or neutron.

nucleus The positively charged core of an atom that contains almost all its mass.

nuclide A particular isotope of an element, identified by the number of protons and neutrons in the nucleus.

optical isomerism A form of isomerism in which two isomers are the same in every way except that they are mirror images that cannot be superimposed on each other.

orbital An area around an atom or molecule where there is a high probability of finding an electron.

ore A mineral from which a metal or non-metal may be profitably extracted.

oxidation The process by which a substance gains oxygen, loses hydrogen, or loses electrons.

oxidation state The sum of negative and positive charges in an atom.

oxide A compound consisting only of oxygen and another element. Oxides can be either ionic or covalent.

oxidizing agent A substance that can cause the oxidation of another substance by being reduced itself.

oxygen (O) A colorless, odorless gaseous element. It the most common element in Earth's crust and is the basis for respiration in plants and animals..

ozone (O_3) One of the two allotropes of oxygen. A bluish gas with a penetrating smell, it is a strong oxidizing agent.

period The horizontal rows of elements in the periodic table.

periodic table A table of elements, arranged in ascending order of atomic number, that summarizes the major properties of the elements.

periodicity Recurring at regular intervals.

peroxide A compound that contains the peroxide ion O_2^{2-} Peroxides are strong oxidizing agents.

pH A scale from 0 to 14 that measures the acidity or alkalinity of a solution. A neutral solution has a pH of 7, while an acidic solution has a lower value and an alkaline solution a higher value.

pH meter A device that uses an electrochemical cell to measure pH.

phosphorescence The emission of light by an object, and the persistence of this emission over long periods, following irradiation by light or other forms of radiation.

photochemical reaction A chemical reaction that is initiated by a particular wavelength of light.

photoelectric effect The emission of electrons from metals upon the absorption of electromagnetic radiation.

photosynthesis The photochemical reaction by which green plants make carbohydrates using carbon dioxide and water.

platinum (Pt) A soft, shiny, silver metallic transition element that is malleable and ductile.

pollutant A substance that harms the environment when it mixes with air, soil, or water.

polyethene A thermoplastic polymer made by addition polymerization of ethene.

polymer A material containing very large molecules built up from a series of repeated small basic units (monomers).

polymerization The building up of long chain hydrocarbons from smaller ones.

polysaccharide A organic polymer composed of many simple sugars (monosaccharides).

precipitate An insoluble substance formed by a chemical reaction.

product A substance produced during a chemical reaction.

protein A large, complex molecule composed of a long chain of amino acids.

proton The positively charged particle found in the nucleus of the atom.

protostar The early stage in a star's formation before the onset of nuclear burning.

quantum number The number used when describing the energy levels available to atoms and molecules.

racemate A mixture of equal amounts of left- and right-handed stereoisomers of a chiral molecule.

radiation Energy that is transmitted in the form of particles, rays, or waves.

radical A group of atoms forming part of many molecules.

radioactive decay The process by which unstable radioactive atoms are transformed into stable, non-radioactive atoms.

radioactivity The spontaneous disintegration of certain isotopes accompanied by the emission of radiation.

rate of reaction The speed at which a chemical reaction proceeds.

reactant A substance present at the start of a chemical reaction that takes part in the reaction.

reaction A process in which substances react to form new substances.

reactivity The ability of substances to react to form new substances.

reactivity series of metals Metallic elements arranged in order of their decreasing chemical reactivity.

reagent A substance that takes part in a chemical reaction, one that is usually used to bring about a chemical change.

red giant A very large, cool star in the final stages of its life.

redox reaction A process in which one substance is reduced and another is oxidized at the same time.

reducing agent A chemical that can reduce another while being oxidized itself.

reduction A chemical reaction in which a substance gains electrons, looses oxygen, or gains hydrogen. It is the reverse of oxidation.

reforming The conversion of straight chain molecules into those that are branched in order to improve their efficiencies.

residfining The process used on the residue fraction of crude oil to convert it into a usable product.

residue The solid remaining after the completion of a chemical process.

resonance structure In organic chemistry, a diagrammatic tool to symbolize bonds between atoms in molecules.

respiration The chemical reaction by which an organism derives energy from food.

reverse reaction A reaction in which the products are converted into reactants.

reversible reaction A chemical reaction that can proceed in either direction. It does not reach completion but achieves dynamic equilibrium.

R_f value The ratio of the distance moved by a substance in a chromatographic separation to the distance moved by the solvent.

rust A reddish-brown oxide coating on iron or steel caused by the action of oxygen and water.

salt A compound formed from an acid in which all or part of the hydrogen atoms are replaced by a metal or metal-like group. Salts are generally crystalline.

saponification The treatment of an ester (hydrolysis) with a strong alkaline solution to form a salt of a carboxylic acid and an alcohol.

KEY WORDS

saturated A solution where there is an equilibrium between the solution and its solute.

scandium (Sc) Silvery-white metallic element in the lanthanide series found in nature only in minute quantities.

sewage Wastewater from domestic and industrial sources.

shell A group of orbitals at a similar distance from an atomic nucleus.

silver (Ag) A white, shiny, ductile metallic element.

silver nitrate (AgNO₃) A very soluble white salt that decomposes to form silver, oxygen, and nitrogen dioxide on heating.

slag Waste material that collects on the surface of a molten metal during the process of either extraction or refining.

smelting The process of extracting a metal from its ores.

soap A cleansing agent made from fatty acids derived from natural oils and fats.

sodium (Na) A soft, silver-white metallic element.

sodium chloride (NaCl) A nonvolatile ionic compound that is soluble in water.

sodium hydroxide (NaOH) A white, translucent, crystalline solid that forms a strongly alkaline solution in water.

sol A liquid solution or suspension of a colloid.

solid A state of matter in which the particles are not free to move but in which they can vibrate about fixed positions.

solubility A measure of the quantity of a solute that will dissolve in a certain amount of solvent to form a saturated solution under certain conditions of temperature and pressure.

solubility curve A graphic representation of the changing solubility of a solute in a solvent at different temperatures.

soluble A relative term that describes a substance that can dissolve in a particular solvent.

solute A substance that dissolves in a solvent and thus forms a solution.

solution A uniform mixture of one or more solutes in a solvent.

solvent A substance, usually a liquid, in which a solute dissolves to form a solution.

species The common name for entities (atoms, molecules, molecular fragments, and ions) being subjected to investigation.

spectrum The arrangement of electromagnetic radiation into its constituent wavelengths.

starch A polysaccharide with the formula $(C_6H_{10}O_5)$. It is composed of many molecules of glucose.

stationary phase That which the mobile phase moves on. In paper chromatography it is the paper.

stoichiometry The calculation of the quantities of reactants and products involved in a chemical reaction.

subatomic particles The particles from which atoms are made. Neutrons and protons are found in the nucleus of the atom. Electrons form a cloud around the nucleus.

sucrose A disaccharide sugar that occurs naturally in most plants.

sulfate A salt or ester of sulfuric acid.

sulfide A compound of sulfur and a more electropositive element.

sulfur (S) A yellow, non-metallic element that is found abundantly in nature.

sulfuric acid (H₂SO₄) An oily, colorless, odorless liquid that is extremely corrosive.

sulfur dioxide (SO₂) A colorless gas with a pungent odor of burning sulfur. It is very soluble in water.

sulfur trioxide (SO₃) A white, soluble solid that fumes in moist air. It reacts violently with water to form sulfuric acid.

supernova The explosion caused when a massive star dies and collapses.

surface area The sum of the area of the faces of a solid.

suspension A type of dispersion. Small solid particles are dispersed in a liquid or gas.

tensile strength The amount of stress a material can stand without breaking.

thorium Th. A gray, radioactive metallic element used as fuel in nuclear reactors.

thorium series One of the naturally occurring radioactive series.

titanium (Ti) A lightweight, gray metallic element that is very strong and resistant to corrosion.

titration In analytical chemistry, A technique used to determine the concentration of a solute in a solution.

transition metals Metallic elements that have an incomplete inner electron structure and exhibit variable valencies.

triple bond A covalent bond formed between two atoms in which three pairs of electrons contribute to the bond.

ultraviolet Electromagnetic radiation of shorter wavelengths than visible light, but of longer wavelength than X rays.

unit cell The smallest repeating array of atoms, ions, or molecules in a crystal.

universal indicator A mixture of substances that shows a gradual color change over a wide range of pH values.

uranium (U) A hard, white, radioactive metallic element used in nuclear reactors and nuclear weapons.

uranium series One of the naturally occurring radioactive series.

valency The measure of an element's ability to combine with other elements.

vanadium (V) A silvery-white or gray metallic element used as a steel additive and in catalysts.

van der Waals forces Weak intermolecular or interatomic forces between neutral molecules or atoms. They are much weaker than chemical bonds.

viscosity A measure of the resistance of a fluid to flow.

wavelength The distance between two corresponding points on a wave.

white dwarf The small, dense remnant of a star near the end of its period of nuclear fusion.

zinc (Zn) A hard, brittle, bluish-white metallic element used in alloys and in galvanizing.

zwitterion An ion that carries both a positive and negative charge.

Internet resources

There is a lot of useful information on the internet. Information on a particular topic may be available through a search engine such as Google (http://www.google.com). Some of the Web sites that are found in this way may be very useful, others not. Below is a selection of Web sites related to the material covered by this book.

The publisher takes no responsibility for the information contained within these Web sites. All the sites were accessible on March 1, 2006.

About Chemistry
Includes links to a glossary, encyclopedia, experiments, periodic table, chemical structure archive, chemistry problems, and articles.
http://chemistry.about.com

Allchemicals.info
Hundreds of definitions and descriptions from absolute zero to zinc.
http://www.allchemicals.info

Chem4Kids
Accessible information on matter, atoms, elements, reactions, biochemistry, and much more, for grades 5–9.
http://www.chem4kids.com

Chemistry Carousel: A Trip Around the Carbon Cycle
Site explaining the carbon cycle.
http://library.thinkquest.org/11226

Chemistry Central
Offers basic atomic information, information on the periodic table, chemical bonding, and organic chemistry as well as extensive links to a wide variety of other resources.
http://users.senet.com.au/~rowanb/chem

Chemistry.org
Offers publications, career advice, information, and curriculum materials for K–12.
http://www.acs.org/

The Chemistry Research Center
Offers high school students links to useful sites for help with homework.
http://library.thinkquest.org/21192

Chemistry Tutor
Help for high school students with chemistry homework. Includes an introduction to chemistry, equations, calculations, types of reactions, information on lab safety, and links to other sources.
http://library.thinkquest.org/2923

ChemSpy.com
Links to chemistry and chemical engineering terms, definitions, synonyms, acronyms, and abbreviations.
http://www.chemspy.com

Chemtutor
A guide to the basics of chemistry for high school and college students.
http://www.chemtutor.com

CHEMystery
A virtual chemistry textbook, providing an interactive guide for high school chemistry students and links to other resources.
http://library.thinkquest.org/3659

Common Molecules
Information and 3-D presentation on molecules studied in chemistry classes or of interest for their structural properties.
http://www.reciprocalnet.org/edumodules/commonmolecules

Delights of Chemistry
Presents more than 40 chemistry demonstrations and 500 photographs/animations of experiments and chemical reactions.
http://www.chem.leeds.ac.uk/delights

EnvironmentalChemistry.com
Includes a chemical and environmental dictionary; a detailed periodic table of elements; articles on environmental and hazardous materials issues; a geologic timeline.
http://environmentalchemistry.com

Eric Weisstein's World of CHEMISTRY
Online encyclopedia, still under construction, with excellent graphics; good source for chemical reactions.
http://scienceworld.wolfram.com/chemistry

General Chemistry Online
Contains searchable glossary, frequently asked questions, database of compounds, tutorials, simulations, and toolbox of periodic table and calculators.
http://antoine.frostburg.edu/chem/senese/101

INTERNET RESOURCES

IUPAC Nomenclature Home Page
Definitions of terms used in chemistry provided by the International Union of Pure and Applied Chemistry. The "Gold book" is particularly good for basic terms.
http://www.chem.qmul.ac.uk/iupac

The Learning Matters of Chemistry
Offers visualizations of molecules and atomic orbits, interactive chemistry exercises, and links to other resources.
http://www.knowledgebydesign.com/tlmc

The Macrogalleria: A Cyberwonderland of Polymer Fun
An Internet "mall" for learning about polymers and polymer science.
http://www.pslc.ws/macrog

Nuclear Chemistry and the Community
Introduction to nuclear chemistry and its impact on society.
http://www.chemcases.com/nuclear

Open Directory Project: Biochemistry and Molecular Biology
A comprehensive listing of internet resources in the field of biochemistry.
http://dmoz.org/Science/Biology/Biochemistry_and_Molecular_Biology

Open Directory Project: Chemistry
A comprehensive listing of internet resources in the field of chemistry.
http://dmoz.org/science/chemistry

The pH Factor
Introduction to acids and bases for middle school students.
http://www.miamisci.org/ph

PSIgate: Chemistry
Offers interactive tutorials, timeline, and links, in many areas.
http://www.psigate.ac.uk/newsite/chemistry-gateway

Reactive Reports
Web chemistry magazine offering news stories and links to sites.
http://www.reactivereports.com

ScienceMaster
News, information, links, columns, and homework help in all major areas of science.
http://www.sciencemaster.com

Science News for Kids
Science Service Suggestions for hands-on activities, books, articles, Web resources, and other useful materials for students ages 9–13.
http://www.sciencenewsforkids.org

The Science of Spectroscopy
Introduction to spectroscopy with descriptions of common spectroscopic analysis techniques, as well as applications of spectroscopy in consumer products, medicine, and space science.
http://www.scienceofspectroscopy.info

Virtual Chemistry
3-D simulated laboratory for teaching chemistry, with links to an online encyclopedia, tutorials, and close-ups of molecules.
http://neon.chem.ox.ac.uk/vrchemistry

A Visual Interpretation of the Table of Elements
Striking visual representations of 110 elements. Site includes detailed information on the elements and on the history of the periodic table.
http://www.chemsoc.org/viselements

Web Elements™ Periodic Table Scholar Edition
High quality source of information about the periodic table for students. There is also a professional edition.
http://www.webelements.com/webelements/scholar

What's that Stuff?
Explores the chemistry of everyday objects.
http://pubs.acs.org/cen/whatstuff/stuff.html

Index

Index of subject headings.

a

b

c

d

e

f

g

h

i